Lecture Notes in Computer Science 8778

Commenced Publication in 1973
Founding and Former Series Editors:
Gerhard Goos, Juris Hartmanis, and Jan van Leeuwen

T0236197

Minhua Ma   Manuel Fradinho Oliveira
Jannicke Baalsrud Hauge (Eds.)

Serious Games Development and Applications

5th International Conference, SGDA 2014
Berlin, Germany, October 9-10, 2014
Proceedings

 Springer

Volume Editors

Minhua Ma
Glasgow School of Art
Digital Design Studio
Glasgow, UK
E-mail: m.ma@hud.ac.uk

Manuel Fradinho Oliveira
SINTEF Technology and Society
Industrial Management
Oslo, Norway
E-mail: manuel.oliveira@sintef.no

Jannicke Baalsrud Hauge
University of Bremen
Bremen Institute for Production and Logistics (BIBA)
Bremen, Germany
E-mail: baa@biba.uni-bremen.de

ISSN 0302-9743   e-ISSN 1611-3349
ISBN 978-3-319-11622-8   e-ISBN 978-3-319-11623-5
DOI 10.1007/978-3-319-11623-5
Springer Cham Heidelberg New York Dordrecht London

Library of Congress Control Number: 2014948638

LNCS Sublibrary: SL 6 – Image Processing, Computer Vision, Pattern Recognition, and Graphics

Typesetting: Camera-ready by author, data conversion by Scientific Publishing Services, Chennai, India

Printed on acid-free paper

Springer is part of Springer Science+Business Media (www.springer.com)

Preface

As games technologies have become more and more widely available, the ability of games to engage users effectively in specific, designed activities has been seized as an opportunity to use computer games for purposes beyond recreation. Since the term 'serious games' was comprehensively defined in 2002, they have been used as tools to gives individuals a novel way to interact with games in order to promote physical activities, to learn skills and knowledge, to support social or emotional development, to treat different types of psychological and physical disorders, to generate awareness, and to advertize and promote in application areas such as engineering, education and training, competence development, healthcare, military, advertizing, city planning, production, and crisis response to name just a few. Many recent studies have identified the benefits of using videogames for a variety of serious purposes. Serious gaming is a particularly timely subject as there has been recent re-emergence of serious games design and production; one 2010 market study indicated that the worldwide market for serious games was worth €1.5 billion.

The aim of the annual International Conference on Serious Games Development and Applications (SGDA) is to disseminate and exchange knowledge on serious games technologies, game design and development; to provide practitioners and interdisciplinary communities with a peer-reviewed forum to discuss the state of the art in serious games research, their ideas and theories, and innovative applications of serious games; to explain cultural, social and scientific phenomena by means of serious games; to concentrate on the interaction between theory and application; to share best practice and lessons learnt; to develop new methodologies in various application domains using games technologies; to explore perspectives of future developments and innovative applications relevant to serious games and related areas; and to establish and foster a cross-sector and cross-disciplinary network of researchers, game developers, practitioners, domain experts, and students interested in serious games.

The 5th International Conference on Serious Games Development and Applications (SGDA 2014) was hosted by University of Applied Sciences HTW Berlin in Germany and was co-located with the European Conference on Games Based Learning (ECGBL 2014). SGDA 2014 appeared in the sequence of the successes of the First SGDA held at Derby in 2010, the Second SGDA conference at Lisbon in 2011, the Third SGDA at Bremen in 2012, and the Fourth SGDA at Trondheim in 2013.

The Conference was supported by the European GALA Network of Excellence for Serious Games, FP7 TARGET Project, SINTEF, Glasgow School of Art, University of Applied Sciences HTW Berlin, University of Bremen, BIBA-Bremen Institute for Production & Logistics, Technical University of Lisbon, INESC-ID/IST, Norwegian University of Science and Technology, University of

Derby, and a number of prestigious European partners. This year, HTW Berlin hosted the fifth annual conference (SGDA 2014) during 9–10 October 2014.

18 full papers and 1 invited keynote covering a wide range of aspects of serious games design and use were presented at SGDA 2014. Speakers came from 14 countries throughout Europe and around the world, including Canada, Australia, Malaysia and China. The papers are published in the Springer LNCS 8778. The keynote speaker was Dr. Stefan Göbel, Head of Serious Gaming in the Multimedia Communications Lab (KOM), Technical University of Darmstadt, Germany.

We would like thank all the authors, speakers, and reviewers for their contributions to SGDA 2014 and welcome you to participate in our discussions at the conference.

July 2014   Minhua Ma

Organization

SGDA 2014 was hosted by University of Applied Sciences HTW Berlin, Germany, in cooperation with the Digital Design Studio, Glasgow School of Art, UK; SINTEF Technology and Society, Norway; Bremen Institute for Production & Logistics (BIBA), Germany; and IFIP Technical Committee (TC14) Entertainment Computing - Working Group on Serious Games (WG 14.8).

Conference Chair

Minhua Ma   Glasgow School of Art, UK

LNCS Volume Editors

Minhua Ma   Glasgow School of Art, UK
Manuel Fradinho Oliveira   SINTEF Technology and Society, Norway
Jannicke Baalsrud Hauge   Bremen Institute for Production and Logistics,
                               Germany

Program Chairs

Minhua Ma   Glasgow School of Art, UK
Manuel Fradinho Oliveira   SINTEF Technology and Society, Norway
Jannicke Baalsrud Hauge   Bremen Institute for Production and Logistics,
                               Germany

Local Organizing Committee

Martin Steinicke   University of Applied Sciences HTW Berlin,
                               Germany
Jannicke Baalsrud Hauge   Bremen Institute for Production and Logistics,
                               Germany

Program Committee

Björn Andersen   Norwegian University of Science, Norway
Aida Azadegan   University of the West of Scotland, UK
Jannicke Baalsrud Hauge   Bremen Institute for Production and Logistics,
                               Germany
Rafael Bidarra   TU Delft, The Netherlands
Francesco Belotti   University of Genoa, Italy
Riccardo Berta   University of Genoa, Italy

David Bustard	University of Ulster, UK
Paul Chapman	Glasgow School of Art, UK
Ben Cowley	University of Helsinki, Finland
Alessandro De Gloria	University of Genoa, Italy
Tendai Dube	University of Derby, UK
Heiko Duin	Bremer Institute for Production and Logistics, Germany
Abdennour El Rhalibi	Liverpool John Moores University, UK
Sara de Freitas	Curtin University, Australia
Stefan Göbel	TU Darmstadt, Germany
Gabriele Hoeborn	University of Wuppertal, Germany
Lakhmi Jain	University of South Australia, Australia
Matthias Kalverkamp	Bremen Institute for Production and Logistics, Germany
Bill Kapralos	University of Ontario Institute of Technology, Canada
Tanya Krzywinska	Falmouth University, UK
Peter Leong	Singapore Polytechnic, Singapore
Fotis Liarokapis	Coventry University, UK
Minhua Ma	Glasgow School of Art, UK
Timothy Marsh	James Cook University, Australia
Igor Mayer	TU Delft, The Netherlands
Paul Mc Kevitt	University of Ulster, UK
Rob Nadolski	Open University, The Netherlands
Andreas Oikonomouv	University of Derby, UK
Manuel Fradinho Oliveira	SINTEF, Norway
João Pereira	Technical University of Lisbon, Portugal
Sobah Petersen	SINTEF, Norway
Ekaterina Prasolova-Førland	Norwegian University of Science, Norway
Johann Riedel	University of Nottingham, UK
Marco Taisch	Polytechnic University of Milan, Italy
Marcus Seifert	Bremen Institute for Production and Logistics, Germany
Riitta Smeds	Alto University, Finland
Ioana Stanescu	ADL, Romania
Daniel Steenstra	Cranfield University, UK
Klaus-Dieter Thoben	University of Bremen, Germany

Sponsoring Institutions

Glasgow School of Art, UK
SINTEF Technology and Society, Norway
Bremen Institute for Production & Logistics (BIBA), Germany
University of Applied Sciences HTW Berlin, Germany
University of Huddersfield, UK
Norwegian University of Science and Technology, Norway

University of Bremen, Germany
Technical University of Lisbon, Portugal
INESC-ID, Lisbon, Portugal
University of Derby, UK

Table of Contents

Music and Sound Effects

Games for Other Purposes

Game Design and Theories

PhysioVinci – A First Approach on a Physical Rehabilitation Game

Tiago Martins[1], Miguel Araújo[2], Vitor Carvalho[1,2],
Filomena Soares[1], and Luís Torrão[3]

[1] R&D ALGORITMI Centre, University of Minho, Portugal
[2] IPCA – Polytechnic Institute of Cavado and Ave, Portugal
[3] University of Hull, UK

Abstract. Several studies have shown very positive results regarding the use of serious games as rehabilitation tools for individuals with physical disabilities, mainly because the game environment gives them the necessary motivation to continue their treatment with enthusiasm. Thus, the objective of this paper is to describe the first steps on the development of a 3D game for physical therapy of patients with motor disabilities as a result of neurological disorders.

Keywords: Serious games, rehabilitation tools, motor disabilities, motivation, physical therapy, neurological diseases.

1 Introduction

While keeping the entertainment, serious games are designed to solve problems in various areas. Considering the health area, it is possible to highlight the important contribution of these games in physical therapy and rehabilitation of patients with motor disabilities due to several causes, including neurological diseases.

These patients require physical therapy programs appropriate to their problems in order to improve as much as possible, their quality of life. However, the exercises that traditional physical therapy provides are often boring and repetitive, which discourages the individuals, causing them to abandon their programs before they have finished, especially if they do not see short-term improvements [1]. Therefore, such programs should be developed in environments that encourage patients to perform the exercises with enthusiasm, so that positive results can be obtained [2, 3].

The results of several studies show that serious games create environments that encourage patients to perform the exercises with enthusiasm and relaxation, maintaining them increasingly motivated, involved and absorbed in their rehabilitation. Usually, these games integrate feedback forms that increase motivation and satisfaction, stimulating the wish to complete specific tasks and achieve certain goals [4].

Though a number of serious games are presently being used in therapy of patients with motor problems, it has been detected a gap with respect to games that are exclusively intended to a broad spectrum of physical therapy exercises designed to improve the mobility of patients with neurological diseases. Consequently, PhysioVinci is a game in 3D environment, designed to overcome that gap.

M. Ma et al. (Eds.): SGDA 2014, LNCS 8778, pp. 1–9, 2014.

Therefore, in this paper it is referred the motivation that serious games can provide to patients who have to perform repetitive physical therapy leading to an improvement in their mobility. As many of the mobility problems are the result of neurological diseases, some of them will be mentioned here. The exercises selected for monitoring through image processing techniques, the game concept and design and its logical scheme, as well as the development of the first level will also be discussed.

2   Literature Review

2.1   Serious Games as a Motivating Factor for Physical Therapy

There are many individuals whose physical disabilities oblige them to practice physical therapy programs based on repetitive exercises, which discourage them and make them to feel isolated, especially if they do not see immediate improvements [1, 5]. However, as such exercises, though tedious, are essential to improve the quality of life of these patients, it is necessary to develop strategies to motivate and prevent them from prematurely abandoning their treatment. Serious games seem to be the appropriate tool to trigger motivation [2].

Among the many advantages we can withdraw from the use of serious games in physical therapy of patients with limited mobility, we can highlight the control and consistency of the stimuli, the feedback performance in real time, the change of stimuli and responses that depend on the physical abilities of the user, the opportunity for exposure to stimuli in a graduated way, the independent practice, which culminates in patient's motivation [6]. At the same time they entertain the players, reward their victories and reinforce the healthy movements [1].

The pleasant atmosphere created by a serious game and feedback forms such as numerical scores, progress bars, character dialogue, controller vibration/force and sound constitute an incentive and can provide the increase of the patients motivation to complete their programs of physiotherapy [4]. In general, they encourage the user to understand the more difficult exercises as challenges, performing them gradually. Furthermore, the possibility of repetition of an exercise, if it fails, seems to be a motivating factor. There is also the attraction that games usually promote. After starting a game, people are interested in keeping on playing it to improve results [2].

Previous studies show that the use of serious games in physical therapy lead to a longer playing time, a higher interest/enjoyment and an increased effort to complete the game [7].

2.2   Neurological Diseases

As already mentioned, some of motor disabilities are the consequence of neurological diseases. A neurologic disease is characterized by a general degeneration of nerve cells that transmit to muscles the electrical signals to the movement. The transmission stops, the muscles gradually lose activity and atrophy, compromising the mobility. Some examples of neurological diseases are multiple sclerosis, stroke, Friedreich's Ataxia and Parkinson's disease [8].

Multiple sclerosis is a progressive disease in which the immune system develops a self-injuring action of the myelin sheath of the white matter of the central nervous system, leading to the demyelination of nerve cells, impairing the conduction of nerve impulses which may result in disturbances in the motor system and cause serious limitations in day-to-day [9].

A stroke typically occurs when a clot interrupts the blood flow to a part of the brain, resulting in the difficulty in the movement of limbs and also the loss of balance [10].

Friedreich's Ataxia is a rare disease that can be defined as an autosomal recessive degenerative atrophy of the posterior columns of the spinal cord, leading to progressive ataxia [11].

Parkinson's disease is a neurodegenerative syndrome characterized by the death of cells responsible for dopamine production in the substantia nigra, forming intraneuronal filamentous inclusions and emerging an extrapyramidal movement disorder [12].

3   Movements Associated to the Pathology

After analysing the exercises performed in physical therapy sessions to neurological patients, and as mentioned in [2], there were selected the movements that besides being the most common and transversal to several neurological diseases are likely to be monitored by image processing techniques. Therefore, the following exercises were chosen (Fig. 1):

- Glenohumeral joint abduction (Fig. 1.1);
- Radiohumeral joint flexion (Fig. 1.2);
- Pulleys (Fig. 1.3);
- Coxofemoral joint abduction (Fig. 1.4);
- Glenohumeral joint flexion (Fig. 1.5);
- Crossed arms movement (Fig. 1.6).

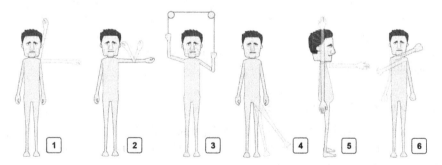

Fig. 1. Set of exercises chosen for the PhysioVinci Game. 1 – Glenohumeral joint abduction; 2 – Radiohumeral joint flexion; 3 – Pulleys; 4 – Coxofemoral joint abduction; 5 – Glenohumeral joint flexion; 6 – Crossed arms movement

The glenohumeral joint abduction can be defined as the movement that occurs in the frontal plane around a horizontal axis directed dorsoventrally, pulls the arm from the midline of the body [13].

The radiohumeral joint flexion also occurs in the frontal plane, consisting of the movement of the forearm towards the shoulder [13].

The pulley consists of a combined movement of glenohumeral abduction and flexion radiohumeral and so it is performed in the frontal plane.

Such as the three aforementioned movements, the coxofemoral abduction joint is performed once more in the frontal plane, around a horizontal axis in anteroposterior direction, and consists of the lateral lifting of the leg [13].

Regarding the glenohumeral joint flexion, it occurs in the sagittal plane, being carried forward and upward, suffering a change from 0° to 180° [14].

The crossed arms movement is a diagonal movement, in which each arm alternately moves forward and upward or downward, trying to reach a target that appears on the opposite side, placed randomly by the physiotherapist.

4   PhysioVinci Game Conception

4.1   Concept and Design of the Game

After the definition of the exercises, it was necessary to idealize the games situations that motivate the performance of those exercises.

In the first place, it is necessary to define the target public for the game. This will be useful, as reported earlier, as an adjunct to physiotherapy of individuals with neurological diseases, in a mild or moderate state. The use of the game may not be indicated for individuals with advanced disease states, since they would not be able to minimally perform the proposed tasks, thus leading them to demotivation, as checked in a previous study [2].

As PsysioVinci is a 3D environment game, the 'Unity 3D' engine was employed in the development. Beyond the acceptability and exponential expansion that it is taking on the market, Unity 3D allows programming in JavaScript and C#, which facilitates the integration of Microsoft Kinect SDK (the Kinect sensor is used to monitor the movements of patients). Another asset of using this software is the compatibility of importing objects from Blender software. Blender was used to build 3D characters, among other game elements.

4.2   Logical Scheme of the Game

As it can be observed in Fig. 2, at a logic level, the game is divided into three main areas: Game (for the player), Backoffice (for physiatrist) and Data Storage serving as an intermediary between both.

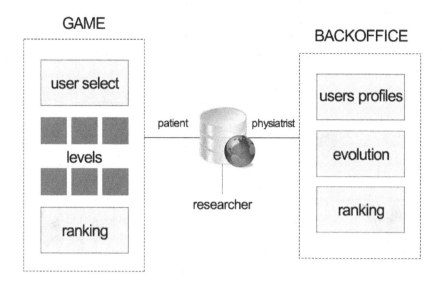

Fig. 2. Simplified Logical Scheme of the Game

The "Backoffice" section is divided into 3 parts: player profiles, statistics and rankings. This area is exclusive to the physiatrist. Here, he/she fills the patient data – player (name, age, weight, type of pathology, degree of pathology, among other relevant personal information). He/she also defines a set of exercises that a particular patient has to perform (eg: Glenohumeral abduction – left arm, bending radiohumeral – left arm, among others.). When the profile is completed, the information is recorded in a centralized server. In this backoffice, the physiatrist may analyze the evolution of a particular patient, compare with other patients, and check the ranking of the best ratings.

The "game" section is divided into three parts: selection of player, game levels and ranking. It is worth noting that the game activity needs a monitor who is responsible for the proper handling of the application and accompanies the player. Thus, before a patient begins to play, the technician must select the correct player.

After selecting the player, there will be a calibration system (Fig. 4.4), to make sure that the patient is prepared to be monitored using the Microsoft Kinect sensor.

After calibration, the player will perform levels (exercises) defined by the physiatrist. At the end of each level the ranking of the ten top-ranked players is presented. These ten players match those that have the same degree of disease that the current player.

Since all the information is centrally stored, in a remote server, researchers/therapists can access the data at any time. The database stores the patient's characterization, such as name, age, gender, pathology, disease status, medical history. Other relevant parameters related to physical therapy he/she is performing, as movements to carry out, responsible physiotherapist, and the patient's progress in the therapy sessions are also registered.

4.3   Levels of the Game

Currently, the game has one level that corresponds to the exercise of glenohumeral joint abduction. The StoryBoard of this level is briefly represented in Fig. 3, which is described next.

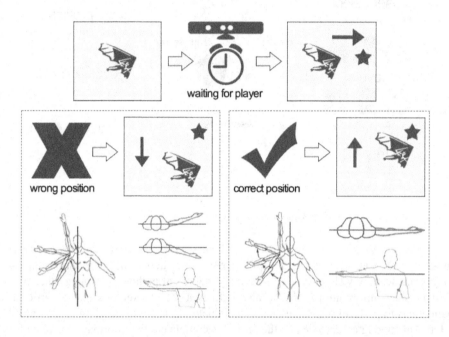

Fig. 3. Simplified Storyboad of the PhysioVinci Level I

This level is based on the Delta Wing invention glide of Leonardo Da Vinci. The reason why it was chosen is related with the similarity between the beating of the Delta Wing of Leonardo da Vinci and the proposed exercise. Theoretically, the player should use both arms to hit the two wings, but since the exercise is performed with only one, the movement of the second wing is replicated (in mirror).

At the beginning of the level the main character follows a stabilized flight with the Delta Wing (Fig. 4.5) until the player takes control of the game (start level). From that moment, the player has to perform correctly the proposed exercise so that the flight continues stabilized and he can catch objects to get points (Fig. 4.6). If the player does not perform the proposed exercise correctly, the flight is destabilized and the glider starts to fall until it touches the ground (Fig. 4.7, Fig. 4.8, Fig. 4.9). If the player is able to correct the exercise before the glider touches the ground, it goes back up to its normal position, accessible to the objects that give score.

This level contains a graph in the upper right corner informing the player if he is properly performing the exercise, indicating the direction of the movement and its percentage of conclusion. Furthermore, it indicates the errors in case that the player is performing wrongly the exercise.

The Kinect Sensor continuously monitors the player position and it is through it that it is possible to check if the user is performing the exercise correctly.

In the specific case of this level the player must perform the exercise correctly according to the descriptions mentioned in the section of the exercises. Theoretically, the player is penalized in the following cases (see Fig. 3): arm-forearm angle lower than 180°; incorrect alignment in the frontal plane or in the sagittal plane; acceleration of execution different from zero.

In fact, due to the anatomy of the human body, we cannot guarantee the values described above, and therefore it is necessary to set some thresholds to ensure that the game has gameplay and does not have an exaggerated precision, which would lead to the disinterest of the player and a consequent demotivation because he was unable to minimally perform the proposed exercise.

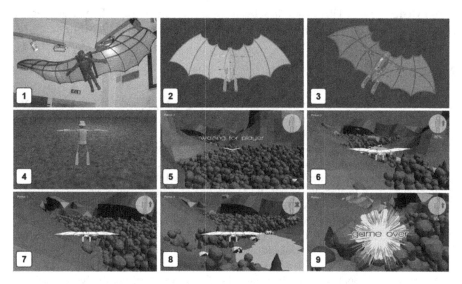

Fig. 4. PhysioVinci, Level I. 1 – Leonard Da Vinci Delta Wind maquette; 2, 3 – 3D model of Leonardo Da Vinci Delta Wind; 4 – Secreenshof of the user calibration system; 5, 6, 7, 8, 9 – Screenshots of de Level I.

5   Results and Final Comments

There are many people with problems associated with neurological diseases, requiring appropriate physical therapy programs. Sometimes these programs become monotonous, leading to the disinterest of patients who eventually abandon them prematurely for lack of motivation. We consider the use of electronic games as a support to physiotherapy as they can trigger the motivation, leading the individuals to comply fully with the respective programs in order to use their quality of life.

Therefore, our research has grown towards realizing, which exercises are most used in physiotherapy for patients with these conditions, in order to adapt them to game situations. For this purpose, we created a story that is based on some Leonard

Da Vinci inventions, which, beyond giving the game a play context, at the same time adds to it a cultural nature.

Presently, the first level of the game is finished. The preliminary tests were performed in laboratory environment with healthy people, to validate the game activity and check for errors. This first tests reveal that players do not show any kind of difficulty either in understanding the performance of the game, either in the effectiveness of the results.

The next step will be to test this game level in the clinics, with patients and physical therapists. When this level is validated, we will proceed to the development of the other levels. We believe that the game offers some advantages regarding other existing games, namely the widest spectrum of diseases to which it can be applied.

Acknowledgements. This work has been supported by FCT – Fundação para a Ciência e Tecnologia within the Project Scope: PEst-OE/EEI/UI0319/2014.

References

1. Ryan, M., Smith, S., Chung, B., Cossell, S., Jackman, N., Kong, J., Mak, O., Ong, V.: Rehabilitation Games – Designing Computer Games for Balance Rehabilitation in the Elderly. ACM, Australia (2009)
2. Martins, T., Carvalho, V., Soares, F.: Application for Physiotherapy and Tracking of Patients with Neurological Diseases – Preliminary Studies. In: IEEE 2nd International Conference on Serious Games and Applications for Health, pp. 1–8. IEEE (2013)
3. Rodrigues, T., Carvalho, V., Soares, F.: Monitoring of Patients with Neurological Diseases: Development of a Motion Tracking Application Using Image Processing Techniques. International Journal of Biomedical and Clinical Engineering (IJBCE) 2(2), 37–55 (2013)
4. Burke, J.W., McNeill, D.J., Charles, D.K., Morrow, P.J., Crosbie, J.H., McDonough, S.M.: Optimising Engagement for Stroke Rehabilitation Using Serious Games. Vis. Comput. 25, 1085–1099 (2009)
5. Carvalho, V., Leão, C., Soares, F., Cunha, M.: Games Development for Pedagogical and Educational Purposes. In: Cunha, M.M.C., Carvalho, V.H., Tavares, P. (eds.) Business Technological and Social Dimension of Computer Games, pp. 1–9. IGI-Global, Hershey (2011)
6. Keshner, E.A.: Virtual Reality and Physical Rehabilitation: a New Toy or a New Research and Rehabilitation Tool? Journal of Neuro Engineering and Rehabilitation 1(8) (2004); BioMed Central
7. Shah, N., Basteris, A., Amirabdollahian, F.: Design Parameters in Multimodal Games for Rehabilitation. Games for Health Journal 3(1), 13–20 (2014)
8. Afonso, Í., Suzart, F.: Carneiro. M., Matos, M., Oliveira, P., Barros, R.: Doenças Neurológicas. Faculdade de São Salvador, Salvador, Brasil (2011)
9. Zanon, R.G., Emirandetti, A., Simões, G.F., Freria, C.M., Victório, S.C., Cartarozzi, L.P., Barbizan, R., Oliveira, A.L.R.: Expressão do Complexo de Histocompatilidade Principal de Classe I (MHC I) no Sistema Nervoso Central: Plasticidade Sináptica e Regeneração. Coluna/Columna 9(2), 193–198 (2010)
10. Gupta, Y.K., Briyal, S.: Animal Models of Cerebral Ischemia for Evaluation of Drugs. Indian Journal of Physiology and Pharmacology 48(4), 379–394 (2004)

11. Pandolfo, M.: Friedreich Ataxia. In: Fry, M., Usdin, K. (eds.) Nucleic Acids and Molecular Biology, vol. 19, pp. 103–119. Springer, Heidelberg (2006)
12. Feany, M.B., Bender, W.W.: A Drosophila Model of Parkinson's Disease. Nature 404(6776), 394–398 (2000)
13. Maciel, A.: Modelagem de Articulações para Humanos Virtuais Baseada em Anatomia. Universidade Federal do Rio Grande do Sul, Porto Alegre, Brasil (2001)
14. Fonseca, F.: Avaliação Clínica do Membro Superior, http://rihuc.huc.min-saude.pt/bitstream/10400.4/1278/1/Avalia%C3%A7%C3%A3o%20membro%20superior%20-%20alguns%20apontamentos.pdf (accessed on April 2014)

A Pilot Evaluation of a Therapeutic Game Applied to Small Animal Phobia Treatment

Maja Wrzesien[1], Mariano Alcañiz [1,2], Cristina Botella[2,3], Jean-Marie Burkhardt[4], Juana Breton Lopez[3], and Alejandro Rodriguez Ortega[1]

[1] Instituto Interuniversitario de Investigación en Bioingeniería y Tecnología Orientada al Ser Humano , Universidad Politécnica de Valencia, Camino de Vera s/n, 46022 Valencia, Spain
[2] CIBER, Fisiopatología Obesidad y Nutrición, CB06/03 Instituto de Salud Carlos III, Spain
[3] Departamento de Psicologia Basica y Psicobiologia Universidad Jaume I, Castellón, Spain
[4] Institut Français des Sciences et Technologies des Transports, de l'Aménagement et des Réseaux, 25 allée des Marronniers, Satory, F-78000 Versailles, France

Abstract. This study presents *Catch Me* game, a therapeutic game for teaching patients how to confront to their feared animals during spider and cockroach phobia treatment, and evaluates whether inclusion of gaming elements into therapeutic protocol does have an added value for the treatment. The *Catch Me* game was designed in order to help patients learn about their feared animals and to learn how to apply adapted confrontation strategies and techniques with the lowest possible anxiety level. In this study, *Catch Me* game was evaluated in terms of knowledge acquisition, anxiety level, self-efficacy belief acquisition, and appeal to both participants and therapists. Data collection consisted of quantitative measures on a sample of 14 non-clinical population. The results showed that the game significantly improved knowledge and self-efficacy belief regarding the feared animal, and significantly decreased the anxiety level of participants. Moreover, both participants and the therapists were highly satisfied with the game.

Keywords: Therapeutic games, augmented reality, phobias.

1 Introduction

Although new technologies have been identified as a potential tool for increasing patient engagement in the therapy and accessibility of the treatment [1], the main reason for treatment failure is lack of patient motivation [2]. Thus, new channels that offer the ability to increase motivation and engagement in the therapeutic process are needed in order to be able to reach a larger clinical population. One possible channel corresponds to the introduction of computer games in the therapeutic environment. Indeed, successful computer games all have one important characteristic in common: the capacity to draw people in [3]. This ability to engage people as well as the wide range of possibilities that new technologies offer can create new, motivating, and engaging therapeutic environments: therapeutic games.

M. Ma et al. (Eds.): SGDA 2014, LNCS 8778, pp. 10–20, 2014.

Despite a growing number of recent studies regarding the use of computer games as a form of therapy, therapeutic games are still under investigation. The aim of this paper is to evaluate the influence of therapeutic game on participants' appeal, knowledge acquisition, anxiety level, and self-efficacy belief for treatment of small animal phobia (i.e., spiders and cockroaches). The paper is organized as follows. Section 2 presents some of the main issues related to new technologies in specific phobia treatment. Section 3 presents issues related to computer games in the therapeutic field. Section 4 presents the methodology undertaken in this evaluation. Finally, Section 5 presents our results, and the remainder of the sections presents the discussion and conclusions that we have drawn from the study.

2   New Technologies in Specific Phobias of Small Animals

Some new therapeutic tools have recently been developed to improve the appeal to phobia sufferers and to cover some drawbacks (i.e., time consuming and logistics problems; a lack of full control of the animal or situation; a low level of acceptance and a high dropout rate) related to the standard therapy for treating specific phobia [4], namely *in vivo* exposure therapy. Virtual Reality (VR) and Augmented Reality (AR) technology offer potentially efficient solutions to the treatment of specific phobias, proposing full control of the phobic object or situation, as well as the immediacy and safety of the environment in which therapists and patients can work. VR has demonstrated to have great potential in different MH applications and has been effectively used in different MH disorders (see [5] for review). Also, AR technology, which has recently been introduced, has become a potential treatment tool for specific phobias such as small animal phobias (e.g. [6]) or acrophobia [7]. However, since some authors [8] demonstrated that these technologies do not necessarily have a direct impact on patient motivation, new channels to motivate and engage patients in the therapy should be addressed. In our opinion, the introduction of serious games in the therapeutic context might be promising. The following section presents the concept of therapeutic games.

3   Therapeutic Games

It has been recognized that computer games are enjoyed by millions of people around the world and that they have come to be an integral part of our cultural and social environment [9]. Even though computer games are known in the MH field for their negative impact on their users (e.g. game addiction, aggressive behavior) [10]; computer games have demonstrated that they can make learning effective, engaging, and inspiring both in the educational field (e.g. [11]), and in the health care field (e.g. [12]). Consequently, in recent years, the use of computer games as a form of therapy has captured the attention of MH professionals (e.g. [13]). The combination of therapeutic content and computer games can be defined as Therapeutic Games (TGs). Specifically, TGs are games that integrate gaming elements with therapeutic objectives. In the MH field, TGs have been applied to autistic spectrum disorder (e.g.

[14]), anxiety disorders (e.g. [15]), language learning impairments (e.g. [16]), cognitive behavioral therapy [17], and solution focused therapy [1].Although TGs have just begun to emerge, and the majority of applications have not yet empirically demonstrated their efficacy and utility, TGs can easily respond to therapeutic requirements. In the case of specific phobia, in order for the exposure to be effective, factors such as repetition [18], the patient's perception of his/her self-efficacy belief [19], and humor [20] all need to be integrated. In our opinion, the introduction of TGs to the therapeutic session with respect to these factors can be beneficial for both the patient and the therapist. A pilot study of a mobile therapeutic game for cockroach phobia treatment has demonstrated this possibility [21]. Botella and her colleagues [21] showed that the mobile TG reduced the patient's anxiety and avoidance (from 10/10 to 7/10) before the therapeutic session started. Moreover, the patient found the use of TG to be very helpful and was willing to use it after the therapeutic session as a homework assignment.

As the above literature review indicates, the enjoyment factor included in TGs seems to be beneficial for patients and can open up a new range of related research. With appropriate design, TGs can be an effective tool in complementing other therapeutic techniques or as a therapeutic tool itself [22]. The aim of this study is to evaluate a therapeutic game, namely *Catch Me* game that aims to be applied in the context of small animal phobia treatment.

4   Methodology

4.1   Research Design

The study evaluates the impact of a therapeutic game on the participants' and therapists' appeal, participants' knowledge acquisition, anxiety level, and their self-efficacy belief that was measures before and after the sessions.

4.2   Participants

9 man and 5 women (M=26.71; SD=6.15 years old) participated in the study. Since the game have not been tested before, due to the ethical issues the pilot evaluation was decided to be performed with non-clinical population. However, the measures and selection criteria of the participants were applied based on the clinical protocol for specific phobia treatment. The participants were selected based on the following inclusion criteria: no prescribed medication use, no current alcohol or drug dependency, no diagnosis of psychological disorder, and no serious medical problems (e.g. heart disease or epilepsy). All of the participants responded to both the spider and cockroach anxiety and avoidance questionnaire. The animal with the highest score determined which animal they were exposed to. The participants that obtained a score greater than 92 out of 126 (N=0) were considered to be potentially phobic subjects and were disqualified from participating in the study due to ethical issues. 6 participants were exposed in the *Catch Me* game to the cockroaches with the higher anxiety and avoidance scores for this animal (M=35.83; SD=24.61), and 8 participants were exposed to the spiders (M=36.13, 22.30).

Also, four therapists with a minimum of 4 years of therapeutic experience with new technologies and phobia treatment participated in the study in order to give their opinion about the therapeutic value and usefulness of the therapeutic game.

4.3   Measures

Spider and cockroach anxiety and avoidance questionnaire
The measure of anxiety and avoidance level was performed by applying the spider and cockroaches fear questionnaire (adapted from [23]). This questionnaire corresponds to 18 questions (on a 7-point Likert scale) that reflect fear and avoidance of a specific animal.

Anxiety assessment
The subjective Unit of Discomfort scale [24] was used to evaluate the level of anxiety during the therapeutic session. Participants were asked at the beginning and at the end of each exposure exercise to indicate their level of anxiety regarding the feared animal (on a 11-point Likert scale).

Knowledge Assessment regarding the feared animal
A knowledge questionnaire was used to evaluate the level of knowledge that the participants had about their feared animal. The participants filled out the knowledge questionnaire at the beginning and at the end of the session; responding to six questions related to the animal, its functions, and its characteristics. 12 questions of equal difficulty (evaluated by one of the researchers) were randomly distributed between pre- and post-knowledge questionnaire.

Self-efficacy belief assessment
The evaluation of the participants' perceived self-efficacy belief toward the feared animal was performed by adapting the Schwarzer & Renner [25] questionnaire. The questionnaire measures with six items (on the 7-point Likert scale) how certain the participant is that he/she can overcome their fear of the animal, at the beginning and at the end of the session.

Participants' appeal assessment
The evaluation of the participants' appeal was performed by applying an appeal questionnaire. The appeal questionnaire developed by our team had close-ended questions and included fifteen items that studied six dimensions: (a) perceived usefulness; (b) perceived therapeutic value; (c) perceived intrinsic motivation; (d) engagement; (e) enjoyment; and (f) intention of use. The participants were asked to rate (on a 7-point Likert scale) the degree to which they agreed with the statement that related to one of these five dimensions.

Therapists' appeal assessment
The evaluation of therapists' appeal was performed by applying an appeal questionnaire. The appeal questionnaire developed by our team included seven items that studied the following dimensions: (a) appeal of the therapeutic game; and (b)

general appeal of the system. The participants were asked to rate (on a 7-point Likert scale) the degree to which they agreed with the statement that related to one of these two dimensions.

4.4   Apparatus and Treatment

a) Projection-based Augmented Reality (P-AR) system
The *Catch Me* game is a part of the Projection-based Augmented Reality *(P-AR)* system. The P-AR system (see [26] for technical details) is a technology-mediated, talk-based, face-to-face therapy that involves direct confrontation with a virtual feared animal in the real environment (i.e., augmented reality). The P-AR system allows the therapist to control the virtual feared animal projected on the table by choosing different functions with the laptop (e.g. increase/decrease the number of animals; increase/decrease the size of animals; make the animal move; stop), and it allows both the therapist and the participant to observe and interact with the projective AR environment using a high resolution projector and ASUS XPro camera.

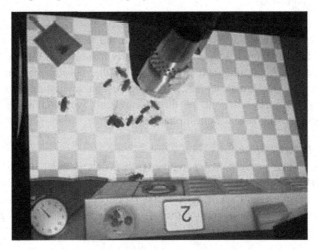

Fig. 1. The participant playing: *Catch Me* game

b) Therapeutic game
The *Catch Me* game described below is an augmented reality therapeutic game that conform to cognitive behavioral therapy protocols. The goal of the *Catch Me* game is to allow small animal phobia sufferers to confront and interact with their phobic animals with the lowest possible level of anxiety in a fun environment. Spiders and cockroaches were chosen as the animals for the project because of the high prevalence of spider and cockroach phobias in the world population.

The purpose and the design motivation of the *Catch Me* game corresponds to active psycho-education. The game aims to encourage active learning of self-efficacy belief and adapted strategies of interaction with feared animals within a highly innovative, fun, and easily accessible, controlled environment. While participating in the games, patients have the opportunity to discover information about the feared animals, to engage themselves in confrontation with the animals, and to test their capacities regarding the animals.

The games correspond to learning adaptive strategies and psycho-educative objectives. The games allow participants to learn information about the animal (e.g. its characteristics such as physical appearance, movement), and how to behave when they are surprised by an animal found in a familiar environment). Specifically, in *Catch Me* game the participant has to catch walking animals with a mug and drag them to the zone where they will stay captured (see Figure 1). Every four animals captured, information about the specific animal appears (e.g. the potential danger of the animal; the particular function of its anatomical characteristics; its function in the ecosystem). More specifically, there are 10 different levels of play (0-9). The highest level corresponds to the highest velocity of animals moving around the virtual kitchen. The velocity increments gradually according to each level. Every 12 seconds 8 new bugs appear. Each game lasts 60 seconds, after which a message appears with a number of captured animals. Also, every 4 bugs a psycho-educative messages are displayed such as "You just feed a tarantula!" or "99% of cockroaches are harmless to man".

The therapist's function is to model the adapted behavior by first demonstrating the interaction with the animal and then guiding the participant through the different parts of the games. The therapist can also change the velocity in which the animals appear so that the exposure to the animals can be gradual.

4.5   Procedure

When the participants arrived to the laboratory, they responded to both a demographic questionnaire and a diagnostic questionnaire (i.e., spider and cockroach fear and avoidance questionnaires). Once the level of anxiety and avoidance of each participant was established, the participants were informed about the objectives of the study, and they completed a consent form, a pre-test self-efficacy belief questionnaire, and a pre-test knowledge questionnaire. Afterwards, they played the game for approximately 2 minutes. The game was played first by the researcher, and then the participant was invited to repeat the exercise. Throughout the game, each participant was asked twice (i.e., at the beginning and at the end of the game) about his/her anxiety regarding the feared animal. At the end of the session, the participants filled out the post-test knowledge questionnaire, the appeal questionnaire, the post-test self-efficacy belief questionnaire. The session lasted approximately 15 minutes.

4.6   Data Analysis

To explore the potential differences in terms of knowledge acquisition, self-efficacy scores, and anxiety level between before and after the game session, a Wilcoxon analysis was used. In order to obtain an appeal score for both participants and therapists, a global score for each dimension as well as a global satisfaction score was calculated and a descriptive analysis was applied. All of the analyses were performed using the SPSS 17.0 application with the alpha level set at 0.05.

5   Results

5.1   Anxiety Level, Self-efficacy Belief, and Knowledge Acquisition

As Figure 2 shows, both self-efficacy belief regarding the capacity of the participants to confront themselves to the phobic stimuli, and knowledge regarding information about the phobic stimuli increased significantly after playing the *Catch Me* game (Z=-2.810; p=.005; and Z=-3.238; p<.001, respectively). Moreover, although the anxiety level of participants in the beginning of the game (M=1.77; SD=1.83) was not very high due to characteristics of the population (i.e., a non-clinical population). Still the anxiety level decreased significantly after the game (Z=-2.414; p=.016) which might show the efficacy of the game as an exposure exercise.

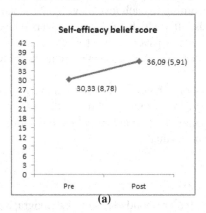
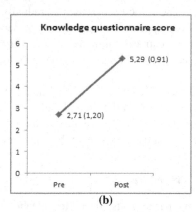

(a)   **(b)**

Fig. 2. (a) Self-efficacy score (out of 42) and (b) knowledge questionnaire score (out of 6) before and after playing *Catch Me* game

5.2   Participants' and Therapists' Appeal

In order to study the impact of the game on the appeal to participants, six scores for each dimension and a global score were calculated for each participant (see Table 1). The results show that, on the general level, participants were highly satisfied with the game.

Table 1. Mean score (out of 7) for the participants' appeal questionnaire

Dimension	Mean (Standard deviation)
Perceived usefulness	6.24 (0.66)
Therapeutic value	6.21 (0.75)
Involvement	6.02 (1.03)
Motivation	5.90 (0.98)
Fun	5.90 (1.07)
Intention to use	6.14 (1.13)
Total satisfaction	6.07 (0.83)

Regarding the therapists appeal, both the system and the *Catch Me* game received very good comments. The therapists strongly agreed (M=6.09 out of 7, SD=1.41) that the system brings some additional value to existent technology-mediated therapies (i.e., VR or AR) or traditional therapy (i.e., in vivo exposure therapy). Moreover, the therapists consider that the system will provide similar clinical efficacy as other therapies (i.e., VR, AR, in vivo exposure therapies), and that it will facilitate their work as therapists (M=6.25 out of 7, SD=0.96; M=6.25 out of 7, SD=0.96, respectively). Regarding the game, the therapists agreed that the game was fun (M=5.50 out of 7, SD=1.23), useful for patients (M=6.00 out of 7, SD=1.16), and that the game brought something new and positive to the therapeutic session (M=6.00 out of 7, SD=1.41) and could motivate patients to participate in the therapy (M=6.25 out of 7, SD=0.96).

6   Discussion and Conclusions

This study presents a therapeutic game and evaluates its influence on appeal, anxiety level, self-efficacy belief, and knowledge acquisition as a part of small animal phobia treatment. The main conclusions and their implications for Mental Health care are discussed below.

First, the evaluation showed a significant influence of the therapeutic game on self-efficacy belief. This allows us to assume that the game migh bring a significant contribution to the therapeutic sessions. Self-efficacy belief is defined by Bandura (1994) as determinant of how people think, behave, and feel. Specifically, one's belief in one's ability to succeed in specific situations such as confrontation with a feared cockroach or spider can play a major role and influence the way in which the person approaches goals, tasks, and challenges [27].

Also, participants' appeal scores were very high (i.e., global satisfaction was around 6 out of 7). The participants strongly agreed that the game was useful, had a therapeutic value for the phobic sufferers, and was fun. Furthermore, in the participants' opinion, the game was motivating, and they were willing to participate more frequently in this type of session if they could. Although the results were obtained only with a non-clinical population we still managed to obtain some interesting results. First, the game significantly increased knowledge about the feared animal, which allows us to conclude that the game is effective in transmitting important information about feared animal characteristics and functions to participants, which responds to the psycho-educative objective of the therapeutic session. Second, the game significantly reduced the feeling of anxiety between the beginning and the end of the game. Although the anxiety scores were not high as in other studies with clinical population (e.g. 9 out of 10 at the beginning of the session; [21]), our results demonstrate a similar tendency to decrease anxiety. Therefore, these results together with the self-efficacy belief results lead us to assume that the game has a potential to be clinically valid and provide an interesting tool to complement the therapeutic session before the exposure or as a homework assignment after the exposure.

This study has certain limitations. First of all, this pilot study should be confirmed with a larger sample. Also, the evaluation of the therapeutic game was performed with a non-clinical population due to ethical issues; thus, before drawing the final conclusions an evaluation with a clinical population must be done. Other issues related to the evaluation of the learning effectiveness should be studied further. In our study, only a declarative type of knowledge (facts) was tested in the knowledge questionnaire. However, the learning process also involves procedures of how to perform the described action, namely procedural knowledge (e.g. how to catch the feared animal) as well as attitudes that correspond to the transfer of learned information to other situations, namely strategic knowledge (e.g. emotional regulation strategies such as respiration exercises during the stressful situation). Thus, learning about the feared animals is not only learning about their characteristics and functions, it is also learning about how to manage the situation when one is confronted with the animal, and how to apply this knowledge to other stressful situations. Finally, a comparative study with a control group would be suitable.

This study shows that *Catch Me* game is a potentially effective tool for helping in the treatment of small animal phobias as well as satisfying, and engaging patients in the therapeutic process. This result is one of the crucial aspects in the learning process of adaptive strategies during the therapeutic process. New technologies used in the Mental Health field must be carefully chosen and applied not only to help the patient to enjoy an emotionally difficult situation a little bit more but also to assist the therapist in supporting and guiding the patient in this task. This pilot study shows that the *Catch Me* game satisfy both potential patients and therapists needs.

Therapeutic games bring new possibilities to the daily practice of therapists and their patients. However, only a few authors have begun to address these issues in empirical studies. Therefore, a deeper understanding of therapeutic games in the mental health field is needed. We believe that this study is a first step in understanding therapeutic game issues in the context of mental disorders.

Acknowledgements. We would like to thank all of the participants for their involvment in the experiment. We would also like to express special gratitude to the therapists (Maria Angeles Pérez Ara; Antonio Riera López del Amo; and Ernestina Etchemendy) for their help in the study. This study was funded by Ministerio de Educación y Ciencia Spain, Project Game Teen (TIN2010-20187). It was also partially founded by the Consolider-C (SEJ2006-14301/PSIC), "CIBER of Physiopathology of Obesity and Nutrition, an initiative of ISCIII" project; and the Excellence Research Program PROMETEO project (Generalitat Valenciana. Conselleria de Educación, 2008-157).

References

1. Coyle, D., Doherty, G.: Clinical evaluations and collaborative design: developing new technologies for mental healthcare interventions. In: Proceedings of CHI, pp. 2051–2060 (2009)

2. Öst, L.G., Ollendick, T.H.: Manual for the one-session treatment of specific phobias in children and adolescents (2001) (unpublished manual)
3. Janett, C., Cox, A.L., Cairns, P., Dhoparee, S., Epps, A., Tijs, T., Walton, A.: Measuring and defining the experience of immersion in games. International Journal of Human-Computer Studies 66, 641–661 (2008)
4. Van Hout, W.J.P.J., Emmelkamp, P.M.G.: Exposure in Vivo Therapy. Encyclopedia of Psychotherapy, 761–768 (2003)
5. Meyerbröker, K., Emmelkamp, P.M.G.: Virtual Reality Exposure Therapy in Anxiety Disorders: A Systematic Review of Process-And-Outcome Studies. Depression and Anxiety 27, 933–944 (2010)
6. Botella, C., Bretón-López, J.M., Quero, S., Baños, R.M., García-Palacios, A.: Treating Cockroach Phobia with Augmented Reality. Behavior Therapy 41(3), 401–413 (2010)
7. Juan, M.C., Pérez, D.: Using augmented and virtual reality for the development of acrophobic scenarios. Comparison of the Levels of Presence and Anxiety. Computers & Graphics 34, 756–766 (2010)
8. St-Jacques, J., Bouchard, S., Bélanger, C.: Is Virtual Reality Effective to Motivate and Raise Interest in Phobic Children Toward Therapy? A Clinical Trial Study of In Vivo With In Virtuo Versus In Vivo Only Treatment Exposure. Journal of Clinical Psychiatry 71(7), 924–931 (2010)
9. Oblinger, D.: The next generation of educational engagement. Journal of Interactive Media in Education 8, 1–18 (2004)
10. Kronenberger, W.G., Mathews, V.P., Dunn, D.W., Wang, Y., Wood, E.A., Giauque, A.L., et al.: Media violence exposure and executive functioning in aggressive and control adolescence. Journal of Clinical Psychology 61(6), 725–737 (2005)
11. Wrzesien, M., Alcañiz Raya, M.: Learning in serious virtual worlds: Evaluation of learning effectiveness and appeal to students in the E-Junior project. Computers and Education 55(1), 178–187 (2010)
12. Baños, R., Cebolla, A., Frías, A., Etchemendy, E., Botella, C., García Palacios, A., et al.: The ETIOBE MATES: A Serious Game platform to improve the learning of nutritional information in children. In: Proceedings of 14th Annual Cybertherapy and CyberPsychology Conference (2009)
13. Ceranoglu, T.A.: Video Games in Psychotherapy. Review of General Psychology 14(2), 141–146 (2010)
14. Parsons, S., Mitchell, P., Leonard, A.: The use and understanding of virtual environments by adolescents with autistic spectrum disorders. Journal of Autism and Development Disorders 34(4), 449–466 (2004)
15. Sharry, J., McDermott, M., Condron, J.: Relax To Win: Treating children with anxiety problems with a biofeedback video game. Eisteach 2(25), 22–26 (2003)
16. Nagarajan, S.S., Wang, X., Merzenich, M.M., Schreiner, C.E., Johnston, P., Jenkins, P., et al.: Speech modifications algorithms used for training language learning-impaired children. IEEE Transactions on Rehabilitation Engineering 6(3), 257–268 (1998)
17. Coyle, D., McGlade, N., Doherty, G., O'Reilly, G.: Exploratory evaluations of a computer game supporting cognitive behavioural therapy for adolescents. In: Proceedings of CHI, pp. 2937–2946 (2011)
18. Foa, E.B., Kozak, M.J.: Emotional processing of fear: Exposure to corrective information. Psychological Bulletin 99, 20–35 (1986)
19. Bandura, A.: Self-efficacy: Toward a unifying theory of behavioral change. Psychological Review 84, 191–215 (1977)

20. Frankl, V.E.: Paradoxical intention: A logotherapeutic technique. American Journal of Psychotherapy 14, 520–535 (1960)
21. Botella, C., Breton-López, J., Quero, S., Baños, R.M., García-Palacios, A., Zaragoza, I., Alcaniz, M.: Treating cockroach phobia using a serious game on a mobile phone and augmented reality exposure: A single case study. Computers in Human Behaviour 27(1), 217–227 (2011)
22. Durkin, K., Barber, B.: Not so doomed: Computer game play and positive adolescent development. Applied Developmental Psychology 23(4), 373–392 (2002)
23. Szymanski, J., O'Donohue, W.: Fear of spiders questionnaire. Journal of Behavior Therapy and Experimental Psychiatry 26, 31–34 (1995)
24. Wolpe, J.: The practice of behavior therapy. Pergamon Press, New York (1969)
25. Schwarzer, R., Renner, B.: Social-cognitive predictors of health behavior: Action self-efficacy and coping self-efficacy. Health Psychology 19, 487–495 (2000)
26. Wrzesien, M., Alcañiz Raya, M., Botella, C., Burkhardt, J.M., Breton-López, J., Ortega, M., Beneito Brotons, D.: The Therapeutic Lamp: Treating Small- Animal Phobias. IEEE Computer Graphics and Applications 33(1), 80–86 (2013)
27. Luszczynska, A., Schwarzer, R.: Social cognitive theory. In: Conner, M., Norman, P. (eds.) Predicting Health Behaviour, 2nd edn., pp. 127–169. Open University Press, Buckingham (2005)

Effect of Ecological Gestures on the Immersion of the Player in a Serious Game

Nicolas Bourgault, Bruno Bouchard, and Bob-Antoine J. Menelas

LIARA Laboratory,
LAIMI Laboratory,
University of Quebec at Chicoutimi (UQAC),
555 boulevard Universite, Saguenay (QC), G7H 2B1, Canada
{Nicolas1.Bourgault,Bruno.Bouchard,bamenela}@uqac.ca

Abstract. In the last decade, several researches have promoted the use of serious games in the medical field. Such solutions are generally played with ecological interfaces in order to attract elderly. It is unclear whether or not these controllers make their respective games more immersive. In this paper, we report the first step of our ongoing research toward the understanding of the relationship between the use of tangible interface with ecological gesture recognition and the immersion level of a serious game adapted for individuals affected by Alzheimer's disease. This first step of our project aimed at investigating the impact of such an interface with healthy people. Initial results suggest that the use of such a controller does not impact the immersion score of the game. Nevertheless, findings indicate it may increase the immersion score when the player has not an extensive contact with video games.

1   Introduction

The world population is ageing at an alarming rate while Alzheimer's disease (AD) becomes a major issue in elder population [1]. Notably, the amount of people diagnosed with AD should quadruple between 2006 and 2015 [2]. This will in turn multiply the cost associated to the support of those afflicted by AD, which had already reached more than 142 billion in 2005 in the United States alone [3]. On the bright side, solutions to slow down the apparition of AD and its impact on cognition or help AD patient to retain their autonomy for a longer period of time may reduce those costs significantly [2]. One of those solutions used in the later case is the use of an Intelligent Habitat (IH) to provide assistance to the cognitively disabled adults [4]. IH allows individuals to remain autonomous longer and also to keep caretakers informed on the situation of the tenant, reducing their burden [5]. The main downside to the IH is its hampered accessibility due to its relatively high cost and the fact that it is mostly a reactive solution. A more accessible and active solution is in the use of a serious game that can slow down the AD's effects on cognition trough training [6]. Guidelines surrounding the design of such games [7] concluded that using a tangible interface with ecological gesture recognition could be beneficial for the user. In particular,

M. Ma et al. (Eds.): SGDA 2014, LNCS 8778, pp. 21–33, 2014.
© Springer International Publishing Switzerland 2014

it is expected that the use of multimodal interfaces may take better advantage of the perceptual capabilities of human beings [8, 9, 10].

It is known that immersion is an important factor in a training game as it helps maintain the interest of the player, making him less likely to stop using it. Considering the definition of immersion proposed by Slater: *"the objective level of sensory fidelity a system provides"* [11], it is plausible to expect that the use of a controller with ecological gesture recognition capabilities will increase the immersion level of a serious game. However, the relationship between the use of such a tangible interface and immersion remains unknown. Our research project aims at investigating this relationship in the context of a serious game adapted to AD patients. This paper reports the first step toward this goal, as we target this point throughout experimentation with healthy people using a serious game originally designed for people suffering from AD. Namely, participants are invited to prepare a cup of coffee in a virtual world either by using mouse interactions or ecological interactions thanks to a Wiimote.

This paper is organized as follows. Section II presents a brief related works regards the used of tangible interfaces in video games. Section III describes our implementation of a serious game adapted to AD patients. Section IV details the tests we have made with the developed prototype in order to evaluate the impact of ecological gestures on the immersion level. Finally, section V concludes this paper with some final thoughts on our work.

2   Related Work

Several researches surrounding serious games that can be played with a tangible interface using gesture recognition happened during the last few years. For instance, Boyle et al. [12] tried to establish if the use of a Wiimote and gesture recognition out of a medical context could help to improve motor skills while performing surgical tasks. To do so, they compared the performance of basic laparoscopic tasks of novices with that of a control group after giving them a week of structured practice sessions playing a game on the Nintendo Wii. The group who had played the Wii has shown a significant improvement over the control group in one of the task that had to be performed. Moreover, while the result were not deemed significant, their overall performance was also better than that of the control group. These results led them to conclude that longer period of training may yield even better results over time.

Another case of serious games using gesture recognition are those developed by Burke et al. [13]. Stroke rehabilitation exercises are usually long and repetitive in nature, leading to some problems with the stroke survivors' motivation and engagement. In order to remedy to this problem, Burke et al. [13] created three immersive games working with a webcam utilising arm gestures recognition and detection. The games themselves were generally played by moving the arms towards an objective on the screen and also had some level of immersion as the player could see themselves in the game as recorded per the webcam. Burke et al. [13] first play tested the game with 10 able-bodied users to obtain feedbacks on their system and fine tune its experience before doing similar tests with three stroke survivors suffering varying degrees of impairment. All three participants agreed that the games were enjoyable (giving them a rating of 9 or 10 out of 10), easy to learn, challenging, sufficiently varied and re-playable. While they did not play test the games with a lot of people, these results show the success of video games using gesture recognition to help motivate and en-gage the players.

In order to study 3D interaction techniques in video games, Katzourin et al. [14] created an immersive game using a virtual reality CUBE system at Brown University. To play that game, users had to use three devices with six degrees of freedom to cap-ture his orientation, the position of his head and that of his hands. All interactions in the game are made using ecological gestures. For instance, swinging your hand lets you swing your sword in the same way in the virtual environment. The goal is to sur-vive as long as possible against waves of ever-spawning enemies. According to Katzourin et al. [14], "more than 50 people" tested the game. Initial reactions to its control scheme were positive, even for people who had no prior experience with vir-tual reality systems and playing video games in general, who were still able to get accustomed to game in roughly five minutes.

In conclusion, current studies tend to show that the use of an interface with ecologi-cal gesture recognition capabilities yields benefit for the users. They can learn to control an immersive game really quick, improve their skills for some types of tasks and be more motivated to exercise via a serious game. We can also note that all the games men-tioned above seemed to have a certain degree of immersion. Many other serious games employing tangible interfaces and ecological gestures recognition exist. A recent re-search, presented by Garcia Marin et al. [15] have listed and analysed over a dozen more of them made to help the physical rehabilitation of stroke survivors. They have described and categorised each of them according to various criteria including the tech-nology used and the methods of interaction employed. However, just like with the previous games presented in this paper, none of them explore the link that may exist between the use of an interface with ecological gesture recognition capabilities and the immersive aspect of the game. Our work aims at studying this aspect.

3   Serious Game with Ecological Gestures

As saw throughout the review, there are quite a few immersive serious games that exploit an interface with gesture recognition capabilities. While realized researches tend to suggest that the use of such a controller may be beneficial, none of them al-lows us to clearly determine what its impacts are on the immersion level of a serious game. To address this issue, we developed a serious game to which we added two different interaction modes. In a previous work, we have described a guideline for the design of serious games specially adapted to patient suffering from AD [7]. This guideline counts four different categories. It covers the following aspects: (i) choosing right in-game challenges, (ii) designing appropriate interaction mechanisms for cogni-tively impaired people, (iii) implementing artificial intelligence for providing adequate assistive prompting and dynamic difficulty adjustments, (iv) producing ef-fective visual and auditory assets to maximize cognitive training. Here we described the developed game.

Figure 1 presents a screenshot of one of our game prototype. This prototype was built using the Unity3D 4.3 game engine. The goal of the game is to add sugar, hot water, milk and instant coffee to the cup before stirring, regardless of the order in which they are added.

Figure 2 shows the action sequences that need to be done in order to complete the game. Trying to interact with the kettle for the first time will activate it. In any other case, interacting with an object in the scene will pick it up in order to use it with another. For instance, interacting with the spoon will pick it up. Trying to interact with the instant coffee pot afterward will start the action to scoop some instant coffee from it. Trying to interact with the background will put the object that was picked up back on the counter. If the player tries to make an interaction between two objects that is not available or useful to complete the cup of instant coffee, a warning message will appear in the darkened zone at the bottom of the screen to inform him of his mistake.

3.1   Proposed Game

Every important action, like scooping some instant coffee with the spoon, is animated. Also, varied forms of feedback are given to inform the player of what is going on in the game. For instance, a timer appears the first time the players clicks on the kettle to indicate it has been activated and is now boiling water. Thereafter, a small sound can be heard and a constant puff of steam can be seen emanating from the kettle's nose to indicate that the water inside is hot. Sound effects have been added for every action in the game to improve its realistic aspect and the appearance of the spoon and cup change visually throughout a game session.

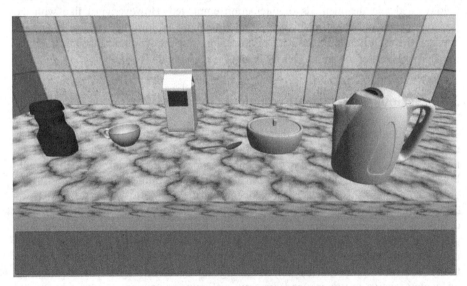

Fig. 1. The serious game prototype

Like we discussed, the kettle emits some steam once activated. The spoon will be empty or filled with grains of coffee or a cube of sugar depending on the player's progression. Finally, the cup will contain models to show all of the components added inside during the play through, as shown by Figure 3.

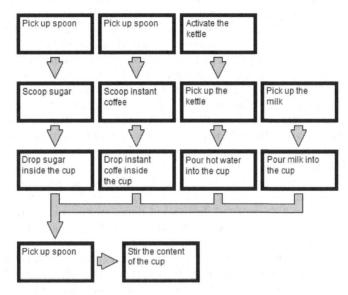

Fig. 2. Action sequence to complete the game

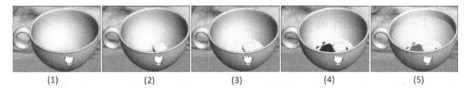

Fig. 3. Some states of the cup in our game: empty (1), containing a cube of sugar (2), containing both a cube of sugar with some milk (3), containing the two previous ingredients plus some instant coffee (4) and finally containing all the required components to complete the game: hot water, sugar, instant coffee and milk (5).

3.2   Interaction Mode

Mouse/keyboard Based Interactions
As the name suggests, this mode exploits a computer mouse and functions with the well know point-and-click paradigm. As such, it is really easy to understand. The user can click on any object to activate it or take it to interact with another.

Wiimote Based Interactions
This mode allows ecological interactions with the help of a *Nintendo Wiimote* and two libraries. The first software we use is *GlovePIE*. *GlovePIE* allows us to interface the *Wiimote's* controls with those of the computer's mouse, saving us the trouble of

interpreting the Bluetooth messages of the remote's button states that will be used in the same way as a simple click. Also, it can send Open Sound Control (OSC) message to other software. The second software we used is a small Java application we called *WiiMotion*. *Wiimotion* implements a gesture recognition engine known as *WiiGee* with a UI to load and save sets of gestures that were trained to be recognised. The WiiGee engine was also modified in order to receive the *Wiimote*'s reports by OSC rather than through Bluetooth communication. Finally, *WiiMotion* can send the results of its gesture recognition to another software through OSC, just like *GlovePIE*.

Figure 4 shows how all of those software interact with each other. *GlovePIE* first connects with the *Wiimote*. Then, it interfaces its control and calculates the cursor's position on screen for the Operating System (OS). The cursor's position is obtained with the orientation of the Wiimote and the data from its infrared camera. At last, *GlovePIE* sends an OSC message to *WiiMotion* containing the *Wiimote's* data report. *WiiMotion* then uses that data to determine whether or not the player is trying to have his gestures recognised. If he does, *WiiMotion* then informs the serious games thanks to another OSC message.

Once inside the game, the controls are as follow. Moving the cursor around is done by pointing at the screen with the *Wiimote*, selecting or activating objects in the scene requires pushing the *Wiimote*'s "+" button and doing an important action requires pressing and holding the *Wiimote*'s "B" button while performing a gesture. The gestures recognised in our prototype are "pouring" a liquid, "scooping" something with a spoon and "dropping" the contents of a spoon. These gestures were selected because they did not impose too much strain on the wrist and felt ecological even while holding a *Wiimote*. Figure 5 shows the *"pouring"* gesture. Each gesture is used at least twice during a play through of the game.

4   Experimentation

In this experimentation, participants were invited to play the game described previously. They were asked to prepare a cup of instant coffee with milk and sugar before being introduced to the game itself and given a short explanation of the controls. We conducted an experiment over two weeks with both interaction modes.

4.1   Participants

A total of 40 healthy participants aged between 19 and 43, with an average of 24 years old, were asked to participate. 11 participants were women and 30 were undergraduate students. Participants were separated into two distinct groups of 20 persons: A and B. Group A has to experiment the mouse and keyboard interaction while those of group B have to play with the *Wiimote* using ecological gesture recognition. This between subjects design was preferred over a within-subjects design to prevent learning effects that would results in playing the game with both interaction modes.

All participants answered a pre-experimental questionnaire in order to determine their level of contact with video games in general and, in the case of group B, their

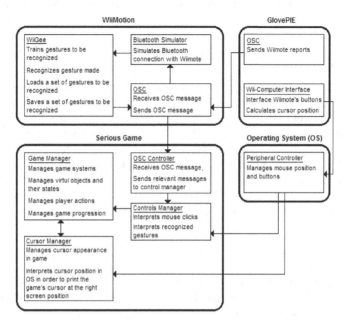

Fig. 4. Serious game with gesture recognition system

Fig. 5. Realisation of the *Pourring gesture*, using the *Nintendo Wiimote*; being a dynamic gesture, three different instants are illustrated.

Fig. 6. Picture of our setup and of a participant using a Nintendo Wiimote with ecological gestures recognition

level of experience with the Nintendo Wii. Figure 7 and 8 present the results obtained. 26 participants had a frequent or very frequent level of contact with video games and 14 participants in group B had at least an average level of experience with the Nintendo Wii.

4.2   Setup

Participants played our prototype using a desktop computer equipped with a 3.2 Ghz Intel Xeon E31235 processor, an NVIDIA Quadro 400 graphic card, a Solid State Drive and 16 Go of RAM. The game ran on a 21 inches widescreen display at a resolution of 1680 by 1050 pixels under Windows 7 (x86) SP1 business edition. To play with the first method of interaction of our game, a Nintendo Wiimote model RVL(M)-2 with a "Wii Motion Plus" extension, a Kinivo BTD-300 Blutooth dongle and a generic USB sensor bar with 6 lights were also used. The sensor bar was tapped under the monitor. The participants using the second method of interaction used a generic Dell computer mouse. Figure 6 shows our complete setup.

4.3   Procedure

Each participant was first met in our lab for a short briefing and explanation of the task to complete. In the case of group B, participants were shown the gesture that could be recognised by the game and got to practice them three times each. The players then had to complete the game. During this period, a supervisor took note of their actions and reactions to the game and was tasked to not help the players unless they were stuck for more than two minutes or outright gave up, ending their play through. Once the game was finished, participants were invited to answer a lengthy form about their experience. Proposed questions were based on the questionnaire developed by Jenette et al. [16] in order to identify the immersion level of a video game. Doing so, we want to assess the impact of using a tangible interface with ecological gestures recognition on the immersive aspect of a serious game.

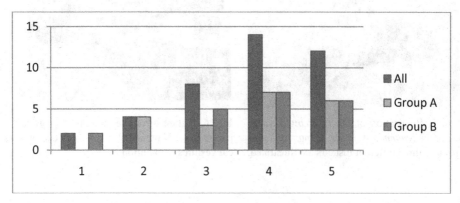

Fig. 7. Level of contact with video games in general among participants

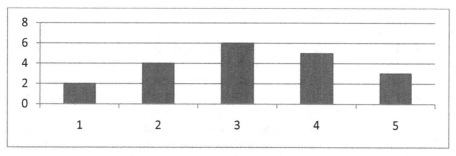

Fig. 8. Level of experience with the Nintendo Wii amongst participants in group B

4.4   Results and Discussion

All participants successfully completed the game without receiving any help despite the fact that 45% of them do not drink coffee or had never before prepared an instant coffee. It is also important to note that the gestures recognition rate was higher than 84% in group B.

Initial results for our experiment showed that the average immersion score (out of 100) was 48,85 for group A and 48,65 for group B. These results would tend to show that there are no relationship between using a tangible interface with ecological gesture recognition and immersion. To make sure, we analysed in detail the results of our questionnaire as well as the immersion score of each group when compared to other metrics we obtained concerning our participants.

Question	1	2	3	4	5	6	7	8	9	10	11
AverageDifference	0,1	0,05	0,35	0,15	0,6	0,1	0,65	0,7	0,4	0,05	0,05

Question	12	13	14	15	16	17	18	19	20	21	22
AverageDifference	0,25	0,1	0,1	0,25	0,15	0,5	0,15	0,2	0,2	0,1	0,3

Question	23	24	25	26	27	28	29	30	31		
AverageDifference	0,4	0,3	0,15	0,25	0,35	0,4	0,45	0,25	0,05		

Fig. 9. Average difference between average answer of both group for each question pertaining to presence in our serious game

The questionnaire pertaining to the immersion score of the game is formed of 31 questions concerning the effect of presence felt by the player during the experiment. This includes questions such as "To what extend did you lose track of time?", "To what extend did you feel consciously aware of being in the real world whilst playing?" and "To what extent did you feel as though you were moving through the game according to your own will?". Answers were on a five points scale. We compared the average results of each group for each question in order to determine if the controllers had a different level of impact on some aspect of presence.

Figure 9 presents the resulting average difference for each question. We noticed that there was no particular difference between the average results obtained for each group. Furthermore, for the questions with the biggest difference in average result, question 7 and 8, results tended to favor the mouse as the most immersive controller. As such, with the tested population, we were not able to establish the relationship between the use of a tangible interface with ecological gesture recognition and immersion by analysing these individual questions' average results.

Figure 10 shows the average immersion score for participants depending on their level of contact with video games. Meanwhile, figure 11 shows the number of participant in each group according to their level of contact with video games. We can see that immersion score was indeed higher in the case of participants with an average level of contact with video games in general. Also, for participants with no contact in group B, we observed that the immersion level is very high when compared to those with a frequent level. Because of the small amount of individuals that were in that category (2 persons), we cannot draw any solid conclusion from that observation. Nevertheless, one has to note that this point has been supported by many previous researches that showed that people with less experience with video games tend to be more likely to give credit in the virtual environment [17]. As such, for people who have been less exposed to video games, such point suggests that proposed ecological interactions may have positive impacts on the level of immersion of the users.

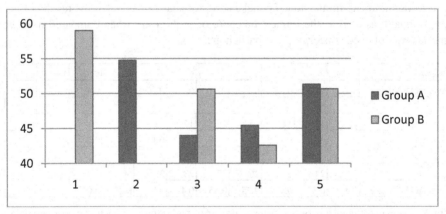

Fig. 10. Average immersion scores depending on level of contact with video games from 1 to 5 (1 stands for no contact and 5 for very frequent contact)

Group/ Level of contact with video games	None	Some	Average	Frequent	Very frequent
Group A	0	4	3	7	6
Group B	2	0	5	7	6

Fig. 11. Number of participants in each group according to their level of contact with video games

Figure 12 presents the average immersion score based on gender for both group. Whereas men and women had average immersion scores of 49,35 and 47,66 respectively in group A, those in group B had scores of 45,26 and 58,8 instead. The difference between scores in this case is different by more than 15% in the case of women. Nevertheless, group A consisted of 6 women and group B of 5 while each of them had even more men participants, numbering at 14 and 15 respectively. As such, these results cannot allow us to conclude with certainty that adding a physical controller with ecological gesture recognition improves immersion amongst women. The results presented may be interpreted in different ways. For one, they show the possibility that the interaction technique used in a game does not bear much of an impact on its immersion score. In that case, it would be normal for the average immersion score of both of our group to be similar. Another possible explanation is that the computer mouse simply affects the immersion level of a game about as much as a *Wiimote* with ecological interaction does. We believe that in our case, the result may have been similar due to the discomfort some of our users may have felt using the *Wiimote*. Even though most of participants in group B had a good level of experience with the Nintendo Wii, a few of them looked like they had some trouble using the controller during the experiment. Such difficulty was not observed with group A. Participants in group B having a harder time using their interface may have led to a diminished experience of the game's immersion. Adjustments should be made to our prototype in order to facilitate the use of the *Wiimote* along with further experiment in order to validate this new hypothesis.

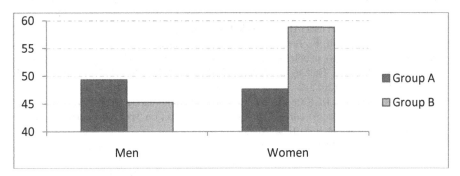

Fig. 12. Average immersion score for both groups depending on gender

5   Conclusion

This work aimed at studying the impact of ecological gestures on the immersion level of the player in a serious game. For this, we have developed a serious game based on the guidelines that we have proposed in previous work. The game supported two interactions mode: using a computer mouse or a *wiimote* controller. 40 young participants have taken part to the realised study. At this stage, it is impossible for us to clearly state the impacts of adding a controller with ecological gesture recognition on the immersion level in a serious game with healthy people. However, our results showed us that it may increase immersion depending on the level of contact that a player has with video games in general. Therefore, further experimentations are needed in order to explore the impact of such controllers when used by elderly and/or AD patients. We believe that immersion is one of the keys needed to make a game interesting and engaging. As such, we hope that this paper will encourage future work studying controller impact on immersion in order for us to better understand all of its aspects.

References

1. Vandewynckel, J., Otis, M.J.D., Bouchard, B., Menelas, B.-A.J.: Training adapted to alzheimer patients for reducing daily activities errors and cognitive decline. In: Ma, M., Oliveira, M.F., Petersen, S., Hauge, J.B. (eds.) SGDA 2013. LNCS, vol. 8101, pp. 28–36. Springer, Heidelberg (2013)
2. Brookmeyer, R., Johnson, E., Ziegler-Graham, K., Arrighi, H.M.: Forecasting the global burden of Alzheimer's disease. Alzheimer's & Dementia 3, 186–191 (2007)
3. Mebane-Sims, I.: 2009 Alzheimer's disease facts and figures. Alzheimer's & Dementia (2009)
4. Bouchard, B., Giroux, S., Bouzouane, A.: A keyhole plan recognition model for Alzheimer's patients: first results. Applied Artificial Intelligence 21, 623–658 (2007)
5. Pigot, H., Mayers, A., Giroux, S.: The intelligent habitat and everyday life activity support. In: 5th International Conference on Simulations in Biomedicine, pp. 507–516 (2003)
6. Imbeault, F., Bouchard, B., Bouzouane, A.: Serious games in cognitive training for Alzheimer's patients. In: 2011 IEEE 1st International Conference on Serious Games and Applications for Health (SeGAH), pp. 1–8. IEEE (2011)
7. Bouchard, B., Imbeault, F., Bouzouane, A., Menelas, B.-A.J.: Developing serious games specifically adapted to people suffering from alzheimer. In: Ma, M., Oliveira, M.F., Hauge, J.B., Duin, H., Thoben, K.-D. (eds.) SGDA 2012. LNCS, vol. 7528, pp. 243–254. Springer, Heidelberg (2012)
8. Menelas, B., Picinalli, L., Katz, B.F.G., Bourdot, P.: Audio haptic feedbacks for an acquisition task in a multi-target context. In: IEEE Symposium on 3D User Interfaces (3DUI) (2010), doi:10.1109/3DUI.2010.5444722
9. Menelas, B.-A., Otis, M.J.-D.: Design of a serious game for learning vibrotactile messages. In: IEEE International Workshop on Haptic Audio Visual Environments and Games (HAVE), October 8-9, pp. 124–129 (2012), doi:10.1109/HAVE.2012.6374446
10. Menelas, B.-A., Picinali, L., Bourdot, P., Katz, B.: Non-visual identification, localization, and selection of entities of interest in a 3d environment. Journal on Multimodal User Interfaces, 1–14 (2014), http://dx.doi.org/10.1007/s12193-014-0148-1
11. Bowman, D.A., Mcmahan, R.P.: Virtual reality: how much immersion is enough? Computer 40, 36–43 (2007)
12. Boyle, E., Kennedy, A.-M., Traynor, O., Hill, A.D.: Training Surgical Skills Using Non-surgical Tasks—Can Nintendo Wii™ Improve Surgical Performance? Journal of Surgical Education 68, 148–154 (2011)
13. Burke, J.W., Mcneill, M., Charles, D.K., Morrow, P.J., Crosbie, J.H., Mcdonough, S.M.: Optimising engagement for stroke rehabilitation using serious games. The Visual Computer 25, 1085–1099 (2009)

14. Katzourin, M., Ignatoff, D., Quirk, L., Laviola, J., Jenkins, O.C.: Swordplay: Innovating game development through VR. IEEE Computer Graphics and Applications 26, 15–19 (2006)
15. Garcia Marin, J., Felix Navarro, K., Lawrence, E.: Serious games to improve the physical health of the elderly: A categorization scheme. In: CENTRIC 2011, The Fourth International Conference on Advances in Human-oriented and Personalized Mechanisms, Technologies, and Services, pp. 64–71 (2011)
16. Jennett, C., Cox, A.L., Cairns, P., Dhoparee, S., Epps, A., Tijs, T., Walton, A.: Measuring and defining the experience of immersion in games. International Journal of Human-Computer Studies 66, 641–661 (2008)
17. Geslin, E., Bouchard, S., Richir, S.: Gamers' versus non-gamers' emotional response in virtual reality. Journal of CyberTherapy & Rehabilitation 4, 489–493 (2011)

Using Serious Games for Cognitive Disabilities

Rita Marques Tomé[1], João Madeiras Pereira[1], and Manuel Oliveira[2]

[1] Instituto Superior Técnico
Rua Alves Redol 9, 1000-029 Lisboa, Portugal
rita.tome@ist.utl.pt, jap@inesc-id.pt
[2] Highskillz, London, United Kingdom
manuel.oliveira@highskillz.com

Abstract. Serious games have increasingly become a good option with regards to professional training. However, the majority isn't appropriate for people with cognitive disabilities, since there are several obstacles when developing for such a heterogeneous population.

This paper's objective is to contribute for the development of serious games for people with cognitive disabilities by presenting a list of recommended design principles, collated from recent literature. A strong emphasis is placed on the adaptability of games since this is an important characteristic that ensures the game can be configured to fit to the needs of each player, minimizing the obstacles encountered and providing a personalized environment for learning.

In some cases cognitive disabilities can have motor control implications and consequently the traditional devices commonly used may not be the most appropriate for this population. In order to help developers choosing an adequate device, this paper also surveys and compares the most common devices used nowadays for serious games.

1 Introduction

Serious games' primary objective is not pure entertainment, but passing some kind of knowledge to the users. Typically they unfold in an environment that is a simulation of the real world, where the player must solve one or more problems.

By using this kind of games, the user can test several behaviours [1] that are considered too risky with undesirable consequences in the real world, either for the user's physical and psychological well-being or that of others. The user learns and develops the best approaches to the problem presented within the game and, as a consequence, when confronted by the same in a real situation, they have a greater probability to act accordingly [2]. Several studies (see section 2) show that there are many benefits from using serious games for rehabilitation of people with cognitive disabilities.

1.1 Serious Games and Cognitive Disabilities

In people with cognitive disabilities have difficulties, the functions of attention, memory, reasoning, language, perception, problem-solving, conceptualizing [3],

M. Ma et al. (Eds.): SGDA 2014, LNCS 8778, pp. 34–47, 2014.

self-regulation and social development [4] are impaired, not allowing the proper knowledge acquisition and competence development. Therefore, they have great difficulty in relating and learning concepts and behaviours. In addition, expressing themselves through writing or speaking is equally challenging, thus having implications at social level. As main examples of cognitive disabilities, we have Fragile X Syndrome, Down Syndrome (also known as Trisomy 21) and autism spectrum disorders (such as Asperger syndrome).

Individuals with such different characteristics than those we are used to deal with, will require, therefore, dedicated attention. Traditional teaching methods often do not apply because learners lose interest quicker and more easily than those not cognitively challenged. Also, we have to take into account that cognitively challenged people do not deal with pressure in the same way as others, being important to provide them not only the pressure-free environments traditional methods typically don't entail, as well as stimulating and innovative environments that capture their attention and motivate them to activities of learning [4,5,6]. This appears to be an untenable paradox, but the use of serious games is a viable solution. However, the vast majority of serious games can not be used by the cognitively challenged individuals because these games take advantage of capabilities that some of them don't have or that are not developed enough, such as reading and writing skills, identification of objects and colours, manual dexterity, among many others. Another barrier is that these games also do not provide the adequate interface and contents of the activities [7]. Even what has been specially developed with this focus is insufficient, since it is mostly simple didactic units and not full games [5], based on 2D graphics [6]. Most of them approach contents in a tightly scoped manner as in the case of like social skills (personal hygiene, appearance, clothes, kitchen utensils and rules), cognitive skills (colours, shapes, order, differences), written language and numeric skills (decimal numeration, addition, subtraction) [6], but let out ore complex situations like everyday work life.

The use of serious games is fairly accepted by this population because they do not feel the pressure existing in the real world, feeling comfortable to explore the virtual world. Furthermore, they feel that there is no risk in testing various behaviours at their own pace, obtaining an immediate feedback on their actions [3,4]. For a person with special needs, the risks are related to insecurity about their abilities, anxiety to deal with various situations and fear of social rejection when they fail to fulfill the tasks proposed. The risks can be disseminated through the repetition of tasks to be mastered, increasing the confidence of the individuals and thus improving the social relationships they establish with other people.

Most users with disabilities also have a (sometimes very high) attention deficit, which greatly hinders learning. The use of serious games has the advantage of being able to capture and keep their attention on the tasks, reducing this problem[1]. In addition to the advantages mentioned, the games allow the development of motor coordination and spatial orientation [2], [5], allow the represented situation to be played under the same conditions, can be adapted to individual person needs, can be interactive and used individually or in groups [4]. Also, since the computer is recognized as an important tool in our society, impaired people feel proud to be using it as well, having increased confidence and self-esteem [8].

2   State of the Art

In 1991, Burt et al. [9] published a report presenting the case studies of four adults with autism that participated in a work-training program, each one with widely varying inabilities to retain a job. Each person had a specifically developed training plan, meaning that the tasks proposed had in mind the inabilities of each one, but also their personality and their qualities. For instance, two people presented a ritualistic behaviour while walking and the approach to each case was quite different: one of the subjects was extremely time-conscious, therefore he was given a detailed task schedule as a form to control his ritualistic behaviours and encourage self-control; for the other subject with ritualistic behaviours, the best approach was to film him and other people walking, so that he could compare both ways. Despite the personalized approaches, both had also a checklist with the desired behaviour and rewards associated, in order to teach them self-control. This report shows us the need for adaptability and personalization of approaches, even if they are aimed for people with the same diagnosed pathologies. For instance, two users with Down syndrome may not react in the same way to a game (even if it is specially designed for people with Down syndrome), which depends on the disabilities they have but also in their interests and existent capabilities. The diagnosis of the pathology is a mere indicator of which characteristics the patients might present, and does not mandate that all patients present all characteristics. Therefore, in the next subsections we survey some recent serious games that define adaptability as an important feature and present the advantages and disadvantages of some of the most common devices.

2.1   Software Applications

eAdventure, by Torrente et al. [2], is a game platform specially designed for the development of games whose objective is to improve professional education of people with cognitive disabilities. In this project, two games were developed with eAdventure: "My first day at work" and "The big party", which are *point-and-click* adventure games. This game genre was chosen because it doesn't present many frequent accessibility barriers and has significant educational potential. Since reflection predominates over action, these games are low-paced and only require simple inputs, specifically mouse clicks. The game genre is an important factor towards a successful learning experience, since the choice of the wrong genre can actually worsen the users' condition. For example, First Person Shooters (FPS) games may have negative effects on people who have attention disorders and impulsivity [1]. It is noteworthy that the platform eAdventure also allows a personalized game experience, where the content and puzzles can be adapted and the complexity and number of objects present can be changed as needed.

In the game "My first day at work", it was noted that participants with severe disabilities had some trouble in remembering short-term goals, which suggested the need for a task-list feature accessible at all times in the game. Also, it was found that many users didn't identify themselves with the game, which is a problem, since they may not be able to play as they wouldn't understand what is going on in the game. The best solution would be to use the players' own images in the virtual avatar, but it was too complex to implement. In the game "My first day at work", the solution adopted for this problem was providing the player a set of avatars with different abilities and characteristics, from which they chose the one with whom they identified the most. As the game "The big party" was a first-person game, the players only chose their gender.

Although the game developed by Cagatay et al. [10] is focused on speech disorder children therapy, it has some interesting aspects, mainly the ability to adapt to the needs of each user, similarly to the work of Torrente et al. [2]. This can be achieved due to the hierarchical structure of the game, where "an object can be added to any scenario part, a scenario part can be added to any scenario, a scenario can be added to any story.". There are several characters available and 25 different objects, including trash can, swing, slide, balls and boats, which have their own functionalities. There are also a variety of scenarios, like a park or a child room. With this game, it is possible to arrange various interaction settings by changing the set of objects and characters to be included in a specific scenario. It is also possible to change the actions each object offers, such as the ball rolling or bouncing and the swing swinging. The variety of functionalities of each object increases the user's attention and avoids him/her getting bored.

A similar work was developed by Hussaan et al. [11], which created a system capable of generating adaptive scenarios taking into account the user's profile and the user's interaction traces. The interaction trace is the history of the user's interactions with a computer and allows to detect the evolution of the user's competence. With it, we can detect if the user is stuck in the game and, if they are, provide adequate help, like hints, or even modify the scenarios. Also, the system can adjust the level of difficulty of the game, so that it is not too simple neither too difficult, and make sure the same exercises are not repeated too many times. The user's profile is also useful to know which kind of resources a user prefers, giving primacy to their placement in the scenarios.

The application Picaa, developed by Fernández-López et al. [7], also allows this adaptation of the game characteristics to the user, specifically "the number of components or concepts to be taught, screen composition, screen position (rotation or not), multimedia used to represent the components, difficulty level (goals of the exercise, working out the punctuation), reinforcements and help to the users. This is done by means of a template, which specifies the adaptations necessary for each user, like in Table. 1.

If and when the activities are tried out don't fit the user needs, the user profile can be changed so that the software can be re-adapted to fit the user's needs.

Table 1. User impairments and possible adaptations [7]

User limitations	Adaptations
Visual	Colors, size, contrast, magnification.
	Do not use color as information
	Conversion of graphical information to text and use of voice synthesis
	User interface components accessible by means of mouse, keyboard or tactile device
Hearing	Alert sounds coded as text or graphic
	Adapted vocabulary
	Use of subtitles and language of gestures
Mobility	Adapted input and output devices
	Alternative selection of components (alt-keys, voice as input, scrolling...)
	Time of scrolling, time for user selection, pace of the application
Cognitive	Simple interface without distracting elements
	Priority use of graphics

Changes include the format of content to be accessible (image, text, sound), interaction with the content (requiring more or less fine motor skill), or screen size.

Bartolomé et al. [12] present a serious game used to promote social skills of people with neurological development disabilities. It is specially developed for people with attention deficit disorder, a very common characteristic in people with cognitive disabilities. An important aspect to consider is how the targeted users react to software: for the younger ones (10-13 years), the most attractive components in the game were the interface and the rewarding system (with medals); for the older adolescents (14-16 years), what was deemed most attractive were the dialogues and social interactions that caused more impact, probably because they were more familiarized with video games than the younger users. Considering the disparity of preferences in a group of children with ages relatively close to each other, one can expect an even greater disparity when considering an adult population, with a wider range of ages (15-64 years). Despite such comparison, designing video games for adults is actually very different from designing them for children, since each group has its own interests and way of thinking. This was clear in the study of Robertson and Hix [8], where the users (men and women aged 25 to 60) were confronted with a child's game. In the whole group, only one user was able to achieve the game objective. Another user didn't even try to play and two other simply said the game wasn't fun. Although, when they switched to Solitary (present in Windows operating system), their reactions were much more favourable, probably due to the fact that they perceived it as a game. Also, Solitaire has a feature that might seem very simple for common players, but that was very attractive to them: each time the cards are dealt, the pattern of the back of the card deck changed. It was a subtle visually attractiveness and, in addition, it also brought something new (but not too new) every time the game was played. It's important to notice that this change was subtle, otherwise some players could feel startled by it and not receptive to the game.

In general, users rejected action-based games and those games where it was required to avoid being attacked (since to their frustration, they were rapidly eliminated) but, on the other hand, Hangman, Wheel of Fortune and Solitaire were popular games among the group.

Total Challenge, by Martins et al. [4], is a serious game developed for people with mild to moderate intellectual disabilities that monitors their evolution with respect to memory, decision-making time, capacity of observation, learning and applying knowledge. It can be played both on-line and off-line. The greatest difference between both modes is that in the on-line mode, the player competes for a place in the on-line ranking, which usually results in higher motivation. In this mode, the rules (that is, maximum time response, number of rounds of each level) are the same for all players, depending on the level. However, for training purposes, the off-line mode is better because it allows the adjustment of the referred rules for a given user. The score acts as an incentive to achieve better results than the prior ones or better than other players, when playing on-line. When the player fails, it receives a motivation message encouraging him to play again and get a better score.

The feedback voice used in this game is friendly and fun and can be male or female, according to user preferences. Each feedback message is complemented with motivation or call attention phrases like "Congratulation, go like this" or "Be more attentive".

The studies presented in this section are briefly summarized in Table 2, thus providing a simple comparison of their main characteristics.

Table 2. Summary

	Game genre	Age range	Educational Benefits	Target pathologies	Adaptability
eAdventure	Point-and-Click	15-64	Professional Education	Cognitive disabilities	Yes
Speech disorder game	—	0-14	Speech therapy	Speech problems	Yes
Project CLES	Adventure	All	Cognitive skills	Cognitive disabilities	Yes
Wii Test Gaming	—	10-16	Social skills	Attention deficit disorder	Yes

2.2 Devices

Building successful games for the cognitively disabled is not only about the software, but also about the hardware that supports the interface. Consequently, it is important to study the usability appropriateness of the more common devices (eg. mouse, trackball and touch-screen) for the target user population. Robertson and Hix [8] revealed that with touch screen the drag-drop times were the fastest, whilst the trackball registered the lowest ones. Nevertheless, all users found the touch-screen tiring and the trackball was difficult to use, since it required participants to use both hands. Consequently, in this study, the mouse was the elected device for this population. However, in the study made by Urturi et al. [13], the participants were asked several questions about their preferences and was found that 70% of them prefer multi-touch screen to a screen with keyboard and 60%

like using tablets with big screens instead of smartphones. A similar situation was detected by Saleh et al. [14], where it was noted that children preferred to use the touch screen feature instead of keyboard and mouse. This means tablet devices were preferred, since they allow multi-touch gestures and engage more than one user at a time, which enriches the social experiences of the users.

Fernández-López et al. [7] introduce software applications for iPod touch, iPhone and iPad, mainly because of their positive features:

- High-quality responsiveness multi-touch screen without the need of a stylus - some cognitive disabled users don't have the necessary skills to work with a pencil or stylus. This can be bypassed by the touch, since it is a natural interaction that requires no learning;
- Mobility - perform activities anywhere at any time;
- Design - just one button at the front;
- Different interactions - rotations or shakes can be interpreted as a user input, thus creating innovating interactions thanks to the built-in accelerometer; make use of forward and backward facing cameras, microphones and multi-point touch-screen capabilities [15];
- Accessibility - devices offer high contrast function, zoom and a gesture-based screen reader;
- Connectivity - peer-to-peer connectivity using Apple Bonjour allows to create an ad-hoc Bluetooth or Wi-Fi network, which is useful in supporting group work;
- Ease of acquisition - can be bought in any shop; their success in the marketplace facilitates continuity over time for this family of devices; relatively inexpensive [15];

It was also pointed out that the iPad allows the use of applications with groups for which the iPod touch-screen was too small. In addition, due to the bigger screen size, there's more room for user interface elements, permitting to show larger items that make it easier to see and touch. Moreover, all of the mentioned devices are socially accepted [15] and have associated an entertainment status, which is crucial to captivate the users. In fact, in some cases, users prefer to use these devices instead of using low-tech options [15].

The review done by Kagohara et al. [15] concluded that iPods, iPhones, and iPads "can be successfully utilized within educational programs targeting academic, communication, employment, and leisure skills for individuals with developmental disabilities". On the other hand, it also indicated that some users showed difficulty in operating these devices with sufficient finesse/motor control to activate the desired functions, thus suggesting that this might not be the most adequate hardware solution for people with significant motor impairments, unless it can be integrated with other solutions.

As an hypothesis to bypass the accessibility obstacles disabled people often face, Alqahtani et al. [16] proposed the use of multimodal applications, which allows the users to choose one method of input between speech, text or point-and-click. The use of speech in applications has advantages like the development of more natural interfaces, hands free access and increased user satisfaction (because it is a multimodal interface). With this kind of interfaces, even the people who lack manual dexterity (a very common characteristic among cognitively disable people), can play the game. This way, the interface also serves as an inclusion tool.

Since video consoles are specifically designed for playing, they present good alternatives to more common devices, like computers or tablets [5]. Hereupon, it is noteworthy the use of the Nintendo™WiiMote, which helps to make the target application seem a video game and not a therapeutic tool and can be used to overcome the small size of some touch screens. It is an easy to learn tool and feels natural to the user, since it uses body movements. Even more important, it allows people with different levels of motor coordination to use the software, another characteristic that also varies a lot between people with cognitive disabilities [12].

In the same line of thought, Nintendo DS™ is also a good alternative to common devices, due to its features: resistant (designed for children - doesn't break or get scratched with ease); has a good autonomy, circa 11 hours; has large memory; and it's not very expensive. In addition it has two screens, which offers more interaction possibilities than only one screen; has wireless connectivity and can be used with other commercial games, thus acting as a reward mechanism [5].

Costa-Pazo et al. [17] compared some other devices according to their suitability for both motor and cognitive disabilities, as we can see, in a summarized way, in Fig.3.

Table 3. Suitability of Interface Devices [17]

Device \ Disability	Motor	Cognit
Trackball	*	*
Touchpad	*	
Joystick	*	*
Head mouse	*	*
Eye mouse	*	
Touch screen	*	*
Actigraph	*	*
Gesture remote	*	*

3   Design Principles

Based the analysis of several studies done in this area, we can establish a list of design principles recommended for an adequate development of serious games for cognitive disabilities, organized in 5 categories. This list aims to help understand which are the components in a video game that could influence the users, thus affecting their performance and their predisposition to learn.

3.1   Interface

(a) Design simply in simple layouts [4], [18,19] to increase concentration of the users in the new information being presented [3];

(b) Use of minimal screen items, since more complex items diminish the acceptance of the software as a game [12];

(c) The icons should be large [19], but not in excess. This helps users with fine motor skills difficulties [3];

(d) If the icons are too large, users are not sure about where to click [12];

(e) Use familiar symbols to the target population [3];

(f) Avoid the use of small objects in the game because they take some time to be recognized by the user [14];

(g) Grouping of icons should be logical and realistic [12];

(h) Icons should be properly spaced to avoid wrong selections [12];

(i) Instructions and buttons should be clearly displayed and always in the same place [3];

(j) Implement a fixed game window, as a way to prevent users from resizing it unintentionally (constitutes a cause of frustration) [12];

(k) The concept of menu bar might not be understood by the users, especially if it contains words, because some users may not be able to read them and understand the concept beyond [12];

(l) Don't use pull down menus, which are not understood by this population, due to motor control and cognitive problems [12];

(m) Colours should be in harmony with the overall interface, while ensuring sufficient contrast for people with limited vision [2], [14], [18];

(n) Changes in colour or graphical environment can help to maintain the user's interest for a longer time [1]. This can be done periodically or as a consequence of some user action;

(o) The game should require only simple commands to change the content easily [7], [19];

3.2   User Control

(a) Give enough time for the users to read and analyze the available information and to make decisions, since they react slowly and move icons with careful gestures [2], [7], [12], [18];

(b) Must be relatively slow games and not require the use of many controls [2];

(c) Should allow users to go back in the game - especially for users who have information processing and/or memory difficulties [3];

(d) Enable user customization based on user preference - enable to slow speed down, use keyboard access, etc. [3];

(e) Help users navigate, by informing them where they are. In order to do this, place navigation information at the same place (ensuring it is consistent and simple), use maps when appropriate, use home and back buttons and provide context information. Emphasis on the use of graphics [3];

(f) Design in ways that minimize the skills and abilities required to navigate [3];

3.3   Identification with the Game

(a) Must give the user a sense of identity, principally through the main character (gender, set of disabilities, physical characteristics, etc) and by creating interesting stories to users. They also evoke empathy and captivate the users [2], [20,21]; An example are the characters developed by Brandao et al. [22], Betinho and the baby Samuca;

(b) The game should provoke emotional reactions [21];

(c) Interaction mechanisms should be designed according to the profile and cognitive limitations of the player. The game should be as configurable as possible in order to meet the needs of everyone [2], [5], [7], [14];

(d) The game should be designed according to the cultural environment of the player [14] ;

3.4   Feedback

(a) Language should be simple (preferentially plain text), clear and direct [2], [18];

(b) Use native language [3];

(c) Avoid dense blocks of text [3];

(d) Every action should have feedback and it should be given through several ways: visual, auditive, subtitles or sign language [2], [18,19];

(e) Feedback can be given by numerical scores, progress bars, character dialogues, sound, vibration of the controller, etc [4];

(f) Since this population has communication difficulties at both vocabulary and comprehension levels, the feedback should use sounds, specifically spoken language [7];

(g) The feedback should take advantages of the stronger intelligences/capabilities of the user, which are used to improve the weaker ones [5];

(h) It must not create any kind of frustration, which is very negative to the player. The errors committed should be corrected without discouraging the user and without repetitively penalizing them for the same failure [5], [18];

(i) The feedback should be used as a rewarding mechanism that can provide the increase of motivation and satisfaction of the user, resulting in a higher desire to complete the tasks [4];

(j) The game should let the user commit errors and learn from them based on the game responses to the user's actions [14], [18], [21];

(k) The player should be recompensed for making the correct actions. This can be achieved by gifting him with things he likes, including: animations, musics, videos, points and objects in game (for example, trophies, clothes for the character, etc.) [1], [4], [5], [14];

(l) The value of the gift should depend on the users performance (based on the time spent on the game, number or correct selections, etc.) [14];

(m) The feedback can be related to the learn action/concept, improving the learning by imitation [5];

(n) Show the user's current results and the next problem to solve [18];

3.5   Transmission of Concepts

(a) Should be given preference to the use of photographs or realistic drawings, due to the difficulty of abstract thinking of this population. If the game is designed in a *cartoon* style, should be complemented with photographs and videos of real environments [2], [6], [12];

(b) The images used should have a large size [14];

(c) It's recommended the use of 3D graphics [6];

(d) The game should have good graphics because it captivates the users and its realism and similarity with reality facilitates the association between virtual and real world [2], [12], [18];

(e) The educational contents must be introduced in the game in a dissimulated way, causing an indirect learning and minimizing the cognitive load pace. This way, the game will be recognized by the users as such, not as an educational software. Therefore, the game should have objectives as a learning tool and objectives as a game [1], [5], [12], [18];

(f) Problem solving in the game must follow the same sequence it would have in the real world, in order to facilitate transfer of learning from the virtual world to the real world [2], [5], [18,19]

(g) The user should be guided step-by-step through the decision making process. This could be achieved using another character of the game, like the director of a Zoo [21];

(h) Actions should reflect real life situations, especially when manipulating objects. For instance, it is more realistic to drag-drop objects to select and move them, than just clicking on them [12];

(i) The learning process should be based in levels or missions, in which the degree of difficulty should increase gradually and the cognitive weakness should decrease [5], [14];

(j) "Work on the association of ideas, building relationships between concepts, sorting sequences of steps" - use the cause and effect paradigm [7];

(k) Including images and the respective name improves retention of the information [12];

(l) Preference is given to approaches with great interaction, contrasting with approaches with a lot of observing to do, but with an answer given with only on interaction (like a mouse click, for instance) [6], [7], [12], [18];

(m) Use animations, but avoid the ones that are too fast. Also, avoid the occurrence of too many actions in rapid succession because they can startle the users [12], [18];

(n) The game should offer a varying range of activities, to minimize fatigue or boredom [14], [18];

(o) Maintain balance between success and challenge [20]

(p) The game should transmit not only functional knowledge, but also social knowledge [14];

3.6   Accessibility

(a) Minimize skills needed to navigate within game [4];
(b) The more suitable game genre is a *point-and-click* adventure, since it has practically no accessibility barriers and has a significant educational potential [2];
(c) Don't include elements that can cause seizures, like elements that flash or have particular spatial frequencies [3];
(d) Use accessibility features, like sign language [18];
(e) Allow the use of different input devices, like mouse, keyboard and speech commands [2];
(f) Provide alternatives to text content, like audio and video, so that it can be changed according to people needs, such as Braille, speech symbols, other languages including sign language [3,4];
(g) Aim for compatibility with assistive technologies, such as screen readers, text-to-speech, zoom features [3];

The presented design guidelines are useful, but to develop effective user interface is required also user testing because "Design guidelines cannot cover the details that need to be dealt with in fitting a user interface into a specific situation of use. Rather, developers must supplement adherence to guidelines with testing with representative users and tasks." [19]. User testing is important because designers and developers don't have much experience in working with this population, lacking real notions about their needs and capabilities.

4   Conclusion

Serious games constitute a great alternative to current therapy/training methods for people with cognitive disabilities. The problem is that there is a lack of appropriate games for this population, hence arising the need for developing new and innovative games that can truly capture the users and help them overcome (some) of their needs. Although, the development of technologies for people with cognitive disabilities finds several obstacles: "difficulty of addressing cognitive issues through technology applications, the underestimation of the needs and abilities of people with cognitive disabilities, or the cognitive disabilities being hidden compared with other conditions." [19].

With the right hardware and software, serious games can become one of the most useful and accepted tools among this population. Despite all pointed out, it should be noted that games can't reverse the users' situation. Games act merely as a tool to help disabled people to acquire knowledge [4], being essential "to achieve greater autonomy so that they can independently perform day-to-day activities. Dependency generates high social and economic costs, and at the same time it generates self-neglect, disinterest and isolation of the individual" [7].

Acknowledgements. This work was supported by FCT (INESC-ID multiannual funding) under the project PEst-OE/EEI/LA0021/2013. The authors also would like to acknowledge to the European funded Project Games and Learning Alliance (FP7 258169) the Network of Excellence (NoE) on Serious Games.

References

1. Griffiths, M.: The educational benefits of videogames. Education and Health 20(3), 47–51 (2002)
2. Torrente, J., del Blanco, Á., Moreno-Ger, P., Fernández-Manjón, B.: Designing Serious Games for Adult Students with Cognitive Disabilities. In: Huang, T., Zeng, Z., Li, C., Leung, C.S. (eds.) ICONIP 2012, Part IV. LNCS, vol. 7666, pp. 603–610. Springer, Heidelberg (2012)
3. Lanyi, C.S., Brown, D.J.: Design of serious games for students with intellectual disability. In: Proceedings of the 2010 International Conference on Interaction Design & International Development, pp. 44–54. British Computer Society (2010)
4. Martins, T., Carvalho, V., Soares, F., Moreira, M.F.: Serious game as a tool to intellectual disabilities therapy: Total challenge. In: 2011 IEEE 1st International Conference on Serious Games and Applications for Health (SeGAH), pp. 1–7 (November 2011)
5. González, J.L., Cabrera, M.J., Gutiérrez, F.L.: Using videogames in special education. In: Moreno Díaz, R., Pichler, F., Quesada Arencibia, A. (eds.) EUROCAST 2007. LNCS, vol. 4739, pp. 360–367. Springer, Heidelberg (2007)
6. Vera, L., Campos, R., Herrera, G., Romero, C.: Computer graphics applications in the education process of people with learning difficulties. Comput. Graph. 31(4), 649–658 (2007)
7. Fernández-López, Á., Rodríguez-Fórtiz, M.J., Rodríguez-Almendros, M.L., Martínez-Segura, M.J.: Mobile learning technology based on ios devices to support students with special education needs. Comput. Educ. 61, 77–90 (2013)
8. Robertson, G.L., Hix, D.: Making the computer accessible to mentally retarded adults. Commun. ACM 45(4), 171–183 (2002)
9. Burt, D.B., Fuller, S.P., Lewis, K.R.: Brief report: Competitive employment of adults with autism. Journal of Autism and Developmental Disorders 21(2), 237–242 (1991)
10. Cagatay, M., Ege, P., Tokdemir, G., Cagiltay, N.E.: A serious game for speech disorder children therapy. In: 2012 7th International Symposium on Health Informatics and Bioinformatics (HIBIT), pp. 18–23 (April 2012)
11. Hussaan, A.M., Sehaba, K., Mille, A.: Tailoring serious games with adaptive pedagogical scenarios: A serious game for persons with cognitive disabilities. In: 2011 11th IEEE International Conference on Advanced Learning Technologies (ICALT), pp. 486–490 (July 2011)
12. Bartolomé, N.A., Zorrilla, A.M., Zapirain, B.G.: A serious game to improve human relationships in patients with neuro-psychological disorders. In: 2010 International IEEE Consumer Electronics Society's Games Innovations Conference (ICE-GIC), pp. 1–5 (December 2010)
13. de Urturi, Z.S., Zorrilla, A.M., Zapirain, B.G.: Serious game based on first aid education for individuals with autism spectrum disorder (asd) using android mobile devices. In: 2011 16th International Conference on Computer Games (CGAMES), pp. 223–227 (July 2011)

14. Saleh, M.S., Aljaam, J.M., Karime, A., Elsaddik, A.: Learning games for children with intellectual challenges. In: 2012 International Conference on Information Technology Based Higher Education and Training (ITHET), pp. 1–5 (June 2012)
15. Kagohara, D.M., van der Meer, L., Ramdoss, S., O'Reilly, M.F., Lancioni, G.E., Davis, T.N., Rispoli, M., Lang, R., Marschik, P.B., Sutherland, D., Green, V.A., Sigafoos, J.: Using ipods ® and ipads ® in teaching programs for individuals with developmental disabilities: A systematic review. Research in Developmental Disabilities 34(1), 147–156 (2013)
16. Alqahtani, A., Jaafar, N., Alfadda, N.: Interactive speech based games for autistic children with asperger syndrome. In: 2011 International Conference and Workshop on Current Trends in Information Technology (CTIT), pp. 126–131 (October 2011)
17. Costa-Pazo, A., Vazquez-Fernandez, E., Rivas, C., Gómez, M., Anido, L., Fernández, M., Valladares, S.: Gesture-controlled interfaces for people with disabilities
18. Lanyi, C.S., Brown, D.J., Standen, P., Lewis, J., Butkute, V., Drozdik, D.: Goet european project of serious games for students with intellectual disability. In: 2011 2nd International Conference on Cognitive Infocommunications (CogInfoCom), pp. 1–6 (July 2011)
19. LoPresti, E.F., Bodine, C., Lewis, C.: Assistive technology for cognition (understanding the needs of persons with disabilities). IEEE Engineering in Medicine and Biology Magazine 27(2), 29–39 (2008)
20. Saridaki, M., Mourlas, C.: Incorporating serious games in the classroom of students with intellectual disabilities and the role of the educator. In: 2011 Third International Conference on Games and Virtual Worlds for Serious Applications (VS-GAMES), pp. 180 181 (May 2011)
21. Szczesna, A., Grudzinski, J., Grudzinski, T., Mikuszewski, R., Debowski, A.: The psychology serious game prototype for preschool children. In: 2011 IEEE 1st International Conference on Serious Games and Applications for Health (SeGAH), pp. 1–4 (November 2011)
22. Brandao, A., Trevisan, D.G., Brandao, L., Moreira, B., Nascimento, G., Vasconcelos, C.N., Clua, E., Mourao, P.: Semiotic inspection of a game for children with down syndrome. In: 2010 Brazilian Symposium on Games and Digital Entertainment (SBGAMES), pp. 199–210 (November 2010)

Atmosphaeres – 360° Video Environments for Stress and Pain Management

Eric Fassbender[1] and Wolfgang Heiden[2]

[1] Atmosphaeres.com, Adelaide, Australia
eric@fassbender.com.au
[2] Bonn-Rhein-Sieg University of Applied Sciences, St. Augustin, Germany
wolfgang.heiden@h-brs.de

Abstract. The Atmosphaeres project aims to reduce sufferers' stress and pain levels by using 360° video environments that are presented in a highly immersive Head-Mounted Display (HMD). Here we report first insights of our prototype combination of the 360° video environments and the Oculus Rift, the HMD used for our project. We find that our 'Atmosphaeres' are capable of truly transporting the user to another, virtually created location, however, there were a number of restrictions with the first system, including image quality and nausea which we hope to eliminate with the system we present in this paper. There are also a number of research questions that need to be considered for the use of the Atmosphaeres in stress and pain management or for general relaxation purposes. These questions include whether 360° video environments are capable of reducing stress and experienced pain and whether changes to the Oculus Rift DK2 do in fact reduce the nausea that was often caused by the DK1. Sound is another important yet often under-considered factor in many Virtual Reality applications and questions we seek to answer revolve around how the quality and type of audio contribute to users' feeling of presence and ultimately their stress and pain levels.

Keywords: Immersive Virtual Environments, Head-Mounted Displays, Restorative Virtual Environments, Stress Management, Pain Reduction.

1 Introduction

The cost of direct workplace related stress for the Australian economy was a staggering $14.81 billion in 2008 with an additional $10.11 billion caused by absenteeism and presenteeism [1]. Newer figures indicate that stress is becoming even worse, with Australians reporting significantly higher levels of stress in 2012 than the year before [2]. Some strategies that people use to deal with stress include watching TV or movies, spending time with friends and family, drinking alcohol or smoking [2]. Arguably, some of these strategies do not seem to be particularly healthy options and an alternative may be to simply go out into nature as there is evidence that being in or looking at images of nature is an effective way to reduce stress [3]-[6]. However, access to nature is not always easy, especially for people who live in big cities where

M. Ma et al. (Eds.): SGDA 2014, LNCS 8778, pp. 48–58, 2014.

constant noise makes it very difficult to find peaceful and quiet places. Travelling to a nearby national park would be a solution, however, often the stresses involved with the effort (traffic jams, travel time, cost, etc.) in fact contribute to the problem rather than solve it. Virtual environments that show peaceful places offer an opportunity to solve this conundrum.

Fig. 1. An early implementation of a stress and pain therapy environment using 3 projectors. Photo: Eric Fassbender.

In Fassbender & De Souza [7] we discussed a low-cost 3-projector display system for use as a relaxation and post-operative restoration environment (see Figure 1). In a newer iteration of the project we have replaced the 3-projector display system with a Head-Mounted Display (HMD) to create the 'Atmosphaeres' 360° video environment. The HMD that we use for this improved system is the Oculus Rift, which removes a great number of restrictions that are affiliated with the 3-projector display system and other similar CAVE-like systems. Figure 2 shows our current Atmosphaeres prototype using the Oculus Rift Head-Mounted Display, Development Kit 1 (DK1). The scene that is shown inside the HMD and on the computer display is a 360° spherical panorama photo of a peaceful tropical creek in the Northern Territory of Australia. The main author wears wireless headphones that play the gurgling sounds of the tropical creek. Note that the computer screen in Figure 2 shows only a 100° slice of the 360° spherical image that is split between the left and right eyes. The remaining scene (260°) outside the user's field of view (FOV) can be explored by turning one's head.

In the following sections we will look at a number of therapeutic Virtual Reality systems and studies that others have developed. We will then describe the advantages of our improved system as compared to the previous 3-projector version and traditional CAVE systems. We will also report some of the restrictions and challenges we face before discussing some of the ensuing research questions.

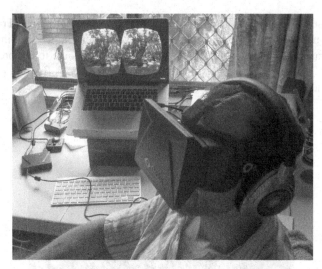

Fig. 2. The main author wearing the Oculus Rift Head-Mounted Display and wireless head-phones. The scene displayed inside the HMD is shown on the computer screen. Photo: Eric Fassbender.

2   Background

Virtual Environments and New Media have ultimately made their way into a great number of healthcare situations. Nowadays it is not uncommon to see children journeying to the operating theatre through a magical, wall-projected forest [8] or the use of tablet computers in radiology departments [9]. There are plenty of examples where new technology is used in a variety of healthcare applications. In the present article we will concentrate on the use of technology for stress and pain treatment as well as general relaxation purposes.

In regards to using virtual environments for stress management, there is very little research, yet the findings from this research show very encouraging results [10]-[15]. For example, Gorini & Riva [11] used Virtual Realities to facilitate the relaxation process of generalized anxiety disorder patients. They found that the use of a virtual relaxation environment "enhances the quality of the relaxing experience" [11] and "showed a significant improvement of the emotional state" [15] of participants.

Annerstedt *et al.* [10] combined a virtual reality forest with sounds of nature and also found evidence for the efficacy of virtual environments as well as nature sounds for stress reduction. While Annerstedt used a wall-projected system similar to our own, earlier approach [7], we are using a HMD for displaying the restorative Atmosphaeres.

One study that used solely the auditory channel to treat stress related issues is Vidyarthi *et al.* [16] who developed the Sonic Cradle, a system that uses participants' breathing to influence sounds that induce a state of relaxation. They found that "reported imagery, bodily sensations, and time distortions, [were] paralleling mindfulness meditators on a 2-week retreat" [17]. Note that Vidyarthi uses sound and breathing for his system and no imagery.

In regards to virtual environments and pain management, Hoffman *et al.* [18] [19] achieved great results with their immersive SnowWorld environment. Amongst other things they found that higher levels of immersion result in a significant reduction of experienced pain for patients who are undergoing burn wound treatment. This reduction of experienced pain is achieved because patients' brains are so engaged with processing the visual and auditory information from the virtual environment that less processing capacity is available for messages sent by the pain receptors of skin areas currently being treated. Thus, fewer pain signals are transmitted to patients' brains, which in turn significantly reduces the amount of pain experienced by patients. The level of immersiveness and quality of the experience is directly related to statistically significant effects in pain reduction. However, in their 2006 and 2011 studies Hoffman *et al.* were possibly limited by the technology at the time with the largest horizontal Field of View (FOV) used by them being 60° horizontally. Current HMD technology in contrast features 100° FOV (e.g. Oculus Rift) and the aim of the Atmosphaeres project is to explore the impact of this increased level of immersion on pain and stress reduction as well as level of overall relaxation as experienced by participants.

These combined results from the various research projects seem to warrant further exploration of using virtual environments for relaxation, pain and stress management. Regardless of academic research, a Reddit user by the name of Futurebrad has already successfully put the distraction/cognitive overload approach with virtual environments into practice to help his son during his cancer treatment (see Figure 3).

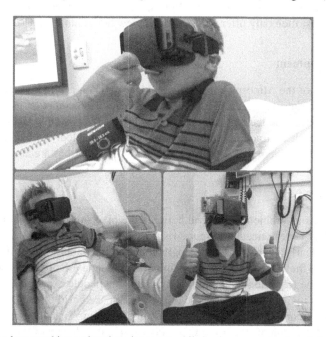

Fig. 3. A young boy watching a virtual environment while having cancer treatment. Source: [20]

3   Prototype Building and Challenges

In contrast to Gorini & Riva [11], Hoffman *et al.* [18] [19] and others [21] [22], we use high-resolution video imagery for the Atmosphaeres, rather than computer-generated imagery. The reason is that the level of detail and realism of the virtual video environment is (currently) higher than that of a purely computer-generated environment, while under most circumstances less effort is required to create high-resolution videos than for a computer-generated environment, in fact, high-resolution 360° videos may be cheaper and faster to produce, depending on the situation. The downside of course is that a video environment is not interactively explorable beyond the limitations of the spherical display. However, exploration of a virtual environment is not directly required for our purposes at this point in time. Besides lacking of interactive exploration, video environments are constrained by realism, whereas computer generated virtual environments allow manipulations which are not limited by realism.

3.1   Advantages

There are many advantages of using a HMD instead of a 3-projector or CAVE system. Firstly, a HMD is much smaller and directly worn by the user, thus it needs a lot less space than a CAVE system, which typically occupies an entire room. Furthermore, a HMD is significantly cheaper (e.g. $350 for the developer version of the Oculus Rift, compared to anywhere upwards of $7000 for a CAVE system) and is easier to install and operate. Furthermore, HMD's offer a head-tracking feature, which enables the user to experience a full 360° spherical environment. In contrast, many CAVE systems often only offer ~180° field of view horizontally and ~60° vertically.

3.2   Development

Programming of the Atmosphaeres is done in Unity 3D on a Windows computer. The executable file runs on Windows as well as on a Macintosh computer using the HDMI connection. While the feeling of immersion and presence is simply astonishing, especially when the head-tracking feature of the HMD is enabled, there are some downsides of the DK1 system that the DK2 and other HMD solutions are aiming to resolve.

3.3   Display Grid

The most obvious problem is the grid between the pixels of the Oculus Rift DK1 display, which is very noticeable. Figure 4 shows one of the lenses of the Oculus Rift. The grid is clearly visible in the photograph and comparable to what it appears like when wearing the HMD. While some similar phenomena are often forgotten after an adjustment time (e.g. the initial odd feeling that some people experience when putting on 3D glasses in cinemas), in the case of the wide-spaced grid of the Oculus Rift, the user's mind is continuously drawn back to this problem. That is, our brains do not 'blend out' this problem, at least not the brains of the developers of the Atmosphaeres prototype.

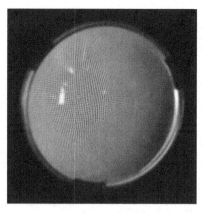

Fig. 4. One of the lenses of the Oculus Rift shows the obvious grid of the display. Photo: Eric Fassbender

3.4   Resolution

Another problem that is rather obvious is the comparably low resolution of 1280x800 of the DK1 developer version of the Oculus Rift. Since Ivan Sutherland introduced the first HMD in the late 1960's [23] the resolution of these displays has increased from around 320x240 pixels/inch in early HMD's to 640x480 in the 1990's. The Rift's 1280x800 resolution is only another approximate doubling of the amount of displayed pixels, which means that display resolution has doubled about every 15 years. In comparison, the number of transistors in computer chips doubles every two years [24]. So clearly there is a rather large divide between the development of computer chips and that of HMD displays. Saying that, the resolution of the DK 2 and the consumer version of the Oculus Rift (expected in 2015) is announced as 1920×1080 pixels. Other hardware developers have announced their consumer HMD's (e.g. GameFace) with 2560x1440 (gamefacelabs.com). So the quality of the image is likely going to improve, however, it remains to be seen whether the distance between the pixels (i.e. the grid) will be reduced to an unnoticeable level.

Low resolution and quality of source video files (1600x800 pixels) has been a problem with our first Atmosphaeres prototype where we used a SpheriCam (spheri-cam.com). However, we have upgraded to a solution of 6 GoPro cameras that are arranged in a Freedom360 (freedom360.us) branded holder that points the GoPro's at very specific angles. The resulting 6 individual video files are then stitched into a single video by using the VideoStitch (videostitch.com) or Kolor Autopano Video (kolor.com) software.

The final output videos are typically rendered at a resolution of 5600x2800 pixels, which is not only a vast improvement over the previous camera (1600x800) but also more than double the vertical resolution that the Oculus Rift is capable of displaying in its current version (1920x1080 pixels).

Fig. 5. Freedom360 mount for 6 GoPro cameras, Source: freedom360.us

3.5   Sharpness

Another problem of the Oculus Rift DK1 is that the sharpness of the display decays towards the edges of the users' FOV. While this loss of sharpness can also be seen in Figure 4, the reduced display quality is not as prominent as it may appear in the photograph. This is because our eyes/brain naturally reduce sharpness for our peripheral vision. Thus, if we look straight ahead in the Rift and use the head-tracking feature to move the spherical environment, the loss of sharpness is not as obvious as it may sound. Still, it is a factor that reduces the level of realism of the displayed virtual environment.

3.6   Nausea

During the prototyping phase and in informal tests with colleagues, friends and relatives, our developers and testers experienced a sometimes high level of nausea when using the Oculus Rift DK1 HMD[1]. This is despite the fact that all of the developers are very used to virtual and 3D environments and don't normally experience much nausea. One reason for this higher than usual level of nausea could be the head-tracking that rotates the virtual world while the body of the users nearly remain in the same location. Furthermore, users do not see their hands or body, which can be irritating and may contribute to the feeling of nausea. The new Oculus Rift DK2 (Development Kit) prototype aims to overcome this problem by using a 'low persistence' display that eliminates motion blur and judder that is experienced with the DK1. By eliminating motion blur, the low persistence of the display supposedly reduces the

---

[1] More formal tests would have been desirable, however, at the time of development of the first Atmosphaeres prototype, this was not possible. Scientifically designed experiments are, however, planned for the second prototype that uses the DK2.

dreaded simulator sickness. As opposed to the 3 degrees of freedom that the DK1 provides (yaw, pitch, roll), the DK2 also provides 6 degrees of freedom by adding the (limited) ability to move the head up and down (heaving), left and right (swaying) as well as forward and backward (surging). If one considers the built-in magnetometer, the Oculus Rift would in fact be considered to provide 9 degrees of freedom. The positional tracking (heaving, swaying, surging) of the DK2 may further help to reduce nausea because the headset now tracks forward and sideways movements of the users' head and adjusts the displayed scene accordingly.

4   Research Questions

Based on the findings of others in the literature and the experiences from our prototyping tests, there are a number of research questions that should be considered when using 360° video environments for the management of stress and pain. These research questions are primarily related to the effects of visual and auditory aspects on users' stress and pain levels as well as related navigation issues and the aforementioned nausea.

4.1   Visuals

One variable we will investigate with the Atmosphaeres is whether a fully interactive (i.e. panable) 360° video is in fact needed or whether a 'static' photo or video that fills the 100° FOV of the user is sufficient to achieve the desired effects. In the latter scenario the user will only see the scene from one point of view, regardless of whether they turn their heads or not. Something we will likely not explore at this point in time, however, that is important to investigate at another stage, is whether 'real' high-resolution photos/videos have a different effect on the dependent variables than computer generated virtual environments. To our knowledge no studies have compared the efficacy of these different display methods on pain and stress relief.

4.2   Audio

In serious games and virtual reality research the visual side of things is well represented, however, the auditory environment often gets left behind. As we argue in [25] the quality of the auditory environment is just as important to the feeling of presence as that of the visual environment. Putting on headphones and adding the natural sounds of a tropical creek to the scene in Figure 2 truly improves the level of immersion of the user. From the authors' perspective the prototype environment (visuals and sound from the tropical creek) really transports the user to another place. However, the question is how much realism of the sound environment is needed to create the illusion of travelling to another place and to which degree the level of audio realism is related to relaxation, pain and stress reduction. Variables we will explore include

- Stereo Sound vs. Mono sound vs. No sounds
- Music vs. Nature Sounds vs. Music + Nature Sounds vs. No sounds

- Realistic vs. Distorted or low quality sound
- Effect of volume on comfort and relaxation (i.e. what is the 'best' volume for sounds at which most people relax?)

4.3   Navigation

Baños (2004) found that using head-tracking of HMD's for navigation might make navigation more difficult for the user. Thus, we will investigate whether the use of the head-tracking feature or a standard joystick is more beneficial to achieve relaxation and pain and stress reduction. Alternatively, the head-tracking feature will be turned off and the user will see a slideshows of 100° FOV images.

4.4   Nausea

Because of the nausea that our beta-testers and developers experienced it is important to explore whether the experienced nausea is worse or better if the head tracking is turned on or off. Additionally, we need to investigate whether nausea is affected by a) still or moving imagery. It might also be interesting to compare the Oculus Rift DK1 and DK2 and investigate what effect the changes to the design of the Oculus Rift (low persistence, positional tracking in DK2) have on the feeling of nausea that is experienced by the user.

5   Conclusions

There are two main areas of investigation for the spherical relaxation environments that are created in this project – stress management and reduction of pain. Very little research has been conducted in using virtual environments for the management of stress, however, the few results that are available uniformly show positive effects. With the new generation of high-quality HMD's, research in this area can now be furthered. The results could have a large impact on our knowledge of the treatment and prevention of stress, which in turn would have far-reaching effects on reducing stress-related costs. The Atmosphaeres project builds on findings from previous research that showed that HMD's can be used to significantly reduce pain during burn-wound treatment. This research also showed that a wider field of view (FOV) has a significant effect on the degree of pain reduction, wider being better. Older HMD's, however, were large and clunky, had a very small FOV of 40° horizontally and 30° vertically and the resolution/quality of the displays were very poor. The HMD used for our research project is the newly developed 'Oculus Rift' DK2, which is very reasonably priced (~$350 for the developer version), has a much larger FOV of 100° horizontally and 90° vertically and the quality of the display is much higher than that of previous HMD's. Furthermore, the Oculus Rift is much lighter (~379 grams) than previous models and there is virtually no 'lag' when users turn their heads, which was another limitation of the previous generation HMD's that greatly impaired users' feeling of being immersed in the virtual environment.

Since a wider FOV is associated with a significant reduction of experienced pain, the hypothesis is that we can further reduce pain and stress of patients who use our 100° FOV Atmosphaeres. If pain and stress levels can be reduced effectively, then recovery times of patients will also improve, which in turn means that patients would free up hospital rooms sooner and be fit again for work, earlier. Thus, costs that accumulate at the hospital and during days away from work are reduced effectively. The low price of the Oculus Rift enables universal use in hospitals and at home, thus allowing the wide-spread use of the Atmosphaeres once our data has been gathered and interpreted.

The findings of this study also affect other application areas for immersive environments. One particular focus may be placed on gaming, which has not been mentioned in our introduction. However, gaming is addressed twofold by our research: one aspect being the optimization of immersive experience in games, the other the consideration of playing games as a means of stress reduction. Although playing challenging computer games extensively may reduce pain by focusing the patient's attention (to a degree positively related to the immersive feeling), the same can easily result in an enhancement of stress rather than a reduction. Immersive interaction within in a storytelling-controlled environment, which includes calming modules in order to prevent reaching an excessive stress level, may be a beneficial combination that may result in even better reduction of both stress and pain.

Acknowledgments. The authors would like to thank John Porte for programming the Atmosphaeres and Jayshree Mamtora for help with article acquisition.

References

1. Medibank Private: The cost of workplace stress in Australia (2008) (accessed April 2013)
2. Casey, L.: Stress and wellbeing in australia in 2012: A state-of-the-nation survey (2012) (accessed April 2013)
3. Alvarsson, J.J., Wiens, S., Nilsson, M.E.: Stress recovery during exposure to nature sound and environmental noise. Int. J. Environ. Res. Public Health 7(3), 1036–1046 (2010)
4. Beukeboom, C.J., Langeveld, D., Tanja-Dijkstra, K.: Stress-Reducing effects of real and artificial nature in a hospital waiting room. The Journal of Alternative and Complementary Medicine 18(4), 329–333 (2012)
5. Ulrich, R.S., Simons, R.F., Losito, B.D., Fiorito, E., Miles, M.A., Zelson, M.: Stress recovery during exposure to natural and urban environments. Journal of Environmental Psychology 11(3), 201–230 (1991)
6. Wells, N.M., Evans, G.W.: Nearby nature - A buffer of life stress among rural children. Environment and Behavior 35(3), 311–330 (2003)
7. Fassbender, E., De Souza, P.: A low-cost 3 projector display system for pain reduction and improved patient recovery times. In: Proceedings of the 24th Australian Computer-Human Interaction Conference, OzCHI 2012, pp. 130–133 (2012)
8. Wainwright, O.: Children journey to the operating theatre through a magical forest (2012), http://www.theguardian.com/artanddesign/architecture-design-blog/2012/dec/12/children-journey-jason-bruges-great-ormond?INTCMP=SRCH (accessed August 2013)

9. Panughpath, S.G., Kalyanpur, A.: Radiology and the mobile device: Radiology in motion. Indian J. Radiol. Imaging 22(4), 246–250 (2012)

10. Annerstedt, M., Jönsson, P., Wallergård, M., Johansson, G., Karlson, B., Grahn, P., et al.: Inducing physiological stress recovery with sounds of nature in a virtual reality forest–results from a pilot study. Physiol. Behav. 118, 240–250 (2013)

11. Gorini, A., Riva, G.: The potential of virtual reality as anxiety management tool: A randomized controlled study in a sample of patients affected by generalized anxiety disorder. Trials 9, 25 (2008)

12. Plante, T.G., Aldridge, A., Su, D., Bogdan, R., Belo, M., Kahn, K.: Does virtual reality enhance the management of stress when paired with exercise? An exploratory study. International Journal of Stress Management 10(3), 203 (2003)

13. Plante, T.G., Cage, C., Clements, S., Stover, A.: Psychological benefits of exercise paired with virtual reality: Outdoor exercise energizes whereas indoor virtual exercise relaxes. International Journal of Stress Management 13(1), 108 (2006)

14. Rizzo, A., Buckwalter, J.G., John, B., Newman, B., Parsons, T., Kenny, P., Williams, J.: STRIVE: Stress resilience in virtual environments: A pre-deployment VR system for training emotional coping skills and assessing chronic and acute stress responses. Stud. Health Technol. Inform. 173, 379–385 (2012)

15. Villani, D., Riva, G.: Presence and relaxation: A preliminary controlled study. Psych. Nology Journal 6(1), 7–25 (2008)

16. Vidyarthi, J., Riecke, B.E., Gromala, D.: Sonic cradle: Designing for an immersive experience of meditation by connecting respiration to music. In: Proceedings of the Designing Interactive Systems Conference (2012)

17. Vidyarthi, J., Riecke, B.E.: Mediated meditation: Cultivating mindfulness with sonic cradle. In: CHI 2013 Extended Abstracts on Human Factors in Computing Systems. ACM (2013)

18. Hoffman, H.G., Seibel, E.J., Richards, T.L., Furness, T.A., Patterson, D.R., Sharar, S.R.: Virtual reality helmet display quality influences the magnitude of virtual reality analgesia. J. Pain 7(11), 843–850 (2006)

19. Hoffman, H.G., Chambers, G.T., Meyer, W.J., Arceneaux, L.L., Russell, W.J., Seibel, E.J., et al.: Virtual reality as an adjunctive non-pharmacologic analgesic for acute burn pain during medical procedures. Ann. Behav. Med. 41(2), 183–191 (2011)

20. FutureBrad: Using the DIVE VR adapter with my son at the hospital (2014), http://imgur.com/7t5DeKB (accessed June 2014)

21. Depledge, M.H., Stone, R.J., Bird, W.J.: Can natural and virtual environments be used to promote improved human health and wellbeing? Environ. Sci. Technol. 45(11), 4660–4665 (2011)

22. Malbos, E., Rapee, R.M., Kavakli, M.: Isolating the effect of virtual reality based exposure therapy for agoraphobia: A comparative trial. Stud. Health Technol. Inform. 167, 45–50 (2011)

23. Sutherland, I.E.: A head-Mounted three dimensional display. In: Proceedings of the 1968, Fall Joint Computer Conference, Part I, December 9-11 (1968)

24. Intel: 60 years of the transistor: 1947 – 2007 (2007), http://www.intel.com/technology/timeline.pdf (accessed July 9 2012)

25. Fassbender, E., Jones, C.M.: The Importance and Creation of High-Quality Sounds in Healthcare Applications. In: Ma, M., Jain, L., Paul Anderson, P. (eds.) Virtual, Augmented Reality and Serious Games for Healthcare 1, pp. 547–565. Springer, Heidelberg (2014)

Sense: An Interactive Learning Application That Visualizes the Nerve Supply of Face

Yeshwanth Pulijala[1] and Minhua Ma[2]

[1] Digital Design Studio, Glasgow School of Art, University of Glasgow, UK
dr.yesh@gmail.com
[2] Digital Design Studio,Glasgow School of Art, UK
m.ma@gsa.ac.uk

Abstract. Human Nervous System is one of the basic yet most difficult topics in medical education. With millions of neurons from varied origins, pathways and types regulating different functions, it is the least understood system of human body. Among all the organs, the face has a dense nerve innervations in a compact area making it a challenge for students to gain the required anatomical expertise. The *Sense* project is an effort made to overcome this challenging task by enabling interactive learning with the help of an intuitive user interface. The ability to learn and test the anatomical knowledge based on a novel three-dimensional head with particle flow animations to visualize nerve impulse propagation makes this application stand out from the conventional and interactive methods of anatomy education. This paper presents the design and development of this application using the Unity 3D game engine. Possible future improvements for evaluation are also discussed.

Keywords: Medical education, 3D visualization, interactive learning, human anatomy, nerve supply of face, Unity 3D, serious games.

1 Introduction

1.1 Innovative Learning Tools in Medical Education

Medical education is a domain where complex learning takes place [1, 2]. Hence, it is extremely important to enhance this learning process using various methods. Revolutionary inventions in the digital technology like the 3D visualizations, simulations, and utilization of technologies like virtual reality and augmented reality in medical education [3, 4], have brought about a clear change in the learning methods. Anatomy is one of the basic life sciences, taught generally in the first year of medicine, dentistry and allied health sciences. Though it has its applications in later part of clinical years, the end of curriculum often means the end of learning anatomy in medical schools. Thus, it is generally perceived that anatomy is all about rote memorization of facts [5]. Especially in case of nervous system of head, it is very common for students to memorize various nerves and the foramina through which they pass. However, the real objective of learning anatomy exists in understanding the proper relation between

M. Ma et al. (Eds.): SGDA 2014, LNCS 8778, pp. 59–67, 2014.
© Springer International Publishing Switzerland 2014

structure and function of an organ [6]. Hence, it needs to be taught in a more innovative and clinically oriented manner for students to understand its relevance [7]. Different models of learning and teaching anatomy currently in practice include lectures, prosected specimens, cadaveric dissections, radiographs, problem based learning [8]and interactive educational aids in the form of animations [9] and serious games [10, 4]. Development of digital technology and increased usage of tablet devices by student community puts animations and interactive applications in the forefront. This brought about a rise in number of medical animations, which are pre-rendered videos without any scope of interactivity. Gaming technologies and interactive animations like Vascular invaders [11] has been tried and found to increase the motivation to study complex concepts. However, topics like nervous system still remained less understood. Sense project is designed and developed to address this problem. We created an interactive application for medical education, which illustrates the nerve supply of face and enhance the learning process.

1.2   The Nerve Supply of the Face

The nervous system in humans is a complex and intricate network of pathways, which assist us to interact with our environment. It is broadly divided into Central nervous system, comprising of Brain and Spinal cord, and Peripheral nervous system consisting of Cranial and Spinal nerves. Based on their function, these nerves are further divided into sensory nerves and motor nerves. The sensory nerves are also called the afferent nerves as they carry information from peripheral receptors to the central nervous system. The motor nerves are also called the efferent nerves as they carry information away from the central nervous system to the rest of the body. [12] Fig. 1 shows an overview of this classification of nervous system.

Human face has a rich vascular supply and dense nerve innervations. This makes it a complex zone for performing procedures like maxillofacial surgery. Anatomically, there are 12 Cranial nerves that arise from the brain, four of which are responsible for the nerve supply of face. They are the Oculomotor (III Cranial nerve), Trochlear (IV Cranial nerve), Trigeminal (V Cranial nerve) and Facial (VII Cranial nerve) nerves [13]. To learn the nature of these nerves, their innervations and pathways, it is of utmost importance for medical and dental students to understand and visualize their internal anatomy. Out of these four cranial nerves, the Sense application demonstrates the structure and functions of only the facial and trigeminal nerves.

The Facial nerve is the seventh cranial nerve. It is responsible for the nerve supply of the muscles that assist in facial expression. It arises in the midbrain, passes through the internal auditory meatus, leaves skull through the stylomastoidformaen, and traverses the parotid gland to supply the face. It is in the parotid gland, where this nerve gives off branches. There are five branches of facial nerve namely, the temporal, zygomatic, buccal, marginal mandibular and cervical branches [14].

The Trigeminal nerve is the fifth and the largest cranial nerve. It is both sensory and motor in nature. It arises from the Gasserian ganglion and divides into the opthalmic, maxillary and mandibular branches. The opthalmic division is sensory in nature and it supplies the eye. The maxillary division, which is also sensory, leaves the skull through foramen rotundum and supplies the maxilla. The third division of the trigeminal nerve, the mandibular division is both sensory and motor in nature. It leaves the skull through the foramen ovale and supplies the various parts of the mandible [15].

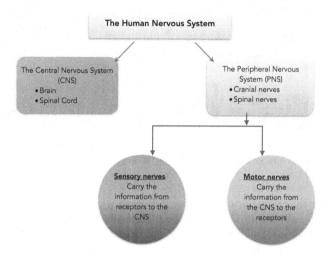

Fig. 1. Classification of Human nervous system

2   The Design and Development of *Sense*

2.1   **Implementing *Sense***

A 3D model of human body is obtained from the Zygote human model [16]. The head and neck regions and their nerve supply are selectively edited from the model using Autodesk 3DS Max software. They are then exported into .obj file format and is imported into Unity 3D software. The interactive elements of the application is implemented in Unity 3D.

The application consists of two major scenes: the learning mode and assessment mode.

Fig.1 shows the learning mode in Sense application. In this scene, students get to learn the anatomy of the Facial nerve and Trigeminal nerve by touching different regions of face. Often the information is presented regarding the nerve and the area they innervate. But here, a flip back model of learning is experimented. According to this model, learning happens from effect to cause. The user gets to know the nerve being responsible for sensation when they touch some part of the face. Based on the zone of the face, the name of the nerve responsible for its innervation appears at the bottom right of the screen. Different fonts are used to differentiate between the Facial and Trigeminal nerves.

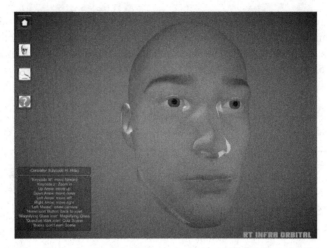

Fig. 2. Scene 1 - Touching any part of the face would reveal its nerve supply at the bottom right. A blue colored font is used for Trigeminal Nerve. A drop down menu showing key controls is also found here.

To facilitate the recognition of a particular nerve when touched, collision detectors (also known as colliders in Unity 3D) are placed all along the pathway of the nerve and a script is enabled which highlights the nerve and changes its color when touched. Anatomical accuracy is maintained all along by having proper references. An ability to interact with the model is added by allowing the user to rotate the skull using "Rotate script". "Zoom" functionality is also enabled to have a closer look at the nerves and their internal anatomy.

To enhance further interactivity, and to help in a deeper understanding regarding the internal anatomy of the skull and its nerve supply, a semi transparent view is used. In this view, when the user touches a zone of the face, not only does its name appear, but the user also gets to see the pathway of the nerve. This way, they get a clear idea regarding where the nerve is coming from in the brain. It is of extreme importance to know the pathway of the nerve, as different levels of nerve defects can cause different debilitating effects. This functionality is achieved by enabling the alpha channel of the skin texture. By reducing the alpha value, the opacity of the overlying skin texture reduces bringing the internal skull and nerves into clear visibility (Fig. 2). By activating this function only upon touching the "skull" icon makes it easy for the user to handle both normal and semi transparent views as per their requirement.

The third functionality of this application is to see the nerves in function (Fig. 3).An interactive animation demonstrating the various parts of ear [17] gave the inspiration for this idea. To achieve this, a duplicate model of the first head is imported into the scene. Particle flow animation is created using Unity Pro's Legacy particle system with mesh particle renderer. This allows the user to see the glowing colors of the particles. A second camera is then placed on the duplicate head to capture the particle flow. Culling view feature is enabled on this camera to make it selectively capture the skull and nerves of the second head. A click on the magnifier button activates this functionality to show the particle flow in the nerves through a magnifying glass. To transfer the second camera's view on to the magnifying glass object,

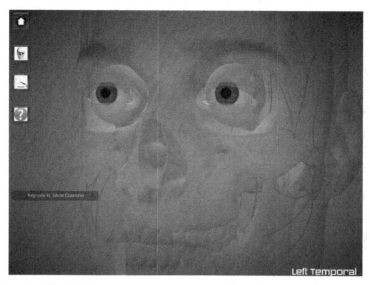

Fig. 2. Scene 1 – The Semi transparent view of the Skull and the Nerves to clearly understand their pathway

which is on the first head, we used the "Render texture" feature in Unity Pro. The varying colors and direction of the particle flow enables the learner to get a better insight into the type of nerve stimulus.

The second scene in this application is a Quiz scene where 10 questions based on what has been explained in the first scene are asked (as shown in Fig. 4). The skull automatically rotates showing up the area of interest in red color. The user can still interact with the skull in three-dimension during the quiz.

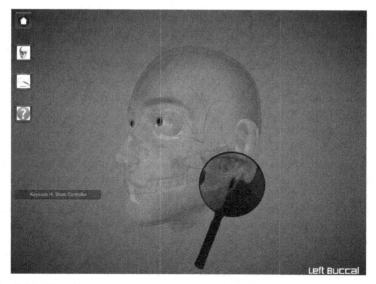

Fig. 3. The Magnifying glass view showing particle flow to depict nerve in function

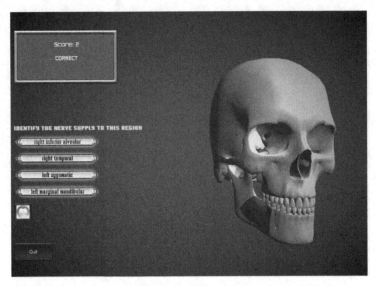

Fig. 4. Scene 2 - Quiz scene. The region of interest is highlighted in red. The *book* button takes the learner back to learning mode.

A quiz script using an array of questions is used to implement this. A correct answer increases the score by one, and an incorrect answer does not change the score. Sound effects are also incorporated to give more feedback to the learner in the assessment. A "book" button placed in the quiz scene enables the user to go back to learning mode in case he feels a need to revisit the nerve supply of that particular region.

2.2   The Standalone Desktop Application

The 3D interactive application is built as a standalone app for Mac and PC. It works effectively on 1024x780 resolution. An introductory scene showing the buttons and their functionality, learning and quiz scenes are built individually. This application when exported to Android platform has a limited functionality as it is basically made for the desktops. For it to work on other platforms, changes need to be made in the script. An evaluation of this software is planned for the future work.

3   Discussion

The use of animations and advanced digital technology in medical education is not a new invention. Various teaching aids are used presently to help medical students understand the details in anatomy, histology and complex processes in physiology. It is reported that virtual reality and simulations have their role in explanation of surgical techniques [18], anesthesia procedures[19] and emergency medicine like cardiopulmonary resuscitation [20]. A literature review done by Ruiz et al. [21] on medical education and role of animation technologies clearly indicated a definite increase in understanding of difficult topics when interactive animations were incorporated into learning methods.

Interactivity and user control were found to develop interest and increase the understanding of complex topics in medicine [22].Sense features a fully interactive model of head, engaging the students in the process of learning. Despite an increased use of animations in education, one issue that needs a serious consideration is to focus when and how animations are needed in order to make an effective impact on the student learning [23]. It is also reported that interactivity with 3D models helps in better understanding than static images that are commonly used in medical education [24]. Sense follows these principles by having an interactive three-dimensional head model with particle flow animations for visualization of the nerve impulse.

It was found that problem based learning [6, 8] helped in improving the critical thinking abilities and also played a vital role in making better judgments, which is very much essential in medical education. Assessment of anatomical knowledge needs to be focused on clinical relevance of the problems. However, most of the assessments are concentrated around retrieval of fragments of information, which are not explained along with their clinical relevance [25]. The quiz scene addresses this problem by guiding students regarding the nerves responsible for the sensation and questioning the region of their innervation. Integrating an interactive 3D model with the questioned area highlighted while presentinga specific questionlinks the knowledge with its visualization. This makes learning student centric. The essence of learning increases when students interactively learn various nerves by clicking, rotating, manipulating the head, and watching animation of the nerve impulse in an interested area. The functionality of magnifying glass immensely helps haptic learners as they get a realistic feel by touching and moving the magnifying glass around to explore various regions of the nerves.

Further improvements that could have been incorporated in this application are to include the Oculomotor and Trochlear nerves in the nerve supply of the face. A further detailed description of the nerves and interactive annotations of the foramens through which they pass would have helped students who are both visual and verbal learners. Additionally, better animation and graphics would make the application work in a more effective manner. Evaluation of this application is planned to improve the system based on user feedback. Further addition of gaming elements and increasing the interactivity by creating a story line as in vascular invaders[12] can be added. Addition of an interactive game on a complex topic like the human nervous system, which leverages on realistic3D models, can improve the existing user interface.

Availability of high-end simulations and animations at the touch of a button and at a low cost when compared to the distant learning courses is further pushing the demand for these applications. With increasing number of students getting their hands on the technological advances like smart devices, and using them for education, it is important to understand what kind of resources would benefit the students most. A major part of the literature review done regarding simulations and games in education focused only on evaluating the innovations in digital technology by comparing them with control groups that do not use any kind of digital technology. This leads to a bias in the results and a missing clarity in what type of visualizations and simulations would actually fit the purposes of medical education [26]. Therefore, it is important to compare different designs of simulations in different learning groups to find out the most suitable kind [21].

4   Conclusion

Changing demands of education are leading to changing methods of teaching. A shift in learning from conventional classroom model to problem-based or clinical case based study [8] would need new advances to supplement the existing educational resources. That is where medical applications like Sense, which convey complex information in an interactive and engaging manner, come into picture. This application could successfully demonstrate the structure and function of the facial and trigeminal nerves and help in problem-based learning. We need more applications like this to be produced for different systems of the body, thereby making learning meaningful and interesting. As every student learns concepts in their own ways, a student centric learning approach with customizable interactive applications available on various platforms would be the ideal way ahead.

References

1. Ifenthaler, D., Eseryel, D.: Facilitating complex learning by mobile augmented reality learning environments. In: Huang, R., Spector, J.M., Kinshuk, D.G.S. (eds.) Reshaping Learning, the Frontiers of Learning Technologies in a Global Context. Springer, New York (2013)
2. de Ribaupierre, S., Kapralos, B., Haji, F., Stroulia, E., Dubrowski, A., Eagleson, R.: Healthcare Training Enhancement Through Virtual Reality and Serious Games. In: Ma, M., Jain, L.C., Anderson, P. (eds.) Virtual, Augmented Reality and Serious Games for Healthcare 1. ISRL, vol. 68, pp. 9–27. Springer, Heidelberg (2014)
3. Kamphuis, C., Barsom, E., Schijven, M., Christoph, N.: Augmented reality in medical education? Perspect. Med. Educ. (2014), doi:10.1007/s40037-013-0107-7
4. Ma, M., Jain, L., Anderson, P. (eds.): Virtual, Augmented Reality and Serious Games for Healthcare 1. ISRL, vol. 68, 650 p. Springer, Heidelberg (2014) ISBN 978-3-642-54815-4
5. Notebaert, A.J.: Student perceptions about learning anatomy. PhD diss, University of Iowa (2009), http://ir.uiowa.edu/etd/312
6. Collins, J.: Modern approaches to teaching and learning anatomy. BMJ 337, a1310, 665–667 (2008)
7. Weatherall, D.: Science in the undergraduate curriculum during the 20th century. Med. Educ. 40, 195–201 (2006)
8. Wisco, J.J., Korin, T.L., Wimmers, P., Stark, M.E.: Integration of PBL cases into gross anatomy laboratory experiences followed by a modified TBL formative assessment: Pedagogy using the best of both worlds. UCLA Health system (2012)
9. Daly, C., Clunie, L., Ma, M.: Using microscope image-based computer generated 3D animations in teaching physiology. In: The 7th Annual University of Glasgow Learning & Teaching Conference: Challenging Conventions, Glasgow, UK, April 10 (2014)
10. Ma, M., Bale, K., Rea, P.: Constructionist Learning in Anatomy Education: What Anatomy Students Can Learn through Serious Games Development. In: Ma, M., Oliveira, M.F., Hauge, J.B., Duin, H., Thoben, K.-D. (eds.) SGDA 2012. LNCS, vol. 7528, pp. 43–58. Springer, Heidelberg (2012)
11. Gauthier, A.: Vascular Invaders: Exploring the motivational impact of a video game inan undergraduate study aid, http://bmc.med.utoronto.ca/bmc/research/masters-projects/ (accessed on July 4, 2014)

12. Scott, K., Kothari, M.J.: Evaluating the Patient with Peripheral Nervous System Complaints. J. Am. Osteopath. Assoc. 105(2), 71–83 (2005)
13. Liersch, K.: Royal Melbourne Hospital Maxillofacial Trauma Learning Package (January 2013)
14. Marur, T., Tuna, Y., Demirci, S.: Facial anatomy. Clinics in Dermatology 32(1), 14–23 (2013, 2014), http://dx.doi.org/10.1016/j.clindermatol.2013.05.022 ISSN 0738-081X
15. Chaurasia, B.D.: Human Anatomy Regional and Applied Dissection and Clinical, 5th edn. Head, Neck and Brain, vol. 3, pp. 351–358 (2010) ISBN 978-81-239-1865-5
16. Zygote Media Group, Inc. (2014), http://www.zygote.com/ (accessed on May 7, 2014)
17. James, B.: The Interactive Ear (2013), http://www.amplifon.co.uk/interactive-ear/index.html (accessed on May 3, 2014)
18. Mehrabi, A., Gluckstein, C., Benner, A., Hashemi, B., Herfarth, C., Kallinowski, F.: A new way for surgical education – development and evaluation of a computer-based training module. Comput. Biol. Med. 30, 97–109 (2000)
19. Anderson, P., Chapman, P., Ma, M., Rea, P.: Real-time Medical Visualization of Human Head and Neck Anatomy and its Applications for Dental Training and Simulation. Current Medical Imaging Reviews 9(4) (2013) ISSN: 1573-4056 (Print), 1875-6603 (Online)
20. Wattanasoontorn, V., Magdics, M., Boada, I., Sbert, M.: A Kinect-Based System for Cardiopulmonary Resuscitation Simulation: A Pilot Study. In: Ma, M., Oliveira, M.F., Petersen, S., Hauge, J.B. (eds.) SGDA 2013. LNCS, vol. 8101, pp. 51–63. Springer, Heidelberg (2013)
21. Ruiz, J.G., Cook, D.A., Levinson, A.J.: Computer animations in medical education: a critical literature review. Medical Education 43, 838–846 (2009)
22. Hu, J., Yu, H., Shao, J., Li, Z., Wang, J., Wang, Y.: Effects of dental 3D multimedia system on the performance of junior dental students in preclinical practice: a report from China. Adv. Health Sci. Educ. Theory Pract. 14, 123–133 (2009)
23. Morrison, J., Tversky, B., Betrancourt, M.: Animation: does it facilitate learning? In: Butz, A., Kruger, A., Olivier, P. (eds.) Smart Graphics: Papers from the 2000 AAAI Spring Symposium, March 20-22, pp. 53–60. AAAI Press, Menlo Park (2000)
24. Garg, A.X., Norman, G., Sperotable, L.: How medical students learn spatial anatomy. Lancet 357, 363–364 (2001)
25. Ramsden, P.: Learning to teach in higher education. RoutledgeFalmer, London (2003)
26. Cook, D.A., Bordage, G., Schmidt, H.G.: Description, justification and clarification: a framework for classifying the purposes of research in medical education. Med. Educ. 42, 128–133 (2008)

Sepsis Fast Track: A Serious Game for Medical Decision Making

Claudia Ribeiro[1], Micaela Monteiro[2] João Madeiras Pereira[1],
Tiago Antunes[1], and Jannicke Baalsrud Hauge[3]

[1] INESC-ID, Lisbon, Portugal
Instituto Superior Técnico, Universidade Técnica de Lisboa, Lisbon, Portugal
[2] Serviço de Urgência Geral Centro Hospitalar Lisboa Ocidental, Lisbon, Portugal
[3] Bremer Institut für Produktion und Logistik,
Hochschulring 20, 28359 Bremen Germany

Abstract. Severe sepsis and sepsis shock are major healthcare problems, affecting millions of people around the world. In order to undermine its potential threat and effect on patients, a medical decision protocol based on evidence was developed to help healthcare professionals to both identify as well as treat these patients in a timely manner. Keeping updated with the algorithm guidelines implies healthcare professionals attending workshop classes, which further complicates the management of resources in an Emergency Department. In this paper we describe the Sepsis Fast Track serious game aimed at teaching healthcare professionals the Sepsis Fast Track guidelines. A set of game mechanics where proposed and developed in order to integrate the guidelines pedagogical goals in the sepsis fast track serious game's gameplay cycle. A case study was conducted in order to validate if these mechanics are appropriate to both teach and refresh healthcare professionals' knowledge.

Keywords: Serious Games, Sepsis Fast Track, Game Mechanics, Work Practices.

1 Introduction

There is a growing interest in serious games as a means to educate and train people [7]. It has been argued that serious games provide powerful and effective learning environments because [9,24]:"(a) they use actions rather than explanations and create personal motivation and satisfaction, (b) they accommodate multiple learning styles and abilities, and (c) they foster decision-making and problem-solving activities in a virtual setting". Recently the field of medicine has also recognized the potential of serious games for medical education. Specifically, Kato et al. [15] and Graafland et al. [10] have described several research works that used serious games in healthcare, both for patient management as well as medical education.

The only games reported in the literature as implemented in clinical practice or formal education are so far virtual reality surgical simulators. The lack of

M. Ma et al. (Eds.): SGDA 2014, LNCS 8778, pp. 68–81, 2014.

adoption of serious games in medical education, and in particular emergency departments (EDs), is related to the lack of consensus on the game attributes supporting learning effectiveness, the process by which games engage learners, and the types of learning outcomes that can be achieved through gameplay [11]. Without this knowledge, game development is a very daunting task mostly dependent on the experience of the game developers and the participation of experts and the target group. In order to provide evidence that serious games could in fact be a fully fledged teaching instrument for medical students and professionals this research gap needs to be tackled.

In this paper we present a case study that involved designing a serious game targeting at medical education and its initial evaluation including a proposition of a set of game mechanics that should be taken into account when teaching the sepsis fast track protocol. Sepsis is a systematic, deleterious host response to infection leading to severe sepsis and septic shock. Currently is among the highest causes of death in the world [20] and was also the most expensive condition seen in U.S hospitals [22]. The speed and appropriateness of therapy administered in the first hour after severe sepsis develops are likely to influence outcome. In order to guarantee the identification and correct treatment of patients a protocol based on evidence has been proposed [3]. This protocol is only useful, if healthcare professionals are aware of its existence and also the specificities of its execution. Due to the high level of healthcare staff mobility this is not always the case. In order to address this challenge on-the-job training sessions accompanied by reading textbooks, as well as attending congresses and participating in practical courses are promoted. This requires a more complex management of resources that are already scarce in a ED's environment. Some of these challenges could be overcome with the adoption of serious games for medical training. Based upon this target, our aim was to understand how medical protocols could be translated to a serious game influencing and instilling healthcare professionals' adherence to the protocol guidelines. Consequently this would impact on their current work practices ensuring production of positive health outcomes.

Section II describes background work related to games and learning and the importance of game mechanics in serious games development process, whereas Section III presents the sepsis fast track serious game for which we used the four-dimensional framework [8] to structure the initial considerations on game design. The section also describes the pedagogical goals and how these where operationalized in terms of game mechanics. Section IV describes the case study conducted where as the results are presented in section V and detailed discussed in Section VI. We finalize with conclusions and future work (Section VII).

2 Pedagogical and Game Constructs

In order to bridge the gap between the learning outcomes and engaging game content it is essential to define the appropriate mechanisms to promote both learning and game play. Salen & Zimmerman argued that the gameplay produced by digital games is not directly attributable to the fantasy context of a game but "the mechanism through which players make meaningful choices and arrive at a meaningful play experience" [21, p. 317]. These mechanisms are commonly referred to by game developers as game mechanics [13]], however it is not clear if concepts applied in entertainment game design can also be directly applied to serious game design.

Lundgern and Björk [16] have defined a game mechanic as any part of the rule system of a game that covers one, and only one, possible kind of interaction that takes place during the game, be it general or specific. A game may consist of several mechanics, and a mechanic may be part of many games. How and when a mechanic is used during a game is defined by the rules of each game using the mechanic. Habgood while investigating the impacts of intrinsic and extrinsic fantasy on learning has defined a game mechanics as the procedural mechanisms of a game that provide the essential interactions required to create a meaningful gaming activity [12].

Dormans, the creator of the Machinations Framework [5] did also discussed the concept of game mechanics. The author stated that within the game design community game mechanics is often used as a synonym for rules which are closer to the implementation of the game. Meaning mechanics need to be accurate enough for game programmers to turn them into code without confusion or for board game players to execute them without failure. McGuire & Jenkins state that "Mechanics are the mathematical machines that give rise to gameplay; they create the abstract game" [17]. With that they point out that mechanics are media-independent: they are amongst those parts of games that are separable from images and sounds and might actually be transposed from one medium to another: a board game might be recreated as a computer game with different art and a different theme without altering the mechanics. Finally, other authors discussed the term "core mechanics" as the mechanics with which the player interacts more often and have the biggest impact on the gameplay [1,17].

The definitions described above were proposed for solving the problem caused by the lack of a game design vocabulary. Consequently, there are many uncertainties related to the characteristics of serious game mechanics as well as if these operate at the same level of abstraction as in conventional entertainment games. Hence, a pedagogy-game mechanic, i.e. serious game mechanic, would be particularly beneficial when considering the purpose and design of serious games. In the context of our work, we define a serious game mechanic as: the building blocks that encapsulate the relationship between game attributes and learning theories and when interconnected form a meaningful gameplay experience which provide the attainment of specific learning outcomes.

3   Sepsis Fast Track Serious Game

3.1   Design Considerations

The main goal of developing a serious game to teach the sepsis fast track algorithm was to provide a tool that help medical professionals to learn or refresh three main aspects of the protocol: sequence of medical interventions, the appropriate therapeutics that should be applied and when; and the interactions between physician-nurse and physician-patient. Since time is a critical factor for sepsis patients, these three aspects has to be done in a timely manner.

Consequently, before starting the game design and development process, it was of the utmost importance to understand the underlying processes and how to integrate both pedagogical considerations and game constructs so as to provide a virtual environment adapted to these objectives. This process included several meetings at the academic hospital involving a multi disciplinary team composed of physicians, a designer and software developers. Inspired by the Four-Dimensional Framework [8], we organized our discussion around four main dimensions, namely the context within which learning would take place, learner profiling, selection of pedagogies and mode of representation. From this discussion, it was decided that the Sepsis Fast Track serious game would be used as a on-the-job-training tool at the academic hospital, it would be targeted at ED physicians and doctors in training and the learning activities and outcomes would be accomplished by implementing different clinical cases with increased levels of difficulty. Regarding Representation [8], it would use a medium level of fidelity, including 3D animated non-player characters (the nurse and the patient).

The next step involved deciding how to structure the game and which game mechanics should be developed in order to accomplish the learning objectives, which is explained in the next sub-section.

3.2 Learning Objectives and Game Mechanics

In the Sepsis Fast Track serious game the player assumes the role of a physician and her/his goal is to confirm if the patient is or is not a case of sepsis, fill out the sepsis fast track form in the hospital IT system and carry out the appropriate medical interventions. The sepsis fast track form is composed of three main parts. The first is concerned with the systemic inflammatory response syndrome criteria, which are the body temperature, heart rate, and respiratory rate and is filled out by the triage nurse. The second part is where the information about the confirmation, or not, of the sepsis case suspicion is registered. It includes the registration of the arterial blood pressure, checked using the game mechanics *Examine ECG Monitor*, the exclusion criteria, checked using the game mechanics *Examine Patient Chart*, the Glasgow coma scale, checked using the game mechanics *Examine Patient*, and the lactate value, checked using the game mechanics *Examine Arterial Blood Gas*. In this part the sepsis fast track activation is also validated. Validating a sepsis case means asserting that the patient identified by the triage nurse is in fact a sepsis case. Finally, the third part of form is concerned with the information about the therapy administered to the patient. This should only be used if a sepsis case is confirmed and validated. Also, the time when the patient had the therapy (hemocultures, antibiotherapy and fluid therapy) should be registered.

The cause of an infection is often confirmed by a blood test. However, a blood test may not reveal infection in people received antibiotics, and consequently such infections will not be discovered by blood tests. In order to do a proper diagnosis and clearly identify the cause of the infection it is necessary to request complementary exams, such as X-ray, CT scan, or ultrasound. The *Request Complementary Exams* game mechanics (GM15) allows to the player to access the IT system and request all the necessary exams. After the request is placed the nurse informs the player of the results for all the requested exams.

Based on thorough discussion with the medical experts and the multidisciplinary team eleven main learning objectives were identified. This was very important in order to be able to define define the game mechanics creating the gameplay in which the player would interact with a sepsis case and correctly learn the protocol. The proposed game mechanics for the Sepsis Fast Track gameplay are described below. The *Examine Patient* game mechanics (GM1) (Fig. 1) allows the player to perform a physical exam of the patient and additionally evaluate his neurological state. In addition to doing a physical exam and evaluating the patients' neurological state, a physician should also ask the patient what are her/his current complaints. The information is available through the *Symptoms Check* game mechanics (GM2) which allows the player to interact with the patient and request information regarding her/his current condition.

The *Check ECG Monitor* game mechanics (GM3) allows measuring the patient's heart rate, respiratory rate, and blood pressure (systolic, diastolic and mean). To trigger this mechanics, the player must click on the ECG Monitor available in the examination room. Evaluating the systolic blood pressure allows the player to evaluate the patient's state of hypoperfusion, which is a condition for confirming the sepsis case. There is a sign of hypoperfusion if the systolic blood pressure is less than 90mmHg.

The *Check Patient's Chart* game mechanics (GM4) allows the player to check the patient's personal and medical information, such as, name, age, complaints registered during the triage, habits and medical history. With the information available in the patient's chart, the player can decide if the patient has any exclusion criteria. Even if a patient has a confirmed sepsis infection and hypoperfusion, if he has any exclusion criteria the antibiotherapy cannot be administered. Therefore, the sepsis fast track must not be validated and the evaluation must end. The patients' chart is represented by a clipboard on the patient's bed.

The *Arterial Blood Gas* game mechanics (GM5) allows the player to perform a blood gas exam. The Arterial blood gas is a blood test that in the sepsis evaluation is used to analyse the blood lactate. If a patient has a lactate value

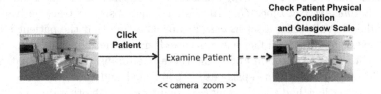

Fig. 1. Examine Patient Game Mechanics (GM1)

of less than 4mmol/L, it is an indication of a possible sepsis case. The blood gas report has the same layout and information as the one used in the real environment.

The *Insert Venous Catheter, Examine Central Venous Pressure* and *Examine Venous Blood Gas* game mechanics (GM6, GM7 and GM9) allows the player to monitor the patient's current central venous pressure. Together with the urine rate (*Examine Urine Flow Rate* game mechanics (GM8)), these values allow the player to assess if the fluid therapy is having the desired effect on the patient.

Almost all kinds of micro organisms from blood can be isolated by hemoculture. Despite its limiting factors (time of sampling, duration of incubation, possible contamination of samples, number of hemocultures), hemoculture is the only method by which the causes of bacteria and sepsis can be isolated. Therefore, it is very important that the physician in charge requests this request in a timely manner. Hemoculture is accessible to the player through the *Request Hemoculture* game mechanics (GM10).

The *Fluid Therapy* game mechanics (GM11) allows the player to initiate fluid therapy (fluid challenge) in patients with sepsis-induced tissue hypoperfusion and suspicion of hypovolemia to achieve a minimum of 30 mL/kg of crystalloids (more rapid administration and greater amounts of fluid may be needed in some patients). However, this game mechanics should be used throughout the gameplay as well as hemodynamic improvement. Therefore, is very important that the physician continually reassesses the patient's current condition.

Once a suspected sepsis case is confirmed, the most important action a physician should do is to administer antibiotic therapy. Therefore, the *Antibiotic Therapy* game mechanics (GM12) is the most important game mechanics of Sepsis Fast Track serious game. It allows the administration of an antibiotic to the patient, which must be made within one hour, since the patient's admission in the Emergency Department. This is critical and if it is not done in time, the patient can die, resulting in a game-over situation.

If fluid replacement is not sufficient to maintain blood pressure, vasopressors can be used. This therapy is available through the *Administer Vasopressors* game mechanics (GM13). When triggered, the player must choose the appropriate vasopressor agent to be administered to the patient. This action starts a real-time cut scene that portrays the nurse administering the chosen vasopressor to the patient.

Patients with a suspicion of sepsis are in a critical condition and must be monitored during the 24 hours after they were diagnosed during triage. Once the patient is given the initial therapeutics (antibiotic, fluid therapy) she/he should be transferred to the intensive care unit where she/he is constantly monitored and attended in order to guarantee that her/his health condition doesn't deteriorate. This would be the ideal scenario but the intensive care unit is an area of the ED that has allocation problems due to crowding. Therefore, transferring a patient is always a difficult task. We have introduced this situation in the gameplay through the *Contact Intensive Care Unit* game mechanics (GM16).

Table 1. Learning Objectives and Game Mechanics

Learning Objectives	Game Mechanics
0 hour	
Confirm suspicion	GM1, GM2, GM3, GM4, GM5
Administer initial therapeutics	GM12, GM13
Register clinical case in the IT System	GM14
Request and interpret the appropriate complementary exams	GM5, GM7, GM8, GM9, GM10, GM15
Transfer patient to the ICU	GM16
After 1 hour	
Reassess patient condition	GM1, GM2, GM3, GM5, GM7, GM8
Perform appropriate therapeutics acts to keep CVP > 8	GM6, GM7, GM11
Transfer patient to the ICU	GM16
After 1 hour and 30 m	
Reassess patient condition	GM1, GM2, GM3, GM5, GM7, GM8
Perform appropriate therapeutics acts to keep MAP > 65	GM3, GM13
Transfer patient to the ICU	GM16
After 2 hour	
Reassess patient condition	GM1, GM2, GM3, GM5, GM7, GM8
Perform appropriate therapeutics acts to keep $S_cVO_2 > 70\%$	GM7, GM9
Transfer patient to the ICU	GM16

The player should contact the intensive care unit between each protocol step in order to successfully transfer the patient.

The relationship between learning objectives and game mechanics is summarized in Table 1.

4   Case Study: Materials and Methods

The main purpose of the case study is to understand if the proposed game mechanics of the serious game have the expected results in healthcare professionals knowledge. In order to assess that we collected two sources of data: the in-game log data and hospital IT data.

Our sample was composed by a group of 15 physicians from which 11 work in the ED Monday to Friday from 8h to 20h and 4 doctors in training who only work in the ED on a weekly basis. Before we started the study we asked the physician to fill out a questionnaires regarding demographic information, her/his gaming habits, previous knowledge regarding the sepsis fast track protocol and experience with serious games. Next they played two clinical cases, one positive and one negative sepsis case. Also in between and at the end of the game session several questions were asked regarding the importance of certain game attributes for learning as well as the suitability of the game to teach this medical procedure both to doctors in training and physicians. After one month, data were retrieved from the hospital IT system containing information about number of sepsis fast track activations and also the data filled out for each sepsis case in the sepsis fast track form. This data only concerned the ED and not the hole hospital. These data comprises the time interval between December 2013 to February 2014, which encompasses the month before the study, the month the study occurred and the month after the study ended.

5   Results

The physicians participating in this study were composed of 11 females and 4 males with an average age of 37 (sd ≈ 11.09) years old and 6 years (sd ≈ 6.59) of previous experience working in an emergency department. Regarding game habits and previous experience with serious games, 50% indicated that they never played games and the other 50% rarely played games (mostly casual games). 56% had previous experience with simulators in medical education (Resuscitation) and 69% of them had previous training on the sepsis fast track protocol in a face-to-face class.

5.1   In-Game Log Analysis

One of the main goals of our serious game is to teach both doctors in training and physicians the sepsis fast track protocol medical acts sequence and appropriate therapeutics that should be administered and when. In order to collect information that allows to measure physicians current knowledge a module was implemented in the game that collects chronological logging data about the decisions made by the physicians in each step of the sepsis fast track protocol while playing the clinical cases. A summary of the right decisions made by both doctors in training and physicians while playing clinical case 8 is presented in Table 2. We only analysed the data from clinical case 8, because clinical case 5 is a false positive meaning, is a patient that has symptoms that indicate a possible sepsis case but in fact it is not.

In the first step of the fast track protocol the physician has to confirm if it is or not a sepsis patient. This involves confirming an infection suspicion, the existence of hipoperfusion and if the patient doesn't have any exclusion criteria (e.g. pregnancy). Once a decision is made the appropriate data should be registered in the hospital IT system which included confirming the activation of the sepsis fast track. As shown in Table 2 both doctors in training and physicians have correctly evaluated the existence of an infection. However, less than half of the physicians started to execute the procedures of the next protocol step without filling out the sepsis form and validating the activation of the sepsis fast track in the hospital IT system.

The next step of the protocol involves administering the initial therapeutics to the patient as well as monitor the patients conditions. This is a very time critical and important step in the treatment. The log data of the game showed that most physicians were unaware of the recommended amount of fluids that should be given in the first hour nor gave priority to administer antibiotic and fluid therapy which are the two therapeutics that can potentially save a patient if administered in a timely manner.

After this initial treatment, the protocol states that the central venous pressure (CVP), mean arterial pressure (MAP) and S_cVO_2 values should be above

Table 2. Medical procedures, number of right decisions during gameplay and game mechanics

	Medical Procedures	Physicians	Doctors in training	Game Mechanics
1	Confirm suspicion	11	4	GM1, GM2, GM5
2	Hipoperfusion?	11	4	GM3
3	Without Exclusion Criteria	11	4	GM4
4	Sepsis Fast Track Activation (IT System)	5	3	GM14
5	Hemocultures	10	2	GM10
6	Complementary Exams?	10	1	GM15
7	Administer Antibiotic Therapy	7	2	GM12
8	Administer Fuild Therapy	7	2	GM11
9	Fluids Quantity	8	0	GM11
10	Contact ICU	6	1	GM16
11	Reassess patient condition	4	1	GM1, GM2, GM3
12	Insert Venous Catheter	5	1	GM6
13	Examine Central Venous Pressure (CVP)	5	1	GM7
14	Examine Urine Flow Rate	5	3	GM8
15	Administer Fluid Therapy	3	1	GM11
16	Contact ICU	0	0	GM16
17	Reassess Patient Condition	9	4	GM1, GM2, GM3
18	Reassess CVP ICU	6	4	GM7
19	Reassess Urine Flow Rate	8	4	GM8
20	Administer Vasopressors	4	4	GM13
21	Contact ICU	0	4	GM16
22	Reassess Patient Condition	11	4	GM1, GM2, GM3
23	Reassess CVP ICU	11	4	GM7
24	Reassess Urine Flow Rate	11	4	GM8
25	Request Blood Venous Gas Exam	11	4	GM9
26	Contact ICU	11	4	GM16

a certain recommended value. To monitor and regulate the CVP the physician has to apply a central venous catheter and according to the CVP value reinforce the amount of fluids currently given to the patient. Checking the urine flow rate is another relevant measure to verify if the fluid therapy is having the desired effect on the patient and although it is not specifically recommended by the protocol we have captured if and when the physicians checked this value. In this particular protocol step the physicians did in general poorly as shown in Table 2. Most of them didn't reassess the patient condition before deciding what to do next and tried to measure the CVP without applying a catheter to the patient or administer fluids without knowing the CVP value.

Monitoring and assessing the MAP current value involves checking the vital signs monitor and according to its value and current patient condition decide if it is necessary to administer vasopressors. In this step most physicians reassessed the patient's current condition before deciding what to do next but in most cases didn't check the current CVP value and as in the previous step didn't tried to contact the ICU to check if there was an opening to transfer the patient.

In the last step of the protocol, which consisted in assessing and monitoring the S_cVO_2 current value, every physician correctly executed the protocol procedures.

Comparing the performance between physicians and doctors in training we noticed that initially all had difficulties both in the sequence of medical interventions as well as choosing the right therapeutics but all showed an improvement towards the end of the protocol, specifically in the two final steps.

5.2 Hospital Data Analysis

Another important goal of our study was to understand if playing the serious game would influence medical professionals' current work practices, namely correctly activating, confirming and executing the sepsis fast track protocol. In order to verify if the serious game had an impact on work practices we have collected the number of sepsis track activations and form completion from December 2013 to February 2014. A summary of this data is presented in Figure 2.

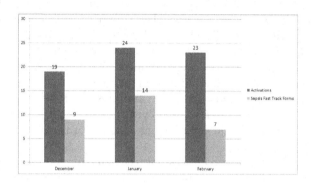

Fig. 2. Number of Sepsis Fast Track Activations and Number of Forms Completed by Physicians

The Hospital IT information includes the number of Sepsis Fast Track forms that were filled out by physicians and also patient's data regarding the sepsis case. This includes the patient's medical condition and the validation, or not, of the Sepsis Fast Track. Analysing this information would allow us to know if there was any impacts on physicians work practices regarding to the registration of the sepsis forms. The registration of these forms is important for better hospital management and ultimately for patient care quality. Also we have collect the number of activation and form completion of December 2013, January and February 2014 so we have comparison measure. The evaluation with the physicians occurred in the beginning of January 2014, the percentage of forms registration of January and February of 2014 are respectively 58.33% and 30.43%. January is 22.70% above the average, and February is 5.2% bellow the average.

Although the results seem promising, there are several factors that may affect the results. Namely, the seasonality and the dynamics of infectious diseases, sepsis in particular [2,4]. Therefore, the results presented may not be conclusive.

6 Discussion

The main goal of our case study was to understand if the proposed game mechanics of the serious game have the expected improvement in healthcare professionals' knowledge. Our in-log analysis showed that although physicians have a had previous training in the sepsis fast track protocol and also practical experience in diagnosing and treating sepsis patients their performance wasn't in general superior to the doctors in training. We believe that this result is related to several factors. One is that in general physicians already carry out the process based on previous experience, often including many years diagnosing and treating patients in the emergency department requiring to handle situations differently than the sepsis fast track protocol prescribes. In addition, most physicians stated their in- ability to do multitasking while playing. We also noticed that they did more mistakes by reassessing the patient current condition. In the real environment they are used to have all the relevant information visible and easily accessible. Therefore, having to specifically interact with medical equipment and characters in the virtual environment was not intuitive. This opinion was both shared by physicians and doctors in training.

Another factor was the fact that the physicians didn't really feel in the role of a real physician in the virtual environment. We observed that they often repeated certain decisions (e.g. administering antibiotic) that in a real situation would be very harmful to the patient. We think this was fostered since they new that it would have no consequences, and even though the objective of the game is to train a protocol in a safe environment, this had a negative impact on the learning.

These factors are both related to the how the game mechanics were integrated in the gameplay as well as the representation dimension of the 4-DF, namely how interactive, what levels of fidelity are required and how immersive the experience needs to be. From these results we believe that regarding fidelity, clinical case data and patient condition has to evolve as close as possible to how it would be in real life if the same procedures have been done. In terms of interactivity, the physicians need to interact with the environment around them more closely to what they are used to do. Unnecessary actions (e.g. clicking objects) don't seem to be relevant to them because it is not how the real environment works.

A virtual environment collapses when the game world is inconsistent with player's expectations. Also, we don't perceive a virtual environment as being "real" unless it reacts to us in a "realistic" way - "action is a necessary component of perception" [14]. A similar point was made by Varela [23] "objects are not seen by the visual extraction of features, but rather by the visual guidance of action". Therefore, our understanding is that interactivity and fidelity are critical factors when designing serious games for medical education. Specifically, these factors need to be very well balanced in order to create an immersive virtual environment adapted to the physicians expectations where they can learn from experience as they do in the real world. We believe that this would help increase their willingness to accept these training methods and also help facilitate transferring the knowledge gain from playing the serious game to the real world environment (work practices). Regarding game mechanics, their integration in the gameplay should have into consideration the multitasking nature of physicians work. Therefore, we believe that they would create a more believable and also natural decision-making environment for physicians if they were aggregated in chunks of multi-tasks (tasks that can be carried out in parallel) instead of single-tasks (tasks that can be carried out in sequence).

The in-game feedback and the debriefing phase of the game were also mentioned several times during the interviews as important game attributes for an effective learning experience with the serious game. The importance of feedback and assessment in learning processes have already been stressed by many theories of learning. Nevertheless, implementing effective feedback is still a challenge in the context of serious games. This difficulty arises as a consequence of the need to provide feedback seamlessly alongside an engaging gameplay experience, and balancing these two factors is a considerable design challenge. From the experience derived from this study and also with the Critical Transport serious game [19], both feedback and assessment have to take into account both the pedagogical content being taught as well as to whom it is being taught. In-game feedback has to provide information both to help the player to improve his current strategy (single-loop learning versus double-loop learning) as well as motivate him to continually being engaged in the game activity. Combining these two effects during game play helps increase the probability of learning to occur.

With this aim in mind we have derived, together with physicians, a list of minor and major errors from the sepsis fast track protocol. By providing these two levels of feedback we have create a certain level of flexibility for physicians to try different strategies and also define different feedback frequencies. Major errors are very severe for the current condition of the patient, while minor errors constitute less danger to the patient. When a major error occurs the player is always warned via a pop-up message as well as decreased in available player's lives and current score. In the case of minor errors, how the in-game feedback is given depends on the current number of minors errors and the step of the protocol. Moreover, whenever there is a major or minor error there is also visual feedback associated through the deterioration of patient condition and cues provided by the nurse in the virtual environment. Therefore, the in-game feedback was both evaluative (measure variables) and interpretive (measure variables and model their relationships) [6]. The assessment provided in the debriefing phase on the other hand was of the type understanding [6], meaning it provided the player with a description of the each error made during gameplay with an explanation why it was an error and what would be the correct decision to make in that situation. Moreover, this information is complemented with a visual representation of the sepsis protocol and an indication of in what step of the protocol it has occurred.

After a thorough analysis, we have concluded that the results from the hospital IT system are inconclusive. Therefore, we cannot discuss if the serious game had or not an impact on work practices but we can discuss possible explanations for these results. Physicians with prior sepsis fast track training may have incorrectly presumed that they already knew the material being covered and did not pay as close attention to the serious game sessions, as already point out at the beginning of this section. This same phenomenon was also noted on the study reported by Platz et al. [18]. Doctors in training with no prior training are more likely to recognize their lack of knowledge and therefore pay closer attention to the material being presented. Moreover, the physicians only played one clinical case and we only analysed two months of post-game data. Therefore, we believe further studies should be conducted that perhaps also include a pre/post/retention-test data analysis.

7   Conclusions

In this paper we have described the sepsis fast track serious game developed based on the theoretical work proposed by the 4-DF and the concept of game mechanics. The current version of the sepsis fast track serious games was implemented according to the described game mechanics. The initial evaluation allowed us to point out a set of issues regarding learning and design guidelines that should be taken into account when developing serious games for medical education. The next planned step is to start using the sepsis fast track serious game to teach the sepsis fast track protocol to all the doctors in training working in the emergency department of the academic hospital. With this experience we expected to clearly validate the external validity of our serious game. Also longitudinal retention tests will be conducted in order to understand with which frequency doctors in training should train with the serious game in order to guarantee that the level of knowledge regarding sepsis fast track protocol doesn't decrease over time. Performing this test is very important both to enforce the efficiency of serious games in knowledge retention as well as to provide evidence that using these kind of educational tool could be used as an alternative to face-to-face training.

Acknowledgment. This work was supported by FCT (INESC-ID multiannual funding) under the project PEst-OE/EEI/LA0021/2013. The authors also would like to acknowledge to the European funded Project Games and Learning Alliance (FP7 258169) the Network of Excellence (NoE) on Serious Games.

References

1. Adams, E., Rollings, A.: Fundamentals of Game Design. Pearson Education, Inc., Upper Saddle River (2007)
2. Altizer, S., Dobson, A., Hosseini, P., Hudson, P., Pascual, M., Rohani, P.: Seasonality and the dynamics of infectious diseases. Ecology Letters 9(4), 467–484 (2006), http://dx.doi.org/10.1111/j.1461-0248.2005.00879.x
3. commitee, s.: Surviving sepsis campaign: International guidelines for management of severe sepsis and septic shock: 2012 (2012), http://www.sccm.org/Documents/SSC-Guidelines.pdf
4. Danai, P., Sinha, S., Moss, M., Haber, M., Martin, G.S.: Seasonal variation in the epidemiology of sepsis. Critical Care Medicine 35(2), 410–415 (2007)
5. Dormans, J.: Engineering Emergence Applied Theory for Game Design. Ph.D. thesis, University of Amsterdam (2012)

6. Dunwell, I., De Freitas, S., Jarvis, S.: Four-dimensional consideration of feedback in serious games. In: Digital Games and Learning, pp. 42–62 (2011)
7. Durkin, K.: Videogames and young people with developmental disorders. Review of General Psychology 14(2), 122–140 (2010), http://dx.doi.org/10.1037/a0019438
8. de Freitas, S., Oliver, M.: How can exploratory learning with games and simulations within the curriculum be most effectively evaluated? Computers & Education 46(3), 249–264 (2006), http://www.sciencedirect.com/science/article/pii/S0360131505001600
9. Garris, R., Ahlers, R., Driskell, J.E.: Games, motivation, and learning: A research and practice model. Simulation & Gaming 33(4), 441–467 (2002)
10. Graafland, M., Schraagen, J.M., Schijven, M.P.: Systematic review of serious games for medical education and surgical skills training. British Journal of Surgery 99(10), 1322–1330 (2012), http://dx.doi.org/10.1002/bjs.8819
11. Guillén-Nieto, V., Aleson-Carbonell, M.: Serious games and learning effectiveness: The case of it's a deal! Comput. Educ. 58(1), 435–448 (2012), http://dx.doi.org/10.1016/j.compedu.2011.07.015
12. Habgood, M.P.J.: The Effective Integration of Digital Games and Learning Content. Ph.D. thesis, University of Nottingham (2007)
13. Habgood, M.P.J., Overmars, M.: The game maker's apprentice: Game development for beginners. APress, Berkley (2006)
14. Held, R., Hein, A.: Movement-produced stimulation in the development of visually guided behavior. J. Comp. Physiol. Psychol., 872–876 (1963)
15. Kato, M.P.: Video games in health care: Closing the gap. Review of General Psychology 14(2), 113–121 (2010)
16. Lundgren, S., Björk, S.: Game mechanics: Describing computer-augmented games in terms of interaction. In: Proceeding of TIDSE 2003 (2003)
17. McGuire, M., Jenkins, O.C.: Creating Games: Mechanics, Content, and Technology. A.K. Peters, Ltd., Wellesley (2009)
18. Platz, E., Liteplo, A., Hurwitz, S., Hwang, J.: Are live instructors replaceable? computer vs. classroom lectures for {EFAST} training. The Journal of Emergency Medicine 40(5), 534–538 (2011), http://www.sciencedirect.com/science/article/pii/S0736467909007550
19. Ribeiro, C., Antunes, T., Monteiro, M., Pereira, J.: Serious games in formal medical education: An experimental study. In: 2013 5th International Conference on Games and Virtual Worlds for Serious Applications (VS-GAMES), pp. 1–8 (2013)
20. Russel, J.: The current management of septic shock. Minerva Medica 99(5), 431–458 (2008)
21. Salen, K., Zimmerman, E.: Rules of play: Game design fundamentals. The MIT Press, Cambridge (2004)
22. Torio, C., Andrews, R.: National inpatient hospital costs: The most expensive conditions by payer, 2011. hcup statistical brief #160. Tech. rep., Agency for Healthcare Research and Quality, Rockville, MD (August 2013)
23. Varela, F.: The Embodied Mind. MIT Press (1991)
24. Wrzesien, M., Raya, M.A.: Learning in serious virtual worlds: Evaluation of learning effectiveness and appeal to students in the e-junior project. Computers & Education 55(1), 178–187 (2010), http://www.sciencedirect.com/science/article/pii/S0360131510000060

iBUAT: Paper Prototyping of Interactive Game Design Authoring Tool for Children

Laili Farhana Md Ibharim and Maizatul Hayati Mohamad Yatim

Computing Department, Faculty of Art, Computing and Creative Industry,
Sultan Idris Education University, Malaysia
life_farhana@yahoo.com and maizatul@fskik.upsi.edu.my

Abstract. There are variety of authoring tools for game design in our market nowadays that can be accessed via online or software installation. However, the main question is if the authoring tools are child-friendly, especially in using the touch screen device? This paper describes the preliminary development process of authoring tool for game design known as paper prototyping with children aged between 7 and 12 years old. The evaluation applied the Think Aloud technique in observation and semi structured interview. This study focused on the seven elements of usability, which are i) interface design; ii) features and functionality; iii) interaction; iv) satisfaction; v) effectiveness; vi) efficiency; and vi) learnability of the authoring tool.

Keywords: Authoring tool, children, creativity and skill, game design.

1   Introduction

Children nowadays are known as the digital generations. They live in a ubiquitous environment in which technology has always been around them. Children's lives today are driven by technological advances which promote laptops, tablets, smartphones and other gadgets as their toys. Digital games are also familiar to them. In fact, digital games have contributed to multibillion-dollar industry and will continue to grow rapidly in line with demand. This encourages the implementation of digital games in various fields of knowledge and skills to support learning and knowledge across disciplines.

In drawing the development of knowledge in terms of creativity and skill, children do not only play the role as a digital games player. In fact, they are perceived to have great potential to create, design and develop their own digital games [1, 2, 3]. Game designing is considered as a novelty activity among the society these days, but not impossible to implement. In this study, the researchers conducted a usability test to an authoring tool for game design, especially for children, namely iBUAT (Invention Board Unique Authoring Tool). This authoring tool is believed to be an interactive digital tool that improves children's development in terms of cognitive, emotion, personality, social, and inventiveness.

M. Ma et al. (Eds.): SGDA 2014, LNCS 8778, pp. 82–92, 2014.
© Springer International Publishing Switzerland 2014

The perception and acceptance of children for interactive product are quite different than adults especially in user interface layout [4]. Therefore, in order to obtain a product that is appropriate for children, developers must understand their nature, behaviour, and needs. The methodology used in the Human Computer Interaction field to design multimedia product specifically for children, known as Child-Centred Design, is adapted from User-Centred Design. Children are actively involved in the design process to get information more clearly and accurately about their needs as a user. Interaction Design and Children should be put highly recommended in the product for its core interface, functionality, and features

In this study, the researchers conducted a low fidelity testing using paper prototyping for iBUAT. Using paper prototyping enables a developer to save time, money, and risk to test the interface of the product before the real product development. Other than that, this method allows for easy modification to improve the existing design in the early phases of designing [5]. This method is primarily used by established computer companies, such as IBM and Microsoft, to develop their products [6].

2   Children as Game Designer

The development and proliferation of digital games today do not only allow children to play. Indirectly, they are able to produce their own fantastic ideas, comments, and suggestions in making the game more fun and to meet their expectations based on their experience and observation while playing. Children have vast potential to be game designers. This is fully supported by Kafai as she urged the children to become producers rather than consumers for computer games [2]. Previously, Druin has established four main roles of children in designing of new technology, especially in the development of interactive multimedia products [7]. The involvement of children as i) users; ii) testers; iii) informants; and iv) design partners varies according to the task and the goal of the adult designer in the design process for new technology.

Based on previous studies involving children in digital games, a number of researchers have taken one step further to expand the role of children as designers, especially in the learning process in the classroom [1], [3], [8]. Designing activity for digital games has brought a variety of learning approaches practice in the classroom especially in term of creative process. This circumstance is believed to bring positive impact on intellectual and attitudes of children in the study. The approach is also dependent on Bloom's Digital Taxonomy which places creating as the highest order thinking skill [9]. Here, the term 'creating' refers to children create their own digital games using appropriate authoring tool and technology. This view is also recommended in the constructionism learning theory that states learning becomes more meaningful when children learn to construct their own artefacts actively [10]. Furthermore, the game design approach can facilitate the exchange of knowledge among students and provide students a fun learning environment, depending on the requirement of the 21st century skills [8]. Besides, creativity and skills of children can be generated and developed via the integration of technology in the learning process.

3   Game Design Authoring Tool for Children

Authoring tool has been one of the software applications that have received favourable response among users to facilitate their tasks, such as photo editing, song composing and game making. Practitioners, especially in the field of entertainment, advertising, media presentation, and education, have taken advantage from a variety of authoring tools in our market nowadays to develop multimedia applications and products more conveniently, economically, and fast. With the involvement of authoring tool for game designing and development for children, it can be referred to as a software based on the principles and guidelines of constructivism that allow children to design and develop their own digital games without high technical and programming knowledge [11]. Most of the authoring tools use three types of techniques, which are card or page base (tool book and hypercard), icon base (provided in the gallery), and time base (timeline). Children are able to explore the objects and features available to design their games with their own creativity and intention.

Authoring tool for design digital games is beneficial to users to generate concepts and game content through the gamification and support collaborative development among children [12]. Great selection of authoring tool is important to assist the young designers to produce good digital games [11]. Statement of the National Association for the Education of Young Children (NAEYC) in 1996 also emphasized that the software (authoring tool) that correspond to a child's development offers opportunities for them to play, learn and create. The main aspects highlighted for a good authoring tool are consistency, child-friendliness, degrees of functionality, staying in the flow, reflection, familiar conceptual models, and familiar steps for programming [4], [11]. Furthermore, it also must emphasize interactions involved in the design process and allow children to independently explore and manipulate to expand their creativity, experience, and skills.

4   Methodology

4.1   Participants and Location

In usability testing of a system and multimedia products, Nielsen has stated that 5 participants are sufficient [13]. Thus, the researchers have conducted tests on 8 children (5 boys and 3 girls) aged between 7 and 12 years old in this usability test. According to Piaget, the children chosen are in the concrete operational stage where they fit the criteria to highlight their skills and creativity more clearly and accurately [14], and have experience with the authoring tool and technology to facilitate the usability test conducted [5]. The participants were randomly selected as these children voluntarily joined the testing during Games Day carnival organized by Digital Games Associates, Faculty of Art, Computing and Creative Industry. The background of the participants, such as sex, religion, and race, were not asserted in this usability test. The involvement of these participants also was with written permission from their parents. The usability test also involved the researchers as testers to guide the participants through the task and prompted for the users' thoughts; two research assistants acted as observers to take down notes based on the observation checklist and facilitators as 'computer' to facilitate the researchers with the components laid for quick access of iBUAT GUI components.

The testing was conducted in an open space at a corner of the hall where the Games Day activities were held. This location was chosen so that the participants were still in the mood to play after they had tried and enjoyed all kinds of games and activities during the Games Day. Besides, this was also to avoid the children to feel depressed as if they were being evaluated in a laboratory [5].

4.2   iBUAT Paper Prototyping Design

Previously, the same researchers have conducted a heuristic evaluation towards a few game developments with authoring tools for children [4]. Based on the findings, the researchers found that the authoring tools that met almost all the requirements in the heuristic evaluation set have had similar interface layout.

The iBUAT is the acronym of Invention Board Unique Authoring Tool. The iBUAT is essentially a game authoring tool that is geared towards children, allowing them to design and play their own games. Children have to create their story for the games using characters and objects provided. The iBUAT has three main menus; i) Play Game: Users play the game they have designed; ii) Design Game: Users design new games or edit games they have designed, and iii) Tutorial: Users learn how to design their own games using the features and functionality provided in the iBUAT.

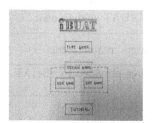  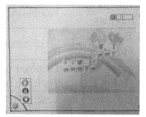

Fig. 1. Menu interface for paper prototype of iBUAT   **Fig. 2.** Design Game interface for paper prototype of iBUAT   **Fig. 3.** Play Game interface for paper prototype of iBUAT

The iBUAT emphasizes the elements of educational technology within its development design. Apart from the fun, engaging, and motivational aspects, the iBUAT content must meet the characteristics contained in education, such as pedagogy and learning theories. Experience, creation, and sharing are the core elements injected in the iBUAT content. As iBUAT is specifically designed for children to design their games on touch screen display, the researchers found that the iBUAT required simple but complete interactive interface display with objects, features, and functionality that were easy to be accessed by children. In addition, the characters and objects available in the gallery that were applicable to the concept of an adventurous storytelling had to be diversified so that the children would be able to create their games creatively.

4.3   Instruments

The usability testing was carried out using paper prototyping with observation and interview methods [5]. Observation was conducted using an observation checklist and video recording as reference for data analysis phase. The observation checklist was adapted from the Post Study System Usability Questionnaire (PSSUQ) [15]. It contains two parts; i) demographic information of the participants involved, and ii) observation criteria that contains 16 items based on seven usability elements, as shown in Table 1.

Table 1. Observation checklist elements

Element	Description
Interface (4 items)	To observe the convenience of layout, icons, objects and navigation on screen display for iBUAT.
Functionality and features (2 items)	To observe the features and functionality provided in the iBUAT gallery in order to meet users' expectation in performing tasks.
Interaction (2 items)	To observe the users' perception with the icons and navigation buttons used in iBUAT.
Satisfaction (2 items)	To observe the users' engagement and enjoyment using the iBUAT to design their desired games.
Efficiency (2 items)	To observe the users' ability to handle the iBUAT on their own.
Effectiveness (2 items)	To observe the ability of iBUAT to fulfil users' requirements.
Learnability (2 items)	To observe the necessity of tutorial features provided by iBUAT to teach the users.

The purpose of semi-structured interview for each participant was to find out more details and deep meaning about the testing session that cannot be seen by our naked eyes [5]. Thus, the interview focused on four important aspects to ensure the usability of iBUAT, which are; i) the difficulties faced by the participants while using the prototype; ii) favourite objects, tools, features, and functions of the prototype; iii) the commands on the interface and the layout of the prototype, and iv) suggestions to improve the prototype. The data gathered was analyse using Atlas.ti according to themes and categories to study.

4.4   Testing Procedure

The usability testing was conducted individually. The researchers handled the testing session based on the Guidelines for Usability Testing with Children [16]. The Think

Aloud technique was applied in this testing because in a usability test, verbal protocols are claimed to uncover the cognitive processes of the participants [5]. Furthermore, this technique has been flexible, especially for agile project to evaluate the users' interface with any form of technology.

5   Result and Discussion

The researcher and the two research assistants discussed what they had observed and heard after each participant had completed their test. This was done to avoid personal perception from the researchers on the data gathered. Based on the data collected from the observation checklist, and interview transcription and recording, the summarized results are as in the following:

5.1   Findings from Observation

Interface: All the participants were comfortable with the iBUAT layout, icons, objects, and the navigation on the screen. The children were more attracted to the simple interface display that was easy to understand [4], [11]. However, the children were a little confused with some of the forms and functions of the icons that are rarely used in gameplay activities, such as 'save' and 'edit' icons. This is because these icons are usually used in game design activity. Hidden functions too made the children helpless in finding the icons. Hence, the interface design should be clear, aesthetic, and the children must be familiar with the environment used in the authoring tool.

Functionality and Features: The iBUAT has all the features and functions that are required by the participants to complete the task of playing, designing or editing. The gallery provided by iBUAT is composed by a selection of objects, such as characters, tools, awards, and obstacles, to design a game. Some participants had problems in recognizing objects in the tool gallery and they could not relate the function of the tool in the storyline of their game. This occurred because they did not have any experience in using the tools, such as skateboard, magic wand, and axe. Therefore, the children's experience with their routine in real life plays an important role in the development of their cognitive and model mental [14]. Thus, the tools and objects portrayed should be close to their environment and daily use.

Interaction: The participants were able to interact with the iBUAT using the icons and the navigation on the screen. They also explored the iBUAT seamlessly. This is because, the iBUAT interface design is referred to interaction design principles, especially on mobile application for children such as visual design and technology use [17], [18]. In order to understand children's needs and perceptions of the product, the developer should emphasize on the type of interaction and the interaction style to ensure that they are able to control the authoring tool and device.

Satisfaction: Engagement is an important element to measure the success of products, especially for children [5]. The participants enjoyed designing their games using iBUAT from the signs of facial and speech expressions. They also agreed that iBUAT was easy to use and the objects in the gallery were easy to be remembered to help them design an interesting digital games.

Effectiveness: The participants had no problem in playing the games because all of them had experience, but none of them had experience in game designing. The researchers had to show some samples as reference. Furthermore, paper prototype is a static medium that cannot simulate the action and function. Some participants could not imagine how to design the game. As a solution, the researchers asked them to create a story and implement it in their design using the Think Aloud approach [5]. As a result, the participants managed to design their own games using iBUAT. Even though the game produced was incomplete and unable to play, the children felt proud of their work. With the advent of iBUAT, it is believed that the creativity of children can be enhanced and developed.

Efficiency: iBUAT is used on touch screen devices, such as tablets, iPads, and smart phones. Children at the concrete operational stage can manipulate things [14]. Children nowadays have been exposed to the technology and devices [19]. Their motor skills in handling devices using touch gesture have been trained informally while they play game application on the touch screen. Designing games using an authoring tool was quite unfamiliar for them. The researcher had to guide them while giving opportunity to explore iBUAT on their own. Despite this being only a paper prototype, the imagination and skills shown by the children in their game story design had been really amazing and interesting.

Learnability: As mentioned earlier, game designing activity is quite new for children. Video tutorial, somehow, may assist the participants to design their games using the features and functions provided by iBUAT because children may be attracted to video rather than text based. Hence, the iBUAT should consider educational video for human factors and interaction design content [20]. The video content should be easy to follow to avoid children from feeling confused and bored.

Fig. 4. Observation session as the participants explored the prototype on their own

Fig. 5. Interview session with the participants after they had completed the task and were satisfied with their game design using the prototype

5.2   Findings from the Interview

The difficulties faced by the participants while using the prototype
> **Question: What is your difficulties and limitation while designing your game using iBUAT?**
>> Participant 1: "I do not know how to start the design"
>> Participant 2: "The prototype is not easy to handle"
>> Participant 3: "I do not understand what to do"
>> Participant 4: "I am not sure which tool to use"
>> Participant 5: "I can use it"
>> Participant 6: "It is ok with me"
>> Participant 7: "Where to start, huh?"
>> Participant 8: "This button is for what?"

Finding Summary: Most of the participants had difficulties to start their design task because they had no experience before. Some of them had problems in recognizing the icons and their functions.

Implication: Model mental and experience might have helped them to explore the prototype [11]. Therefore, the video tutorial with animate instruction may help them to understand the iBUAT. Their curiosity led them to overcome the limitation, and finally, they produced their game design.

Favourite objects, tools, features and functions of the prototype
> **Question: Which is your favourite part in iBUAT?**
>> Participant 1: "The character is so cute!"
>> Participant 2: "I like to play the game rather than design the game"
>> Participant 3: "I like to custom my character"
>> Participant 4: "I like all"
>> Participant 5: "The fruit character looks yummy, hehehe"
>> Participant 6: "I like to decorate my character to look like me wearing a cap and a pair of spectacles"
>> Participant 7: "I want to watch the video tutorial"
>> Participant 8: "I like the background"

Finding Summary: The objects for game design (characters, obstacles, rewards, and etc.) provided by iBUAT attracted the participants' attention and interest. The customize features enhanced the participants' creativity to make their games different from others. Furthermore, side features, such as play game and tutorial video, were made interactive so that the participants could explore more.

Implication: Children and adult is different type of user. Design guidelines is important especially to develop product for children [17]. Developer have to put highly attention about children perception, acceptance and interaction design to develop interesting and usable product.

Comments on the interface and the layout of the prototype

Question: What do you think about the interface and layout of iBUAT? Do you like it?

Participant 1: "I feel comfortable with the interface and layout"

Participant 2: "Sometimes I feel confused with the icon buttons and navigation, I cannot find the delete button…"

Participant 3: "I do not know what to comment.."

Participant 4: "The stage to design is too small, I wish it is wider so that I can put more objects on my game design"

Participant 5: "There are no controllers on the screen. So, how can I play my game?"

Participant 6: "The interface and layout are quite simple"

Participant 7: "The interface is not colourful… I feel bored.."

Participant 8: "I like the interface and the layout"

Finding Summary: The participants are quite confuse about their role as designer while using iBUAT. They also have lack skill and knowledge in using authoring tool. They still need assistant and guidance using the iBUAT.

Implication: The products would have to meet the characteristics for children [7]. The interface and the layout had to be simple and easily recognized, especially for the icons and navigation. A developer would have to follow the interaction design principles, especially on mobile application. Thus, the interface and the layout would be able to drive the participants to use the prototype confidently.

Suggestions to improve the prototype

Question: If you want to design your game using iBUAT, what do you want iBUAT provide to you?

Participant 1: "I wish there were more features to make my games powerful, such as I can compete with my friends"

Participant 2: "Please add sounds to this prototype"

Participant 3: "I need more characters"

Participant 4: "I want guidance to assist me design my game"

Participant 5: "More characters would be better"

Participant 6: "Standardize the icon and navigation forms"

Participant 7: "I think that the level features were not appropriate because I did not use them at all"

Participant 8: "Give more options for customized features"

Finding Summary: The participants need verity of selection and features to design their games. The prototype can be improved in terms of the selection of objects, tools, features, and functions to fulfil the participants' requirements and expectations.

Implication: A developer would have to give serious attention on the requirements of authoring tool for children, especially the usability elements, the design of the interface, and the users' perceptions, as suggested in [4] and [11]. Thus, the iBUAT can be used as a powerful tool in education, especially to provide active learning environment.

6   Conclusion

Learning by design and learning by doing are believed as powerful approaches for children in enhancing their creativity and skills when the children are given opportunities to be directly involved in the designing process of digital games. Children have the advantage to explore the world and take a broader knowledge in creating and designing their own products. The development of iBUAT is one of the researchers' efforts to achieve the objective above. Therefore, it is hoped that the findings from this study would be able to provide some overviews to develop the real iBUAT. All the improvements would have to be made to make sure that the iBUAT is unique, usable, and has a positive impact on the children's development, especially in implementing technology into their education and daily lives.

Acknowledgement. The researchers would like to thank the children who took part in the study for sharing their thoughts and for being such an inspiration to us, and also to the Games Day committee that give full support to us to conduct the test successfully.

References

1. Baytak, A., Land, S.M., Smith, B.K.: Children as educational computer game designers: An exploratory study. TOJET 10(4) (2001)
2. Kafai, Y.B.: Playing and making games for learning: Instructionist and constructionist perspectives for game studies. Games and Culture 1(1), 36–40 (2006)
3. Prensky, M.: Students as designers and creators of educational computer games: Who else? British Journal of Educational Technology 39(6), 1004–1019 (2008)
4. Laili Farhana, M.I., Maizatul Hayati, M.Y.: Heuristic evaluation of children's authoring tool for game making. Journal of Education and Vocational Research 4(9), 259–264 (2013)
5. Markopoulos, P., Read, J.C., MacFarlane, S., Hoysniemi, J.: Evaluating Children's Interactive Products: Principles and Practices for Interaction Designers. Morgan Kaufmann, San Franscisco (2008)
6. Snyder, C.: Paper Prototyping: The Fast and Easy Way to Design and Refine User Interfaces. Morgan Kaufmann, San Franscisco (2003)
7. Druin, A.: The role of children in the design of new technology. Behaviour and Information Technology 21(1), 1–25 (2002)
8. Kamisah, O., Nurul Aini, B.: Teachers and students as game designers: designing games for classroom integration. In: de Freitas, S., Ott, M., Popescu, M., Stanescu, I. (eds.) New Pedagogical Approaches in Game Enhanced Learning: Curriculum Integration, pp. 102–113. Information Science Reference, Hershey (2013)
9. Churches, A.: Bloom's taxonomy blooms digitally. Tech & Learning (2008)
10. Papert, S.: Situating construction. In: Harel, I., Papert, S. (eds.) Constructionism, pp. 1–12. Ablex Publishing, Norwood (1991)
11. Maizatul Hayati, M.Y.: Children, Computer and Creativity: Usability Guidelines for Designing A Game Authoring Tool for Children. PhD Dissertation, Otto-Von-Guericke University of Magdeburg, Germany (2009)

12. Mehm, F., Konert, J., Göbel, S., Steinmetz, R.: An Authoring Tool for Adaptive Digital Educational Games. In: Ravenscroft, A., Lindstaedt, S., Kloos, C.D., Hernández-Leo, D. (eds.) EC-TEL 2012. LNCS, vol. 7563, pp. 236–249. Springer, Heidelberg (2012)
13. Nielsen, J., Landauer, T.K.: A Mathematical Model of the Finding of Usability Problems. In: Proceedings of the INTERACT 1993 and CHI 1993 Conference on Human Factors in Computing Systems, pp. 206–213. ACM (1993)
14. Sharifah Nor, P., Aliza, A.: Belajar Melalui Bermain: Prinsip Utama Kurikulum Pendidikan Awal Kanak-Kanak (Learning Through Play: Curriculum Key Principles of Early Childhood Education). Utusan Publication & Distributors, Kuala Lumpur (2013)
15. Lewis, J.R.: Psychometric evaluation of the PSSUQ using data from five years of usability studies. International Journal of Human-Computer Interaction 14(3-4), 463–488 (2002)
16. Hanna, L., Risden, K., Alexander, K.: Guidelines for usability testing with children. Interactions 4(5), 9–14 (1997)
17. Hourcade, J.P.: Interaction design and children. Foundations and Trends in Human-Computer Interaction 1(4), 277–392 (2008)
18. Pratt, A., Nunes, J.: Interactive Design: An Introduction to The Theory and Application of User-Centered Design. Rockport Publishers, USA (2012)
19. Laili Farhana, M.I., Norhayati, B., Maizatul Hayati, M.Y.: A Field Study of Understanding Child's Knowledge, Skills and Interaction Towards Capacitive Touch Technology (iPad). In: 2013 8th International Conference on Information Technology in Asia (CITA 2013). IEEE (2013)
20. Nielsen, J., Landauer, T.K.: A Mathematical Model of The Finding of Usability Problems. In: Proceedings of the INTERACT 1993 and CHI 1993 Conference on Human Factors in Computing Systems, pp. 206–213. ACM (1993)

A Review of Serious Games for Children with Autism Spectrum Disorders (ASD)

Hanan Makki Zakari[1], Minhua Ma[1], and David Simmons[2]

[1] Digital Design Studio, Glasgow School of Art, Glasgow, UK
H.Zakari1@gsa.ac.uk, M.Ma@gsa.ac.uk
[2] School of Psychology, University of Glasgow, Glasgow, UK
David.Simmons@glasgow.ac.uk

Abstract. This paper reviews 40 serious games designed for children with autism spectrum disorders (ASD) and these games/studies are classified into four categories; technology platform, computer graphics, gaming aspect and user interaction. Moreover, the paper discusses serious games designed for the improvement of communication skills and social behavior, social conversation, imaginative skills, sensory integration and learning accounts in ASD children. The children usually interact with these games by ordinary IO (input/output) e.g. keyboard and mouse or touchscreen tools. Previous researches show the effectiveness of playing serious games on mobiles or tablet devices in helping ASD children to express their feelings and improve the level of engagement with others. However, there are limitations in designing games for helping autistic children with sensory processing disorder (SPD), improving imaginative play, and teaching first aid. Further, there is not much research that addresses repetitive behavior in ASD children.

Keywords: Serious games (SG), Autism Spectrum Disorder (ASD), Education and therapy, Interactive tools, Technologies platforms, Computer graphics.

1 Introduction

Autism Spectrum Disorder (ASD) is described as a serious neurodevelopmental disorder, which involves delay in the development of many basic skills including the ability to socialize and communicate [1], as well as the ability to speak [2]. Nowadays, (ASD) is considered as a "paediatric health issue" as it has been shown that 1 in 88 children in the USA [3], 1 in 100 children in the UK [4] and 1 in 625 children in Malaysia [5] have diagnosis with ASDs. Moreover, recent research suggests that the percentage of people who have autism has grown in recent decades [6]. Hence, it is important to identify effective ways to help them communicate and participate in their society more easily, with a view to improving their quality of life.

Autistic individuals have a limited range of interests, and struggle to bond emotionally with their parents and those around them, and also have repetitive behaviors and sensory processing disorders (SPDs), such as being sensitive to sound, sight, touch etc. Having said that there is also considerable heterogeneity within those diagnosed with ASD [6],[7]. Over the years, many researches have been conducted on how to improve the lives of individuals affected by ASDs. Different technologies

M. Ma et al. (Eds.): SGDA 2014, LNCS 8778, pp. 93–106, 2014.

have been developed to assist autistic children in developing social skills, communication skills, vocabulary building and vocalization; as well as classroom visual support systems [6]. Surprisingly, children with this disorder interact well with technology, however they find it hard to relate to their environment. This has led to a lot of research being conducted which focuses more on how to improve their communication and social interaction skills. Interrelating important areas associated with this disorder will not only open a door to a better future for children with this disorder, it will also increase their chances of becoming independent upon adulthood. Children's brains are still under development and the chances of improving their social and communication skills are greater compared to adults, because they are not fully exposed to the harshness of society [8].

Several articles have reviewed serious games for ASD; [9] have investigated the use of Virtual Reality (VR) studies from 1996 to 2010 and reviewed their examined studies (age, number of patients, and results). Moreover, [5] have reviewed articles focusing on serious games for ASD children between 2002 and 2011 in different aspects (technology classification and purpose of serious game). However, this paper provides a review of existing research studies in serious games for ASD from 2004 to early 2014. It is structured in four sections: technology platforms, computer graphics, gaming aspect, and user interaction used in serious games.

2   Sensory Processing Disorder

Kanner saw abnormal behaviors in response to sensory stimuli in many children with ASDs [10]. Additionally, recent studies have increasingly recognized sensory signs in children with ASDs, which means there may be links between ASDs and SPDs, such as vision, smell, auditory, etc. [11], [12]. Most children with ASDs have exhibited "hyper-and hypo-sensitivities in multiple domains" [13]. Yet, there are unclear reasons behind sensory processing disorders in ASD. [10], [11], [14] point out there may be correlations between sensory processing symptoms and ASD, such as repetitive behavior, anxiety, restrictiveness, self-injuring and inattentiveness. For example, anxiety symptoms are more correlated with sensory hypersensitivity, while attention difficulties are more likely to be related to sensory hyposensitivity [14].

We summarize the SPD symptoms based on Kranowitz [15] in Table1, which could indicate to parents the signs of sensory processing dysfunction as they appear in children. However, this SPD checklist may not show all the characteristics of sensory abnormality symptoms. Furthermore, these symptoms may appear stronger on some days compared to others. Also, these characteristics are not standard criteria; it is educating parents to observe these symptoms in their children [15].

There is only serious game that targets sensory disorder in ASD children and vision only [16]. Thus there is a need for deep understanding of sensory symptoms in children with ASDs to treat these symptoms [10], [17]. In addition, more research is required to determine the efficacy of serious games on ASD children with sensory dysfunction [14]. Hence we suggest that those who are interested in developing serious games for ASD people should take into account dysfunctional sensory processing. Our consideration is developing a serious game for ASD children who suffer from sensory disorders, in order to enhance effective games that can improve their communication skills and which can be related to their environments.

Table 1. Sensory Processing Disorders

Poor functioning Tasks

Auditory-Language Processing Dysfunction:
- Unable to locate the source of a sound
- Difficulty discriminating between sounds/words; i.e., "dare" and "dear"
- Difficulty reading, especially out loud (may also be dyslexic)
- Difficulty articulating and speaking clearly
- Difficulty putting ideas into words (written or verbal)
- Difficulty filtering out other sounds while trying to pay attention to one person talking
- Difficulty attending to, understanding, and remembering what is said or read
- Often ask for directions to be repeated and may only be able to understand or follow two sequential directions at a time
- Looks at others to/for reassurance before answering
- If not understood, have difficulty re-phrasing.

Poor Tactile Perception and Discrimination:
- Difficulty with fine motor tasks such as buttoning, zipping, and fastening clothes.
- Not be able to identify which part of their body was touched if they were not looking.
- Afraid of the dark.
- Be a messy dresser; looks disheveled, does not notice pants are twisted, shirt is half un tucked, shoes are untied, one pant leg is up and one is down, etc.
- Difficulty using scissors, crayons, or silverware-continues to mouth objects to explore them even after age two-has difficulty figuring out physical characteristics of objects; shape, size, texture, temperature, weight, etc.
- Not be able to identify objects by feel, uses vision to help; such as, reaching into backpack.

Poor Muscle Tone and Coordination:
- Have difficulty turning doorknobs, handles, opening and closing items
- Difficulty catching themself if falling
- Difficulty getting dressed and doing fasteners, zippers, and buttons.
- Have poor body awareness; bumps into things, knocks things over.
- Poor gross motor skills; jumping, catching a ball, jumping jacks, climbing a ladder etc.
- Poor fine motor skills; difficulty using tools (pencils, silverware, combs, scissors etc.)
- Difficulty licking an ice cream cone.
- Unsure about how to move body during movement, for example, stepping over something

Table 1. (*continued*)

	Hyposensitivity (Under-responsively)
Auditory: - Often does not respond to verbal cues or to name being called - Love excessively loud music or TV. - Seem to have difficulty understanding or remembering what was said. - appear oblivious to certain sounds. - Appear confused about where a sound is coming from. - Talks self through a task, often out loud. - Needs directions repeated often, or will say, "What?" fre-	**Tactile:** - Needs to touch everything and everyone. - Not bothered by injuries, like cuts and bruises. - Crave vibrating or strong sensory input. - Frequently hurts other children or pets while playing. - Be self-abusive; pinching, biting, or banging his own head thoroughly enjoys and seeks out messy play.
Vestibular: - Over being tossed in the air. - Could spin for hours and never appear to be dizzy - Loves the fast, intense, and/or scary rides at amusement parks. - Always jumping on furniture, trampolines and spinning in a swivel chair. - Love to swing as high as possible and for long periods of time. - Always running, jumping, hopping etc. Instead of walking. - Rock body, shakes leg, or head while sitting - Like sudden or quick movements, such as, going over a big bump in the car or on a bike. - In constant motion, cannot seem to sit still.	**Vision:** - Difficulty telling the difference between similar printed letters or figures; i.e., p & q, b & d, + and x, or square and rectangle. - Difficulty locating items among other items; i.e., Papers on a desk, clothes in a drawer. - Difficulty controlling eye movement to track and follow moving objects. - Difficulty telling the difference between different colors, shapes, and sizes - Difficulty finding differences in pictures, words, symbols, or objects - Difficulty with consistent spacing and size of letters during writing and/or lining up numbers in math problems - Have a hard time seeing the "big picture"; i.e., focuses on the details or patterns within the picture - Often loses place when copying from a book or the chalkboard. - Often loses their place while reading or doing math problems - Make reversals in words or letters when copying, or reads words backwards; i.e., "was" for "saw" and "no" for "on" after first grade - Complain about seeing double. - Tend to write at a slant on a page - Confuse left and right - Fatigue easily with schoolwork.
Oral Input: - Lick, taste, or chew on inedible objects. - Prefer foods with intense flavor; i.e., excessively spicy, sweet, sour, or salty. - Excessive drooling past the teething stage. - Frequently chews on hair, shirt, or fingers. - Act as if all foods taste the same. - Love vibrating toothbrushes and even trips to the dentist.	**Olfactory:** - Difficulty discriminating unpleasant odors. - Drink or eat things that are poisonous because they do not notice the noxious smell. - Do not notice odors that others usually complain about - Unable to notice or ignore unpleasant odors. - Make excessive use of smelling when introduced to objects, people, or places - Use smell to interact with objects.

Table 1. *(continued)*

Hypersensitivity (Over-responsively)	
Auditory - Distracted by sounds not normally noticed by others; i e., humming of lights or refrigerators, fans, heaters, or clocks ticking. - Distracted by background environmental sounds; i e., lawn mowing or outside construction. - Frequently asks people to be quiet. - Runs away, cries, and/or covers ears with loud or unexpected sounds. - Fearful of the sound of a flushing toilet (especially in public bathrooms), vacuum, hairdryer, squeaky shoes, or a dog barking. - Refuse to go to movie theaters, parades, skating rinks, musical concerts etc. - Decide whether they like certain people by the sound of their voice.	Tactile: - refuse to walk barefoot on grass or sand - Avoid touching certain textures of material (blankets, rugs, stuffed animals) - Dislike messy play, i e. sand, mud, water, glue, glitter, slime, shaving foam etc. - Complain about having hair brushed.
Vestibular: - Prefer sedentary tasks, moves slowly and cautiously, avoids taking risks. - Dislike elevators and escalators. - Dislike playground equipment; i e., swings, ladders, slides, or merry-go-rounds. - Afraid of heights, even the height of a curb or step. - Afraid of being tipped upside down, sideways or backwards. - Fearful of feet leaving the ground. - Fearful of walking on uneven surfaces - Difficulty riding a bike, jumping, hopping, or balancing on one foot. - Loses balance easily and fearful of activities which require good balance - Avoids rapid or rotating movements.	Vision: - Enjoy playing in the dark. - Sensitive to bright lights; will squint, cover eyes, cry and/or get headaches from the light. - Difficulty keeping eyes focused on tasks/activities that require appropriate amount of time - Easily distracted by other visual stimuli in the room; i e., movement, decorations, toys, windows, doorways etc. - Rub they eyes, have watery eyes or get headaches after reading or watching TV. - Avoid eye contact.
Oral Input - Lick, taste, or chew on inedible objects. - Picky eater, often with extreme food preferences; i e., limited repertoire of foods, resistive to trying new foods or restaurants. - Dislike about toothpaste and mouthwash. - Difficulty with sucking, chewing, and swallowing. - refuse going to the dentist - Only eat hot or cold foods	Olfactory: - Offended by bathroom odors or personal hygiene smells. - Bothered by smell of perfume or cologne. - Bothered by household or cooking smells. - Like someone or some place by the way it smells. - Tell other people (or talks about) how bad or funny they smell - Refuse to eat certain foods because of their smell.

3   Autism Games Reviewed

During recent decades, serious games development has utilized a range of technologies for ASD children with 2D and 3D graphics, including different platforms, learning objectives and modes of interaction (i.e. input/output devices). Table 1 presents 40 ASD games and case studies, which have been designed for various learning objectives targeting children with ASDs. For each game or case study, we list the platform that it runs on, computer graphics in terms of two-dimensional or three-dimensional representation, learning objectives, gaming aspects and interaction methods. Table 2 is also sorted by the purposes (learning objectives) of the games.

Table 2. Case studies in Serious Games for Children with ASD

Author	Year	Technology Platform	Computer Graphics	Purposes/ Objectives	Gaming Aspect	User Interaction
Lányi and Tilinger [18]	2004	Desktop/laptop	2D&3D	Education: Teach shopping & transportation	Yes	Ordinary IO
Pares et al. [19]	2005	Large screen	3D	Education: Interact with environment	No	Camera-based
Barakova et al. [20]	2007	Desktop/laptop	2D	Education: Social behavior	Yes	Ordinary IO
Finkelstein et al. [21]	2009	Desktop/laptop	2D&3D	Education: Teach Emotion Recognition	Yes	Ordinary IO
Battocchi et al. [22]	2009	Tabletop	2D	Therapy: collaboration & social interaction	Yes	Touch-screen
Arya et al. [23]	2009	Desktop/laptop	3D	Education: facial expression and emotion	Yes	Ordinary IO
De Leo et al. [24]	2010	Mobile	2D	Education: Improve communication skills	Yes	Touch-screen
Tsai et al. [25]	2011	Desktop/laptop	2D	Education: teaching facial emotion & communicate	Yes	Camera-based
Miranda et al. [26]	2011	Desktop/laptop	3D	Education: Teaching Facial Emotions	Yes	Ordinary IO
Artoni et al. [18]	2012	Desktop/laptop	2D	Therapy: eLearning environment	Yes	Ordinary IO
Abirached et al. [27]	2012	Desktop/laptop	2D	Education: Teaching emotion	No	Ordinary IO
Hourcade et al. [28]	2012	Tablet	2D	Education; Social skills	Yes	Touch-screen
Bereznak et al. [29]	2012	Mobile iPhone.	2D	Education: Teach Vocational & daily living skills	No	Touch-screen
Jain et al. [30]	2012	Desktop/laptop	3D	Therapy: Teaching facial expression	Yes	Ordinary IO and camera-based
Hulusica & Pistoljevic [31]	2012	Desktop/laptop	2D	Education: Teach basic skills	Yes	Ordinary IO
Hansen et al [32]	2013	Mobile	2D	Education: Learning facial expressions	Yes	Touch-screen
Piana et al. [33]	2013	Desktop/laptop	2D&3D	Education: Learning emotion expression	No	Ordinary IO and camera-based
Chukoskie et al. [34]	2013	Desktop/laptop	2D	Education: Natural social engagement.	Yes	Camera-based
Chen [35]	2013	Tablet	2D	Education: Develop social skills	Yes	Touch-screen
Bertacchini et al. [36]	2013	Tablet	3D	Education: Emotional learning environment	Yes	Touch-screen
Bartolome et al. [37]	2013	Desktop/laptop	2D	Therapy: interaction skills measurement	Yes	Camera-based

Table 2. *(continued)*

Schuller et al. [38]	2014	Desktop/laptop	2D	Education: facial expiration and emotion	No	Ordinary IO & camera-based
Yan [39]	2011	Tablet	2D	Therapy: consideration the emotional and social skills	Yes	Touch-screen
Davis et al. [40]	2007	Desktop/laptop	2D	Education: Narrative	Yes	Ordinary IO
Hoque et al. [41]	2009	Desktop/laptop	2D	Therapy: Learning speech	Yes	Ordinary IO
Sharmin et al. [42]	2011	Desktop/laptop	2D	Therapy: Increase intelligibility in speech	No	Ordinary IO
Frutos et al. [2]	2011	Desktop/laptop	2D	Education: learning speech	Yes	Ordinary IO
Rahman et al. [43]	2011	Desktop/laptop	2D	Therapy: Speech development	Yes	Ordinary IO
Anwar et al. [44]	2011	Desktop/laptop	2D	Education: Increasing fluency in the speech	Yes	Ordinary IO
Hailpern et al.[45]	2012	Desktop/laptop	2D	Therapy: Speech Delays	Yes	Ordinary IO
Al-Khafaji et al. [46]	2013	Mobile	2D	Education: Learning words	Yes	Touch-screen
Zancanaro et al. [47]	2014	Desktop/laptop	2D	Therapy: Teach social conversation skills	No	Ordinary IO
Choi & Lim. [16]	2010	Desktop/laptop	2D&3D	Therapy: Visual motor coordination, social skills, sensory Integration	Yes	Camera-based and a tangible device
Hassan et al. [48]	2011	Desktop/laptop	2D	Education: Learning money concept	Yes	Ordinary IO
Jercic et al. [49]	2012	Desktop/laptop	2D	Education: Emotion training in the context of financial decision-making	Yes	EEG-based
Wang et al. [50]	2010	Desktop/laptop	2D&3D	Therapy: Electroencephalogram (EEG) game	Yes	EEG-based
Bartoli et al. [51]	2013	Console, Xbox 360	3D	Therapy: Understanding motion-based touchless	No	Camera-based
Bai [52]	2013	Desktop/laptop	3D	Education: Imaginative play	Yes	Camera-based
Pomsta et al. [53]	2013	Desktop/laptop	3D	Education: Imaginative skills	Yes	Touch-screen
Ulturi et al [45]	2011	Mobile	2D	Education: Teach first aid	Yes	Touch-screen

3.1   Technology Platforms

Various ASD serious games have been utilized in different technologies, including desktops, laptops, smartphones, large screens and console games. As shown in Fig. 1, about 70% of serious games for autistic children were designed for PCs and laptop platforms.

Playing games on smartphones, pads, and tablets for educational purposes is becoming popular these days for children suffering from ASDs [46], because the small screen size of the device helps with ASD children's attention [39] and the touch screen interface provides a more intuitive interaction.

ASD games played on either smartphones or tablet devices have the next highest percentage at 22%. For example, PixTalki is a smartphone application, in which children can download photos from websites into their smartphones in order to use the photos to express their emotions and desires [24]. Lastly, large screens [19], tabletop [22] and game console [51] have the lowest share (2-3%) of technology platforms for ASD games.

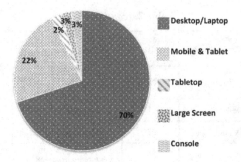

Fig. 1. Technology platforms of ASD games

3.2   Purposes

The general design of video games for ASD tends to achieve two main purposes: education and therapies. Fig. 2 depicts the purpose of serious games for ASD children, showing that there is more attention on developing communication and social skills than other goals. 54% of research focusing on serious games for ASD accounts for studies conducted in the improvement of communication and social skills. The study shows that children can select their favorite characters at the beginning of the game from some faces that have been drawn as cartoon characters: boy, girl and alien. The study shows that ASD players tend to play as a game character which is consistent to his/her real-life identity in terms of gender, i.e. males joining the game chose to play with a boy avatar, while girls preferred to play with a girl avatar. The game also presents a score panel of difficulty levels, so that it is easy for teachers and parents to recognize the children's achievement. However, there are repetitive behaviors in many ASD children; for instance, some selected wrong answers on purpose because they enjoyed the feedback sound. Thus, the study recommends having customization tools so that parents and teachers can control auditory feedback, to avoid such negative behavior.

The next highest percentage (26%) of ASD games relates to social conversation [44], [47], learning words [46] and speech therapy purposes [38], [43], [47]. Games aiming for therapeutic intervention for sensory processing disorders [16], learning first aid [54] and improving imaginative play [53] have the lowest percentage in ASD games. There is a need for more consideration to provide serious games for ASD children with sensory processing disorders, since they are a ubiquitous feature of ASDs and have been important biomarkers for diagnosis and monitoring of therapeutic interventions for the conditions.

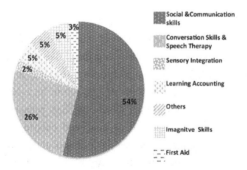

Fig. 2. Purposes

3.3   User Interaction

Figure 3 presents the modes of interaction which have been used serious games for ASDs. The most common interaction in these games is keyboard and a mouse. These ordinary Input/output (IO) devices are used in 45% of games, while the touchscreen is the second highest interactive tool used in serious games. It has been reported that dealing with touchscreen devices is more effective than interacting with a computer using a mouse [39]. Previous literature suggests interfaces like touch devices have the least amount of learning curve due to the implicit direct manipulation in the interaction. Touchscreen devices are more commonly used and favored [35], and this creates greater impact on social interaction and how it reflects positively on autistic life. Camera-based interface is used in 13% of studies, while 10% of studies utilize more than one mode of interaction in their games [46], [39]. An example of a game requiring the use of two interaction modes is the "Interactive therapy system" designed for ASD children [16], which uses a digital camera to capture body movement, and also a tangible device like a 30cm wand for children to break animated balloons. It is worth to mention that a small percent of studies (2%) use electroencephalography (EEG) based brain computer interface in their games [49], [50].

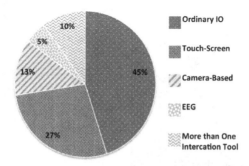

Fig. 3. User Interaction

3.4   Gaming Aspect

According to studies from 2004 to early 2014, video games for ASD children have been developed, examined or analyzed, showing that 80% of studies designed games for playing or assisting applications. Developing a game has three activities in order to improve different skills in children with ASDs, while an e-learning application is just a game which helps autistics to learn words through photos, videos and sounds. The other studies (19%) have only tested or analyzed existing games to understand the autistic needs in serious games, whether for educational or therapeutic purposes, testing several Kinect games to identify the way in which children experience movement-based games with full body interaction.

According to the previous studies there are various gaming aspects in serious games for ASD children; matching or filling (shapes) [51], [31], game level up [34], [16], multiplayer [35], [36] collecting or beating objects [18], 39], constructed shapes [20], [25], 39] and puzzle pictures [22], [26]. Having gaming elements in autism applications is more beneficial to ASD children [22], [35], [53], because collaborative play will enhance social communication and improve level of interaction with others

There are some application games for smartphone in App Store and Google Play that may be used for ASD children with sensory dysfunction. For example, Figure 7 (Blanc ball) is a game requires the player to place the balls in their small colored holes by tilting the device, in order to achieve this the player should avoid obstacles (big holes). The game would be improved the balance in ASD children with vestibular dysfunction, whereas playing the game rely on accurate physical engine. Moreover, Sky Burger game requires the player to catch the right ingredients the full form sky, which may improve level of attention in ASD children.

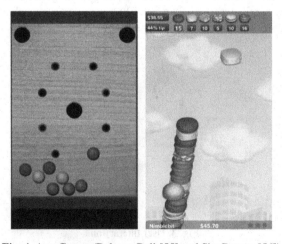

Fig. 4. App Games (Balance Ball [55] and Sky Burger [56])

4   Conclusion and Future Work

This paper has reviewed previous studies (2004-2014) of serious games designed for children with ASDs. As shown by earlier studies, there is only one game for sensory processing disorders; and it focuses on vision only [16]. Due to the nature of multi-sensory stimuli and multimodality of digital technologies, it is possible to combine vision, auditory, and vestibular in serious games for SPDs. There are limitations for simulating other sensory stimuli such as tactile, olfactory and oral input. However, recent advances in computer technology have started exploring the possibility to integrate tactile and olfactory senses using haptics [57] and digital scent technology [58].

In term of designing serious games for ASD children, it is necessary to provide a customization mechanism in these games to allow parents and teachers to discourage certain player behaviors, such as repetitive behaviors. Moreover, ASD children's games could provide a data analysis or visualization tools which presents the progress and development of the child's skills. For future research, our plan is to design and develop a serious game for ASD children with sensory processing difficulties, and to implement it for Android-based touchscreen smartphones, tablets and touchpads, which is the most popular operating system for mobile platforms at present.

References

1. Cross, M.: Children with Emotional and Behavioral Difficulties and Communication Problem. Jessica Kingsley Publishers, London (2004)
2. Frutos, M., Bustos, I., Zapirain, B., Zorrilla, A.: Computer Game to Learn and Enhance Speech Problems for Children with Autism. In: 16th International Conference on Computer Games, pp. 209–216. IEEE, Louisville (2011)
3. Centers For Disease Control And Disorder (2011), http://www.cdc.gov/mmwr/preview/mmwrhtml/ss6103a1.htm?s_cid=ss6103a1_w
4. NHS, http://www.nhs.uk/conditions/autistic-spectrum-disorder/Pages/Introduction.aspx
5. Noor, H., Shahbodin, F., Pee, N.C.: Serious Game for Autism Children: Review of Literature. World Academy of Science, Engineering and Technology 64, 648–652 (2012)
6. Abirached, B., Zhang, Y., Park, J.: Understanding User Needs for Serious Games for Teaching Children with Autism Spectrum Disorders Emotions. In: World Conference on Educational Multimedia, Hypermedia and Telecommunications. AACE, Denver (2012)
7. AHRQ, Effective Health Care Program (2011), http://effectivehealthcare.ahrq.gov/ehc/products/106/709/aut_fin_to_post.pdf
8. Centers For Disease Control And Disorder, New Data on Autism Spectrum Disorders (2014), http://www.cdc.gov/features/countingautism/
9. Bellani, M., Fornasari, L., Chittaro, L., Brambilla, P.: Virtual reality in autism: state of the art. Epidemiology and Psychiatric Sciences 20, 235–238 (2011)
10. Rogers, S.J., Ozonoff, S.: Annotation: What do we know about sensory dysfunction in autism? A critical review of the empirical evidence. Journal of Child Psychology and Psychiatry 46, 1255–1268 (2005)
11. Case-Smith, J., Weaver, L., Fristad, M.: A systematic review of sensory processing interventions for children with autism spectrum disorders. Autism 18, 1–6 (2014)

12. Tomchek, S., Dunn, W.: Sensory Processing in Children With and Without Autism: A Comparative Study Using the Short Sensory Profile. American Journal of Occupational Therapy 61, 190–200 (2007)
13. Marco, E., Hinkley, L., Hill, S., Nagarajan, S.: Sensory Processing in Autism: A Review of Neurophysiologic Findings: Neuropsychiatric Disorders and Pediatric Psychiatry. Pediatric Research 69, 48–54 (2011)
14. Hazen, E., Stornelli, J., O'Rourke, J., Koesterer, K., McDougle, C.: Sensory symptoms in autism spectrum disorders. Harvard Review of Psychiatry 22, 112–124 (2014)
15. Kranowitz, C.: The Out of Sync Child. The Berkley Publication Group, New York (1998)
16. Choi, M., Lim, C.: Interactive Therapy System Design for Children with Autistic Spectrum Disorders. In: International Conference on Kansei Engineering and Emotion Research, KEER, France (2010)
17. Dowson, G., Watling, R.: Interventions to Facilitate Auditory, Visual, and Motor Integration in Autism: A Review of the Evidence 30, 415–421 (2000)
18. Lányi, C.S., Tilinger, Á.: Multimedia and Virtual Reality in the Rehabilitation of Autistic Children. In: Miesenberger, K., Klaus, J., Zagler, W.L., Burger, D. (eds.) ICCHP 2004. LNCS, vol. 3118, pp. 22–28. Springer, Heidelberg (2004)
19. Pares, N., Carreras, A., Durany, J., Ferrer, J., Freixa, P., Gomez, D., Kruglanski, O., Pares, R., Ribas, J., Soler, M., Sanjurjo, A.: Promotion of Creative Activity in Children with Severe Autism Through Visuals in an Interactive Multisensory Environment. In: Conference IDC 2005 Interaction Design and Children. ACM, New York (2005)
20. Barakova, E., Wanrooij, G., Limpt, R., Menting, M.: Using an emergent system concept in designing interactive games for autistic children. In: 6th International Conference on Interaction Design and Children. ACM, Aalborg (2007)
21. Finkelstein, S., Nickel, A., Harrison, L., Suma, E., Barnes, T.: cMotion: A New Game Design to Teach Emotion Recognition and Programming Logic to Children using Virtual Humans. In: IEEE Virtual Reality Conference, pp. 249–250. IEEE, Lafayette (2009)
22. Battocchi, A., Pianesi, F., Venuti, P., Ben-Sasson, A., Gal, E.: Collaborative puzzle game: Fostering Collaboration in Children with Autistic Spectrum Disorder (ASD) and with Typical Development. In: The International Conference on Interactive Tabletops and Surfaces, pp. 197–204. ACM, New York (2009)
23. Arya, A., Dipaola, S., Parush, A.: Perceptually Valid Facial Expressions for Character-Based Applications. International Journal of Computer Games Technology, 13 (2009)
24. De Leo, G., Gonzales, C., Battagiri, P., Leroy, G.: A smart-Phone Application and a Companion Website for the Improvement of the Communication Skills of Children with Autism: Clinical Rationale, Technical Development and Preliminary Results. Journal of Medical Systems 35(4), 703–711 (2011)
25. Tsai, T.-W., Lin, M.-Y.: An Application of Interactive Game for Facial Expression of the Autisms. In: Chang, M., Hwang, W.-Y., Chen, M.-P., Müller, W. (eds.) Edutainment 2011. LNCS, vol. 6872, pp. 204–211. Springer, Heidelberg (2011)
26. Miranda, J., Fernandes, T., Augusto Sousa, A., Orvalho, V.: Interactive Technology: Teaching People with Autism to Recognize Facial Emotions, pp. 299–312. InTech (2011)
27. Artoni, S., Buzzi, M.C., Buzzi, M., Ceccarelli, F., Fenili, C., Rapisarda, B., Tesconi, M.: Designing ABA-Based Software for Low-Functioning Autistic Children. In: Cipolla-Ficarra, F., Veltman, K., Verber, D., Cipolla-Ficarra, M., Kammüller, F. (eds.) ADNTIIC 2011. LNCS, vol. 7547, pp. 230–242. Springer, Heidelberg (2012)
28. Hourcade, J., Bullock-Rest, N., Hansen, T.: Multitouch Tablet Applications and Activities to Enhance the Social Skills of Children with Autism Spectrum Disorders. Personal and Ubiquitous Computing 16(2), 157–168 (2012)

29. Bereznak, S., Ayres, K., Mechling, L., Alexander, J.: Video Self-Prompting and Mobile Technology to Increase Daily Living and Vocational Independence for Students with Autism Spectrum Disorders. Journal of Developmental and Physical Disabilities 24, 269–285 (2012)

30. Jain, S., Tamersoy, B., Zhang, Y., Aggarwal, J.: An Interactive Game For Teaching Facial Expressions To Children With Autism Spectrum Disorders. In: The 5th International Symposium on Communications, Control and Signal Processing, ISCCSP, Rome (2014)

31. Hulusica, V., Pistoljevic, N.: LeFCA: Learning Framework for Children with Aut-ism. Procedia Computer Science 15, 4–16 (2012)

32. Hansen, O.B., Abdurihim, A., McCallum, S.: Emotion recognition for mobile devices with a potential use in serious games for autism spectrum disorder. In: Ma, M., Oliveira, M.F., Petersen, S., Hauge, J.B. (eds.) SGDA 2013. LNCS, vol. 8101, pp. 1–14. Springer, Heidelberg (2013)

33. Piana, S., Stagliano, A., Camurri, A., Odone, F.: A set of Full-Body Movement Features for Emotion Recognition to Help Children affected by Autism Spectrum Condition. In: IDGEI International Workshop (2013)

34. Chukoskie, L., Soomro, A., Townsend, J., Westerfield, M.: Looking' Better: Designing an at-Home Gaze Training System for Children with ASD. In: 6th International IEEE Conference on Neural Engineering, pp. 1246–1249. IEEE, San Diego (2013)

35. Chen, C.: Developing a Tablet Computer Game with Visual-Spatial Concept Jigsaw Puzzles for Autistic Children (2013), http://design-cu.jp/iasdr2013/papers/2197-1b.pdf

36. Bertacchini, F., Bilotta, E., Gabriele, L., Vizueta, D., Pantano, P., Tavernise, A., Vena, S., Valenti, A.: An emotional learning environment for subjects with Autism Spectrum Disorder, pp. 653–659. IEEE, Kazan (2013)

37. Bartolome, N., Zorrilla, M., Zapirain, G.: Autism Spectrum Disorder Children Interaction Skills Measurement Using Computer Games. In: 18th IEEE International Conference on Computer Games: AI, Animation, Mobile, Interactive Multimedia, Educational & Serious Games, pp. 207–211. IEEE, Louisville (2013)

38. Schuller, B., Marchi, E., Cohen, S., O'reilly, H., Pigat, D., Robinson, P., Daves, I.: The State of Play of ASC-Inclusion: An Integrated Internet-Based Environment for Social Inclusion of Children with Autism Spectrum Conditions. In: CORR, 1403 p (2014)

39. Yan, F.: A SUNNY DAY: Ann and Ron's World an iPad Application for Children with Autism. In: Ma, M., Fradinho Oliveira, M., Madeiras Pereira, J. (eds.) SGDA 2011. LNCS, vol. 6944, pp. 129–138. Springer, Heidelberg (2011)

40. Davis, M., Otero, N., Dautenhahn, K., Nehaniv, C., Powell, S.: Creating a Software to Promote Understanding About Narrative in Children with Autism: Reflecting on the Design of Feedback and Opportunities to Reason. In: 6th International Conference on Development and Learning, pp. 64–69. IEEE, London (2007)

41. Hoque, M., Lane, J., Kaliouby, R., Goodwin, M., Picard, R.: Exploring speech therapy games with children on the autism spectrum. In: INTERSPEECH, pp. 1455–1458 (2009)

42. Sharmin, M., Rahman, A., Ahmed, M., Rahman, M., Ferdous, S.: Teaching Intelligible Speech to the Autistic Children by Interactive Computer Games. In: Symposium on Applied Computing. ACM, New York (2011)

43. Rahman, M., Ferdous, S., Ahmed, I.: Increasing Intelligibility in the Speech of the Autistic Children by an Interactive Computer Game. In: International Symposium on Multimedia, Taichung, pp. 383–387. IEEE, Taichung (2010)

44. Anwar, A., Rahman, M., Ferdous, S., Ahmed, S.: A Computer Game based Approach for Increasing Fluency in the Speech of the Autistic Children. In: 11th IEEE International Conference on Advanced Learning Technologies, pp. 17–18. IEEE, Athena (2011)
45. Hailpern, J., Harris, A., La, B.: Designing visualizations to facilitate multisyllabic speech with children with autism and speech delays. In: Designing Interactive Systems Conference, pp. 126–135. ACM, New York (2012)
46. Al-Khafaji, N., Al-Shaher, M., Al-Khafaji, M.: M-Learning Application for Autistic Children using Android Platform. In: Future Trends in Computing and Communication (2013)
47. Zancanaro, M., Giusti, L., Zviely, N., Eden, S., Gal, E., Weiss, P.: NoProblem! A Collaborative Interface for Teaching Conversation Skills to Children with High Functioning Autism Spectrum Disorder. In: Interfaces that Invite Social and Physical Interaction, pp. 209–224 (2014)
48. Hassan, A., Zahed, B., Zohora, F., Moosa, J., Salam, T., Rahman, M., Ferdous, H., Ahmad, S.: Developing the Concept of Money by Interactive Computer Games for Autistic Children. In: IEEE International Symposium on Multimedia, Dana Point, pp. 559–564 (2011)
49. Jercic, P., Astor, P., Adam, M., Hilborn, O.: A Serious Game Using Physiological Interfaces For Emotion Regulation Training In the Context of Financial Decisionmaking. In: ECIS, 207 p. (2012)
50. Wang, Q., Sourina, O., Nguyen, M.: EEG-based "Serious" Games Design for Medical Applications. In: International Conference on Cyberworlds. IEEE, Singapore (2010)
51. Bartoli, L., Corradi, C., Garzotto, F., Valoriani, M.: Exploring Motion-Based Touchless Games for Autistic Children's Learning. In: 12th International Conference on Interaction Design and Children. ACM, New York (2013)
52. Bai, Z.: Augmenting Imagination for Children with Autism. In: 11th Interaction Design and Children, pp. 327–330. ACM, New York (2012)
53. Porayska-Pomsta, K., Anderson, K., Bernardini, S., Guldberg, K., Smith, T., Kossivaki, L., Hodgins, S., Lowe, I.: Building an Intelligent, Authorable Serious Game for Autistic Children and Their Carers. In: Reidsma, D., Katayose, H., Nijholt, A. (eds.) ACE 2013. LNCS, vol. 8253, pp. 456–475. Springer, Heidelberg (2013)
54. de Urturi, Z.S., Zorrilla, A.M., Zapirain, B.G.: A Serious Game for Android Devices to Help Educate Individuals with Autism on Basic First Aid. In: Omatu, S., Paz Santana, J.F., González, S.R., Molina, J.M., Bernardos, A.M., Rodríguez, J.M.C. (eds.) Distributed Computing and Artificial Intelligence. AISC, vol. 151, pp. 609–616. Springer, Heidelberg (2012)
55. Balance Ball, https://play.google.com/store/apps/details?id=com.sumadagames.balanceBall
56. Sky Burger,
https://itunes.apple.com/gb/app/sky-burger/id311972587?mt=8
57. Changeon, G., Graeff, D., Anastassova, M., Lozada, J.: Tactile Emotions: A Vibrotactile Tactile Gamepad for Transmitting Emotional Messages to Children with Autism. In: Isokoski, P., Springare, J. (eds.) EuroHaptics 2012, Part I. LNCS, vol. 7282, pp. 79–90. Springer, Heidelberg (2012)
58. Tillotson, J.: Scentsory Design: Scent Whisper and Fashion Fluidics. In: Adams, R., Gibson, S., Müller Arisona, S. (eds.) DAW/IF 2006/2007. CCIS, vol. 7, pp. 403–417. Springer, Heidelberg (2008)

Jumru 5s – A Game Engine for Serious Games

Natascha Schweiger[1], Katharina Meusburger[1],
Helmut Hlavacs[1], and Manuel Sprung[2]

[1] Research Group Entertainment Computing,
Faculty of Computer Science, University of Vienna, Austria
{natascha.schweiger,katharina.meusburger}@gmx.at,
helmut.hlavacs@univie.ac.at
[2] Clinical Child and Adolescent Psychology,
Faculty of Psychology, University of Vienna, Austria
manuel.sprung@univie.ac.at

Abstract. An increasing number of children are suffering from autism or other psychological disorders. These children have difficulties in social interactions or communications, i.e. interpreting emotions or non-verbal expressions. In the framework of the Games4Resilience Lab at the University of Vienna we developed a computer game for autism therapy, as a joint effort between Clinical Child Psychology and Computer Science. Since none of the existing HTML5-based game engines proved to be usable, we implemented our own web game engine Jumru 5s based on HTML5, CSS3 and JavaScript, having been especially developed for serious games. Furthermore, we introduce the serious game EmoJump,being implemented with our framework and aiming to improve emotion recognition skills.

1 Introduction

In 2012 the Autism and Developmental Disabilities Monitoring (ADDM) Network published statistics on the development of children with Autism Spectrum Disorders (ASDs) in the United States, showing that the number of children suffering from an ASD is increasing [4]. ASDs are various disabilities in a child's development that complicate their social life due to deficits in communication or behavior. Though there is no cure for ASDs, research shows that the symptoms can be relieved by an appropriate treatment [5].

People with ASDs have problems at different degrees, for example interpreting facial or generally non-verbal expressions. A major issue for them is also to keep focus on eye gaze and eye contact. All these factors lead to difficulties in emotion recognition [5], [3].

Though ASDs may appear in different ways, we focus solely on *emotion recognition* and how to train this ability [5].

To be able to develop appropriate game technologies to help children recognize emotions, we have implemented our own game engine especially designed for developing serious games.

M. Ma et al. (Eds.): SGDA 2014, LNCS 8778, pp. 107–118, 2014.

2   Related Work

Abirached et al. [3] evaluate some design principles and user needs for developing serious games that deal with emotion recognition. These principles include a certain level of *customization*, allowing the game to fit specific user needs. Customization means character or language selection, changing audio settings or other feedback elements.

Adaptability and customization are important factors to increase the user's attention. Finkelstein et al.[2] describe the influence of these aspects on the user's concentration. The higher the level interactivity and adaptability is, the more attentive a user gets. If the interface fits the personal interests, the user is more attracted to the game.

In their work, Abirached et al. [3] further complain that existing approaches in computer-based tools assisting children with ASDs are too static in their game play. They state that *"the fundamental need for a system to assist children with ASDs in recognizing, understanding, and generalizing facial expressions of emotions using an interactive computer-game approach has not been sufficiently addressed"*.

Obviously developers are missing some features that should enable proper game development. Arising requirements as customization, interactivity, and adaptability should also be addressed by a game engine.

The architecture of an engine itself consists of some components to simplify game development. Though there exists no standard list of features a game engine must provide, we shortly mention basic components an engine should fundamentally include.

Generally an architecture is divided into manager or subsystems that are responsible for a specific area, but interact with each other. In his book, Alan Thorn lists following components that constitute a game engine, being also relevant for our work [7]:

1. **Asset management**: A manager tool that is responsible for loading game assets, supporting multiple types.
2. **Rendering**: After an asset-manager has loaded game data, the game engine must also provide functionality to render these assets on screen.
3. **Media management**: As the game engine should support multiple media types like image, video and audio, some management system to correctly play and pause media tracks is necessary.
4. **Scene or stage management**: Loaded game data is composed and structured in layers or nodes. Some functionality must enable traversing or manipulating the game's stages.
5. **Physics engine**: The laws of physics like gravity or other forces must be included. If a player jumps or an element is thrown into the air, physical laws bring it automatically back to earth.
6. **User input**: This feature includes catching user input and process it according to the current game mode.
   In case of developing a game engine for serious games, an important and mostly unadressed feature is the following one:

7. **Logging**: Especially for serious games some sort of mechanism to collect and log data about the player is necessary. This component should enable analysis of the game experience by storing data of the game context at specific events. Sometimes logging in serious games can include further tools like emotives or other psychophysiological tools that match the user's emotional state against the game experience [8].

Therefore a game engine is good if it provides some functionalities to keep the game code simple. To what extent existing frameworks or game engines[1] meet these requirements is presented in the following section. Some of these engines are also mentioned as tools on the SEGAN[2] website and often came across our mind during the development. All of the presented engines are designed for the web and are open source. They are based on HTML5 and JavaScript technologies and enable 2D game development.

Quintus[3] is a modular HTML5 game engine with a syntax similar to jQuery. Different modules can be included into the engine, but you can also extend it by own components. Quintus provides modules for asset or audio management and sprite creation, which are the basic elements in the engine. Sprites live inside a scenes module and scenes can be staged independently on top of each other. A 2D module enables collision detection and applies physics to sprites. The engine allows the creation of tiled backgrounds or animations and tweenings. Both desktop devices and mobile devices are supported (button and touch input).

The *Crafty*[4] engine has some similarities with the Quintus engine. It also has a jQuery-like syntax and is based on different components or modules that can be added on entities. Crafty enables preloading of audio and images, sprite (keyframe) animations and key-, mouse- and touch input devices. It further supports both canvas or DOM rendering. Crafty provides modules that apply physics and allow collision detection. Lastly it implements storage mechanisms to persist data even if the browser window is closed.

PandaJS is a modular engine[5], and supports both mobile and desktop devices. It is based on *PixiJS*[6], a WebGL/Canvas rendering engine. PandaJS supports dynamic asset loading between the scenes, sprite-creation and debugging options, like visualizing the bounding box (provided by the physics module). It also allows to build own modules and has a lot of animation features, like tweenings or a particle engine. PandaJS further provides local storage mechanisms, to play the game if the website is down.

---

[1] Examples from `http://html5gameengine.com/`
[2] Serious Games Network `http://seriousgamesnet.eu/tools`
[3] `http://html5quintus.com/` developed by `http://cykod.com/`
[4] `http://craftyjs.com/` developed by Timothy J. S. Martin and contributors
[5] `http://www.pandajs.net`, developed by Eemeli Kelokorpi
[6] `http://www.pixijs.com/`

EnchantJS[7] is an object-oriented engine that handles code asynchronously, which means execution is shut down and resumed if user input is captured again. EnchantJS consists of a core library that can be extended through further plug-ins managing avatars, user inputs and interface elements, webGL or box2D. Basically the core library contains a basic entity object, from which all other entities inherit functionality. The engine supports DOM or canvas rendering, provides animations and the creation of tiled backgrounds.

We started developing our serious game with *LimeJS*[8], an engine that uses the Google closure library[9] to build and minify projects. LimeJS is built upon a basic `lime.Node`-element, from which every other object in the scope is derived. The root element is composed of scenes that contain an arbitrary number of layers, sprites or shapes. Nodes get their physics component of the box2D library. The engine supports DOM or canvas rendering, to enable desktop and mobile devices. In contrast to the other engines, it does not offer any asset preloading mechanisms. Nevertheless it provides keyframe animations and further CSS3 animations like scaling or rotating. User input is realized by mouse-clicks that are captured by a button-element. Further components processing user input have to be implemented by the developer using the engine.

Though LimeJS provides several tutorials and has a supportive community, we stopped working with it when we experienced difficulties, for example while resizing the window. Suddenly the sprite animation of our player running on the ground froze, animations did not stop correctly or we had to hack elements like the `PauseScene`, which is shown while the game is paused. Finally we decided to implement an own engine for serious web games.

As we can see existing JavaScript and HTML5 game frameworks and engines provide basic functionality for developing games, but none of them is especially designed for serious gaming. None of them incorporated a logging module or some type of logging feature. To be able to work with an engine that fits our needs and serves as an engine for serious games, we have implemented an own web game engine, which is the basis for our game.

Table 1 shows a comparison between our engine and the game engines mentioned above.

3   Jumru 5s – A Game Engine for Serious Games

In our project we developed a serious game for the web, based on HTML5, CSS3 and JavaScript. The game *EmoJump* should train the emotion recognition skills of autistic children at the age of 5-12. Therefore we are working in a close collaboration with the Department of Clinical Child and Adolescent Psychology of the University of Vienna, which use the game in a training study. Our game engine,

---

[7] http://enchantjs.com/ developed by Ubiquitous Entertainment Inc.'s Akihabara Research Center http://www.uei.co.jp/

[8] http://www.limejs.com/ developed by http://www.digitalfruit.ee/eng/

[9] https://developers.google.com/closure/library/

Table 1. Comparison of web game engines

	Quintus	Crafty	PandaJS	EnchantJS	LimeJS	Jumru 5s
Asset preloading	yes	yes	yes	yes	no	yes
Rendering	canvas	DOM or canvas	webGL or canvas	DOM or canvas, webGL through plug-in	DOM or canvas	canvas
Media	audio	audio	audio	audio	audio	audio and video
Compos. (scene, stage)	modules	compo-nents	modules	prototypes plug-ins	prototypes	prototypes
Physics	2d module	gravity compo-nent	physics module	basic module, box2D	box2D	bounding-box, gravity
User input	button, touch, keyboard	button, touch, keyboard	button, touch, keyboard	button, touch, keyboard, plug-ins	button	keyboard, button
Animation	keyframes, tweenings	keyframes, tweenings	keyframes, tweenings, spine, flash	keyframes, tweening, plug-ins	CSS3, keyframes	CSS3, keyframes
Logging	/	/	/	/	/	Logger

called *Jumru 5s (**Jump** and **Run** Framework for HTML**5 S**erious Games)*, is based on HTML5, CSS3 and JavaScript technologies.

Therefore we define a namespace-object called jumru that builds a scope, in which all the framework objects and functions are encapsulated. Figure 1 provides a basic overview on the core elements of the framework, that are explained in the following section.

3.1   Architecture

Our engine is generally based on the composite pattern. By using this pattern we create a tree-based hierarchy of nodes, consisting of composites and leaves. Applying the tree-based structure onto our engine, we always have the jumru.Stage, called gamestage in the code, as the root node that encapsulates all other nodes in the tree. Multiple jumru.Scenes are lying on the next level,

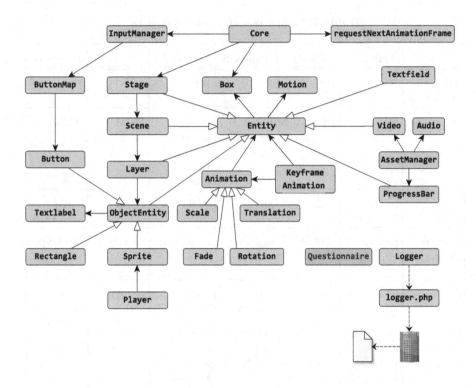

Fig. 1. Jumru 5s - Overview

directly under the stage, but just one scene is active at time. This approach enables switching between existing scenes so just one scene is as an `activeScene`. Just this scene is shown and drawn, all other scenes are invisible and therefore ignored (not updated). A scene on the other hand consists of an arbitrarily number of `jumru.Layers`. Layers encapsulate elements of type `jumru.ObjectEntity`, that represent drawable nodes. Object-Entities are leaf-nodes and can not contain any children. Stage, scene and layer are `<div>`-container, whereas object-entities are `<canvas>`-elements that draw images or shapes.

The main node from which nearly every other node in the framework is derived is the `jumru.Entity`. This element just serves as a main node providing basic functionality. When speaking of basic functionality we mean features like positioning, size and resizing, visibility and activity, traversing mechanisms or collision detection. Therefore an entity can contain a bounding box being used for collision detection. `jumru.ObjectEntity` represents a drawable item like images, sprites, shapes or button-elements. An element can be moved through the canvas by applying a `jumru.Motion`. Such movements are relevant for a scrolling background, a moving game-element or implementing a parallax effect. A motion-element calculates an offset value in each game loop step and translates the element by this value.

The engine also provides a standard `jumru.Player` that can contain multiple `jumru.Sprites`. A sprite is also an object-entity and consists of sprite-sheets. These sprite-sheets are split into frames that are drawn after another. The standard player also has a bounding-box and provides a jump-function.

According to the necessary game engine components we also incorporate a `jumru.AssetManager` that can correctly preload images, audio and video elements before further game play is processed. An asset-manager also contains a `jumru.ProgressBar` that visualizes the preloading progress. For video and audio our framework provides functions for playing, pausing media elements or other media relevant controlling mechanisms. Beside the asset-manager, the engine also contains a `jumru.InputManager`. By using the input-manager developers can add a specific handler by passing three arguments: a key-event (i.e. `keydown` or `keyup`), the game mode to consider and a game code-specific function to call. It also enables toggling mechanisms if a `jumru.ButtonMap` is defined, which can be used for defining different buttons for a menu selection.

In addition to these basic engine components, we define some standard CSS3 Animations like scaling, rotating, translating or fading of entities. All of these animations can be put together to a CSS3 keyframe-animation. We also pay attention to different browser vendors, currently Mozilla Firefox and Google Chrome are supported.

The heart of our game engine is the `jumruCore`, a global object that provides the *gamestage*, which encapsulates all tree-objects. It further contains constants like game-width and game-height and is responsible for looping the game. By using the engine, we can define a *loop*-function in our game code and specify what should happen in the game, i.e. do something according to a game mode, let the player jump or collide with object-entities, etc.. After creating the *loop*-function, we can pass it to the `jumruCore`. The `jumruCore` now handles updating and drawing the elements and also calls the specified loop of the game developer in each game loop-step inside the engine.

3.2 Game Loop

The game loop controls the game play and contains functions for calculating frames per second (fps), looping the game's loop (which is set by the developer) and updating and drawing the **gamestage**, respectively the gamestage's **activeScene**.

We are looping the game by using **requestNextAnimationFrame**[10], which lets the browser decide when to call the next frame, instead of using the old-fashioned **setInterval()**-method, which would use a constant update rate. How the gameloop of the engine is implemented is shown in the code script below.

---

[10] `http://www.ibm.com/developerworks/java/`
`library/j-html5-game2/index.html#raf`

```
jumru.Core.prototype.gameloop = function(now) {
    if(jumruCore.isPlaying) {
        jumruCore.fps = jumruCore.calculateFPS(now);
        jumruCore.loop();
        jumruCore.gamestage.draw();
        jumruCore.requestId =
        requestNextAnimationFrame(jumruCore.gameloop);
    }
};
```

calculateFPS() In each game loop step, we calculate the amount of time that has passed since the last `animationframe`. The fps should always be between 30-60, to get a smooth visible game play, otherwise the game starts jittering [1]. Furthermore we also successively calculate the average of all fps values computed before. The average frame rate can be used for displaying it to the user or for logging [6].

loop() After setting the frames per second, we call the gameloop defined by the user by calling `jumruCore.loop()`. Afterwards the actual updating and drawing of the framework elements used in the game takes place.

draw() By calling `jumruCore.gamestage.draw()` we force the `gamestage` to update and draw the `activeScene` and all its children. The basic draw-method is implemented in `jumru.Entity`.

Because the draw-operation itself is very cost-intensive, we mark every element as `active`. If we explicitly set an element non-active, for instance after drawing it once like a never changing background image, it will not get updated and drawn again. The same goes for object-entities and layers. To save performance we also mark object-entities as *dirty*, if their position or size changes, or the element has an active motion. Just the minimum dirty area of the canvas is marked dirty, so not the whole canvas is cleared and redrawn, but just the previously defined dirty area.

3.3   Features for Serious Games

A special feature for serious gaming and a further engine component is the *logging mechanism*. Our engine provides a basic `jumru.Logger`, that holds a multidimensional array, which contains several log-entries, also arrays. The first log-entry is always reserved for the final file name, that is used to store a .csv file on the server via php. Therefore we implemented a `logger.php` that receives the log in JSON format, decodes it and outputs it as a .csv file. The JavaScript Logger is just a basic logger, that can be extended by the game coder, to define more specific functionalities, according to the game type. For example we extended the framework logger in our game code to be able to log specific data about each level and the player (collected items, lost lives, etc.).

For further evaluation mechanisms and as a future task we develop a *questionnaire component* that builds and prints a form based on a XML file. This tool should be simple to use in order to enable domain experts the possibility to add or change the questionnaire's content easily.

4   Case Study: EmoJump

As mentioned before, our game with the name EmoJump, which is based on the game engine Jumru 5s, is developed in cooperation with students of psychology. EmoJump is a serious game for emotion recognition, so at the one hand it should help children to train their visual perception of emotions and on the other hand, the game delivers logging information about the children's game play for further analysis of the psychologists. The game is developed as an endless runner game, where the player has to collect emotional faces, which are displayed as coins. Additionally the player sees a thought bubble, showing a simple scenario. The child should interpret, understand an reconstruct the emotions and feelings presented in the scenario. Afterwards it has to collect emotion coins that match with the feelings shown in the thought bubble.

A main aspect of the game is the gamestage, which is separated into several scenes, representing different game modes. Every scene has its own layers, which include several object -entities like images, buttons or input fields. The first active scene is used for displaying the menu and shows the logo and the first interactive elements of the game. It further offers the user the possibility to change some options of the game like language (english/german), background music or sound effects.

The menu scene guides the player from the start screen to the player selection, where he can choose between two different characters, to offer the child some sort of customization and adaptability. In a further step, the player can type his name, which is also important for further analysis and logging to identify the player. Afterwards the screen switches to the level selection with three main levels, whereupon every main level has 12 sublevels. Before the player can start the game he is introduced into the game play by an instruction video explaining how he has to handle EmoJump in a correct way.

After selecting a sublevel, the game switches into the preloading-scene. Meanwhile all important data for the chosen level is loaded and the game is built up in the background. A XML parser reads in informations about barriers, grounds, emotions and further data, that are necessary for the level. A ground is a dynamic element which is randomly set and constantly moved through the visible area and contains barriers that the player has to avoid. Next to barriers, grounds contain emotions, presented as collectable coins. All these elements are randomly set, if a ground moves out of the screen. Barriers, grounds and emotions are combined in one layer that is set in motion. An example on how the game looks like in each level is shown in Figure 2.

There is one important object in EmoJump called `emoGame` which stores the most important game elements like game modes, player and level data to call them at every point in the code. This object is similar to the `jumruCore` in the framework.

The player in EmoJump is derived from the framework player and extended for specific characteristic and options, which are important for EmoJump. Beside the player, we also defined a derived logger, that logs information about the game:

Fig. 2. 3 Level of EmoJump: left: Level1, center: Level2, right: Level3

1. **sublevel**: date, time, time played, speed, fps, etc.
2. **player**: played thought bubbles, collected items (correct, wrong), crashes, score, etc.

Handling of the game focuses on playing with the keyboard, but it also supports navigation with the mouse.

Currently the game is still in development and not yet completed, so we tested the game at different operation systems by randomized game plays and logged the fps in each game loop step. Analysis of our tests show how the game with the engine behind deal with the frames per second and how the look and feel of the game is during playing.

5   Experimental Evaluation

5.1   Experimental Setup

To gain first insights into the performance of the engine we tested the game on various devices with different platforms and browsers (Firefox 28.0, Chrome Version 34.0.1847.131). Therefore we played level 1.1 and logged the fps-value in each game loop-step. For comparison reasons we have calculated some statistics using R^{11}.

5.2   Results

Figure 3 shows average fps values on Firefox and Google Chrome. Orange bars represent Firefox results, green bars show the values calculated for Google Chrome. The bars represent the average frame rate, the segments in the middle visualize the standard deviation as error bars. We took care on outliers and limited fps values to 0 and 300. We tested the game on different operating systems: Windows 8.1, Windows 7 Home Premium, OS X Mavericks 10.9.2 and Linux Knoppix 7.2.0.

The target testing environment of our game is going to be Windows with Firefox. We see that we reach an average fps of 60 in Firefox for Windows 8.1 and OS X. In Chrome we also have an average frame rate of 60 for Windows,

---

[11] http://www.r-project.org/

FPS OVERVIEW

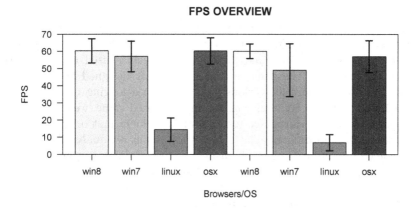

Fig. 3. Average FPS received in Firefox and Google Chrome on Windows 8.1, Windows 7, OS X 10.9.2 and Linux (Knoppix 7.2.0)

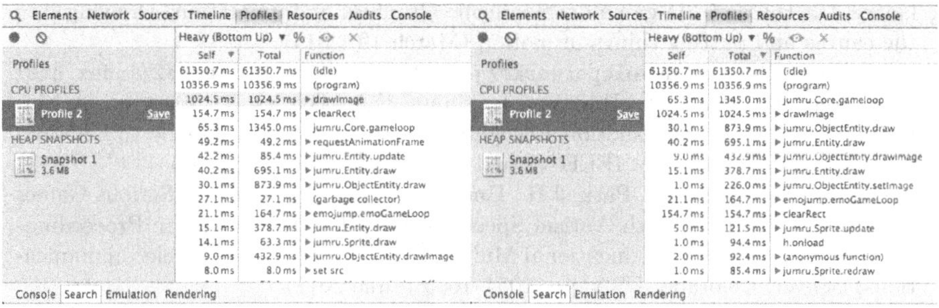

Fig. 4. CPU Profile Google Chrome. Left: Sorted by self-time, Right: sorted by total-time

but for OS X its a little less and we achieve an average value of 56. Windows 7 shows some lower values for Firefox (57) and Chrome (49) than Windows 8.1, which may also occur because of different devices. Unfortunately for Knoppix our frame rate is low - in Firefox we can still play the game at a fps of 14, whereas on Chrome we could not play the game due to a fps lower than 10. On Linux we could not activate hardware acceleration, which causes these low values. We also used Google Chrome's profiling mechanisms to evaluate performance bottlenecks. Taking a CPU profile while playing the game visualizes which functions take the most time during the execution, which is shown in Figure 4. By listing the most heavy functions in execution time (self and total ordered) shows that the `drawImage()` and `clearRect()` methods are very time consuming, because operations directly affecting the canvas are very expensive.

6 Conclusions

In this paper we provided an overview on basic game engine components for developing serious games for the web. We introduced our developed web game engine *Jumru 5s*, its structure and possibilities, which is used as framework for our game *EmoJump*. The game engine is especially designed for jump and run games and furthermore for serious games due to a logging module and a questionnaire component. By analysing the implemented game, we outlined the engines potential. The performance tests should provide a first overview about the games execution on different platforms. Additionally we analysed the game using Google Chrome's profiling mechanism and studied the execution time. The purpose of this project is the development of an engine for serious games which should not only help to design games which make fun, but also train and treat people properly to cope with their disabilities.

References

1. Geary, D.: HTML5 2D game development: Graphics and animation. Drawing into the canvas and putting things in motion (March 19, 2014),
http://www.ibm.com/developerworks/java/library/j-html5-game2/index.html
2. Finkelstein, S., Nickel, A., Harrison, L., Suma, E.A., Barnes, T.: cMotion: A New Game Design to Teach Emotion Recognition and Programming Logic to Children using Virtual Humans. In: IEEE Virtual Reality, pp. 249–250 (2009)
3. Abirached, B., Zhang, Y., Park, J.H.: Understanding User Needs for Serious Games for Teaching Children with Autism Spectrum Disorders Emotions. In: Proceedings of World Conference on Educational Multimedia, Hypermedia and Telecommunications, Denver, Colorado, USA, pp. 1054–1063 (June 2012)
4. CDC, Centers for Disease Control and Prevention: Autism Spectrum Disorders (ASDs) - Data & Statistics (March 9, 2014),
http://www.cdc.gov/ncbddd/autism/data.html
5. CDC, Centers for Disease Control and Prevention: Autism Spectrum Disorders (ASDs) - Facts About ASDs (March 10, 2014),
http://www.cdc.gov/ncbddd/autism/facts.html
6. Wikipedia: Cumulative moving average (March 19, 2014),
http://en.wikipedia.org/wiki/Moving_average#Cumulative_moving_average
7. Thorn, A.: Game Engine Design and Implementation. Jones & Bartlett Learning (2011)
8. Nacke, L., Lindley, C., Stellmach, S.: Log Who's Playing: Psychophysiological Game Analysis Made Easy through Event Logging. In: Markopoulos, P., de Ruyter, B., IJsselsteijn, W.A., Rowland, D. (eds.) Fun and Games 2008. LNCS, vol. 5294, pp. 150–157. Springer, Heidelberg (2008)

Serious Music Game Design and Testing

Szu-Ming Chung

Department and Institute of Digital Content Design, Ling Tung University,
Taichung, Taiwan, ROC
smc2006312@hotmail.com, szuming@teamail.ltu.edu.tw

Abstract. This experimental research intends to design a serious music game for preoperational children. Based on Piaget's cognitive developmental theory, Kodály and Orff's approach, the researcher integrates the Taiwanese folk tunes and folksongs materials, the western music system, and multi-touch screen technology to create serious music games. These games are developed as mobile applications to run an experimental study with 21 preschoolers from a local private kindergarten. The testing process collects data by participant observation, video recording, and learning records on tablet PCs. This paper presents the exploration and discussions of the problems and solutions for developing a valid serious game testing for preschoolers.

Keywords: serious music game, preschoolers, android system, interface design, qualitative research.

1   Introduction

This experimental research intends to design serious music games to motivate and inspire musical interests in preschoolers. As an individual from Taiwan with a strong background in traditional Chinese culture mixed with Ho-Lo, Hakka, aboriginal tribal, and mainland Chinese cultures, the researcher integrates the Taiwanese folk tunes and folksong materials and Western music teaching ideas to create music games for 4-5 year-old children. It is based on the highly developed Western music educational approaches, Bruner's knowledge map, and Piaget's developmental theory [1]. Considering user ages, psychological causes, interface usability, testing validity and credibility, the researcher experiences many evolutionary stages, such as refining and implementing audible musical audio signals, integrating visual animation with effective music sounds, developing smooth gameplay flow of an effective serious game, establishing a standard pre-testing and testing process, and video taking and progressive data recording on tablets. For the purpose of accomplishing a desirable serious music game, the researcher explores and discusses the serious music game design, cognitive and musical development in preoperational children, musical material selection, methodology, game interface design, testing design, and participant observation results in the following sections.

M. Ma et al. (Eds.): SGDA 2014, LNCS 8778, pp. 119–133, 2014.
© Springer International Publishing Switzerland 2014

2   Related Study

2.1   Serious Music Game Design

Broadly saying, serious game design involves the teacher, student, and learning. Such learning includes formal and informal learning, games, play, communication and multimodality, and pedagogical theories [2]. Digital game-based learning (DGBL) is a sub-section of serious games [3, 4]. Distinguished from traditional teaching with a strong constructivist theory, the DGBL engages students in a learning process [5, 6, 7], which motivates them to solve problems and overcome challenges [8]. The educational use of DGBL has certain advantages (integration, hypermedia, interactivity, immersion, narrativity, etc.) and disadvantages (addiction, violent behaviors, etc.). To improve DGBL, the research or educator should focus on critical factors, such as clear relative advantages, increased compatibility, and reduced complexity [9]. Designing serious music games requires consideration of embodiment of musical ideas with pedagogical theories and a teaching approach, which includes musical development and cognitive skills, visual and listening skills, and interactivity and kinesthetic coordination [1].

2.2   Cognitive Development

Piaget's idea about developmental stages is that they occur in a consistent order [10]—sensorimotor, preoperational, concrete operations, and formal operation. The development usually occurs in a sequential order just like we crawl before we can walk and run. Furthermore, the developmental changes occur in almost all children according to a fairly standard timetable [11]. During the early childhood years, 2–8 years of age, the child is rapidly developing the symbolic function, or semiotic function in cognitive concepts, representational thought, time, space, and movement and speed [10]. As the child develops, there are two basic functions: organization and adaptation. Every act is organized and the dynamic aspect of organization is adaptation. *Assimilation* and *accommodation* describe how the organism utilizes something from the environment and incorporates it. At the same time, the organism responds to stimulus and actively changes it internally. These "functional invariants" occur continuously in cognitive development in a balancing manner. When assimilation is more than accommodation, the child is playing. When accommodation is more than assimilation, the child is imitating. When they are in balance, the most adaptive condition (*equilibration*) is displayed. Cognitive development also consists of a succession of changes whose structural units are called *schemata*. Cognition develops continuously, however, the results are discontinuous and termed as sequential periods, subperiods or stages by Piaget [12]. 4 and 5 year old preschoolers fall under the stage of preoperational subperiod of concrete operations. The preoperational child:

- Can differentiate signifiers of words, images, etc.;
- Can classify images according to their content or structure (visual, auditory, etc.) [10];
- Is egocentric in their representational thought and cannot take another individual's point of view;

- Tends to focus on the successive states of a display;
- Lacks the reasoning ability of cause-and-effect and a hierarchy of categories [12].

These characteristics can be influenced by several factors, such as maturation, physical experience, logicomathematical experience, social experience, and equilibration [13].

2.3   Musical Development

Young children in their first three years of life can perform more consistent beats in their babble and singing when they can perform smoother movements [14]. Another study shows that mere listening to piano music can activate auditory information and the motor cortex (responsible for body movement, including preparation, sensory guidance, and control of movement) [15]. This indicates that sound mapping is in parallel with motor activities in the musical brain. Based on Elliott's analysis and the figure of types of representations, the genuine representation (physical experience) and symbolic representation (communicative experience) interact between the corporal movements and musical sounds, verbal words, and visual signs [14]. In early childhood, physical activities and practical experience usually enhance and stimulate genuine mental representation. Such development is also found true in music learning. Genuine musical representation can only be achieved by musical doing. As language ability is acquired by communicative process, the development of musical knowledge can only be assessed through music activities, such as singing, performing, improvising, conducting, and so on.

Some children younger than 3 years old can sense the beat of music [14, 16]. More than half of 3 year olds can tap to a steady beat, based on tests with computerized rhythmic performance conducted in the United States, South Africa, and Australia [17, 18]. Some research found that pitch matching accuracy is correlated with vocal range. Early childhood children can match pitch well within their vocal range [19]. Some studies report that most preschool children have limited vocal range from the middle C to an octave higher [20, 21] and that vocal range will expand with age [22, 23].

2.4   Musical Materials

Based on Kodály method [24], Orff approach [25, 26], and their concepts combined [27], music learning is sequential learning of rhythm, melody, songs, and other musical elements with preparation of duple meter rhythmic patterns, pentatonic scales, two songs, singing with movements, and improvising in folk tunes and folk songs with which children are familiar with in their culture and daily life. Demographics show that the majority of the people in Taiwan are ethnically Han (Holo 73.3%, Hakka, 18.1%, and others 6.2%) [28]. Shü [29] studied traditional Taiwanese music and songs by key, range, interval, melodic contour, construction, performance manner, and features of lyrics whose results are written in *Fu-Lau-Si-Ming-Ker*. These are represented by

27 different genres of folksongs. Chung [30] analyzed these songs and found that the major constructs include musical elements of duple meter and common time, pentatonic, intervals of seconds and minor thirds, up-and-downward major minor seconds and thirds, sectional musical, and through-composed music. Through applying the well-established Western music system and well-developed music teaching methods (Kodály and Orff), the researcher believes that the Taiwanese folksong elements are the optimal choice for establishing this experimental research.

2.5   Qualitative Research and Validity

The researcher attempts to find new patterns or meanings from situated phenomena (gameplay/game-based learning) by observed or recorded data (video recording and computers). It is clear the superficial quantity data collected on tablet PCs cannot show deeper understanding that occurs in a learner's mind. Video records offer evidence of the verbal or physical behavior exhibited by participants. The empathetic insight depends on the observer/the researcher's expert interpretation. The challenge for qualitative researchers is how to use descriptive observation data to attain validity. Lincoln and Guba [31, 32] proposed criteria (credibility, transferability, dependability, and confirmability) to judge the soundness of qualitative research and techniques for establishing them. Unlike quantitative researchers, qualitative researchers intend to offer readers a credible account and a vicarious experience for substantiation or modification of existing generalizations based on uniqueness of personal understanding [33].

3   Methodology

The purpose of exploring Piaget's theory is to design age appropriate games with consideration of musical intelligence and physical capacities of young children. The researcher does not intend to interpret that almost all children develop in this broadly defined theory. In this respect, the goal of each game is to provide the opportunity of experience and challenge (Table 1) but not to attain standardized testing of knowledge and skills. The testing process collects data by ways of participation observation, video recording, and learning records on tablet PCs for analyses. The participation observation is based on the observer's personal interpretation of participants' behavior that occurred in the testing process. The learning records are pre-determined and assigned to each game and then recorded after every gameplay episode. Since the sample size is small, to attain valid results, two researchers will produce codes to analyze the collected data in three dimensions: attitude, interaction, and problem solving. After comparing analyses of the two researchers, the results will provide the validity of this qualitative study. Table 2 displays the criteria of coding.

Table 1. Goals and Learning Records

Game	Goal	Learning Records
Steady beat game	Know and feel steady beats	Record succeeded times and missed bests
Pitch matching game	Know and feel second and third intervals in pentatonic scale	Record missed intervals
Up-Down melodic game	Experience and feel up-down melodies	Record experience times
Improvisation game	Experience improvisation on pentatonic scale	Record improvised tones and times

Table 2. Tested Dimensions and Sub-Items

Dimensions	Sub-Items
Attitude	Passive/active Showing interest/no interest Emotional
Interaction	Verbal responses Physical responses Responding to visual or auditory cues
Problem Solving	Exploring different way of playing Asking questions

4   Game Interface Design

To provide young children with different tone qualities, A_4 (440 Hz) of different instruments in various instrumental families (woodwinds, brasses, strings, percussions, and piano) are created to play quarter beats of the common meter; the pentatonic scales (C_4, D_4, E_4, G_4, A_4) are used to construct two tone examples (intervals of seconds, minor thirds) and single note improvisation games (16 bests long, 4 measures in common time meter), two octave scale upward from the middle C_4 to compose up-down melodic lines. For the purpose of collecting accurate data, at the start of each game, every player has to choose one instrument of 20 from various instrumental families to represent him/her. To design a playable game interface, every game is constructed by the following principles: (1) Every game plays an instrumental sound by random; (2) Every music example plays at a tempo of 1 beat per second; (3) Every game has a demonstration; (4) Repeat and pass icons emerge when the demonstration and the game are over; (5) When all 20 instruments are chosen, meaning when 20 games are successfully finished by players, an icon leads to a database which records the total number of missed games by each player. Figure 1 and 2 show the flow charts

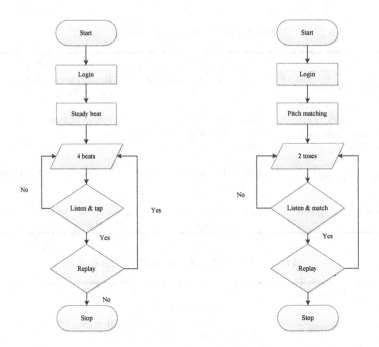

Fig. 1. Flowcharts of Steady beat and pitch matching games

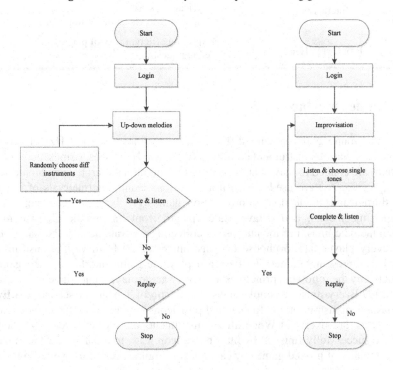

Fig. 2. Flow charts of Up-down melodies and improvisation games

of 4 games. According to these charts, the arrangement of auditory, visual (animation), interactive, and feedback design of each game are listed in Table 3. The sequence of visual design in the steady beat and pitch matching games is displayed as two standard examples in Figure 3 and 4.

Table 3. Auditory, Visual, and Interaction, and Feedback Design on Game Interface

Game Interface	Auditory	Visual (Animation)	Interaction	Feedback
Steady beat game	Instrumental sounds of steady beat (beat per second)	A bouncing crystal ball with a responsive penguin Bridge animation	Tapping to match the beats (bouncing until the player completes a successive 4 beats)	Negative feedback (stop bouncing; "Uh-oh!") Positive feedback (waving; wings making "O"; "Success!")
Pitch matching game	2-tone samples (C_4 D_4, D_4 E_4, E_4 G_4, G_4 A_4, D_4C_4, E_4D_4, G_4 E_4, A_4 G_4, and unisons of 5 tones)	Bridge animation 7 steps on rainbow ladder paralleling C major scale tones Ear icon for listening again	Touching to match 2 tones on rainbow ladder	Negative feedback (silent steps) Positive feedback (playing matched musical sounds and turning to the next sub-game; "Success!")
Up-Down melodic game	Up-down running melody crossing 2 octaves	A marble running on the leveling roads to pick up objects (implying the direction of keyboard melodic lines)	Left-right shaking to experience up-down melodies	Negative feedback (not moving) Positive feedback (picking up the objects) A sleigh carrying all the pickups and entering an igloo
Improvisation game	Single pentatonic scale tones in a random manner	5 color bubbles (pentatonic tones) randomly emerging from the ocean bottom Treble clef icon for listening the entire music Bridge animation	Touching colorful bubbles to improvise a 16 quarter note song	Positive feedback (a treble clef emerged for playing the entire song)

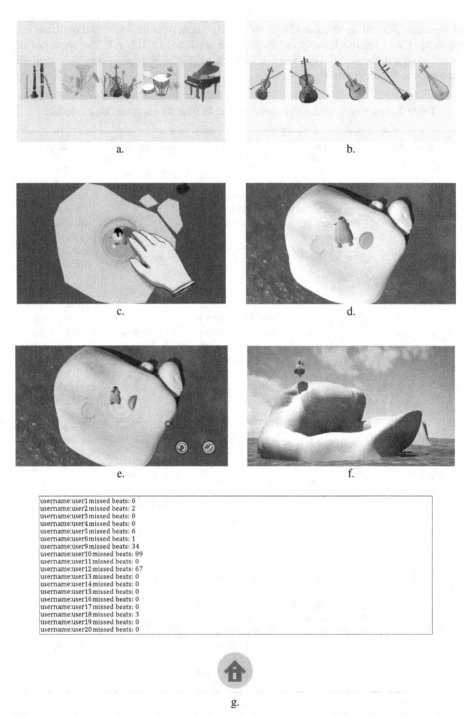

Fig. 3. Steady beat game: a. Login 1; b. Login 2; c. Demo; d. "Uh-oh!" e. "Success!" f. Animation; g. Recorded data (missed beats)

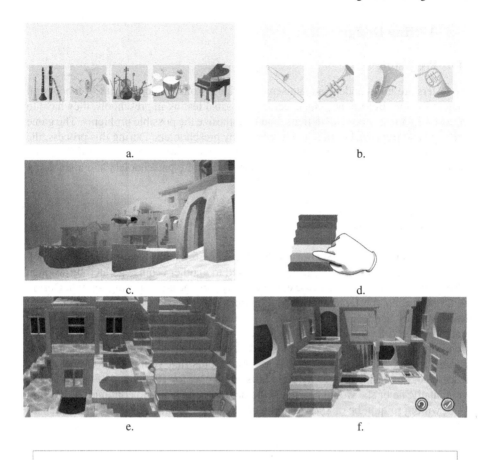

a.   b.

c.   d.

e.   f.

username:user3 first missed intervals: 7 incorrect intervals: re,re,re,do,la,so,mi,mi,so,so,mi,re,la,so correct intervals: 2
correct intervals: so,mi,do,re
username:user4 fourth missed intervals: 36 incorrect intervals: do,re,so,mi,re,re,re,re,la,so,so,so,re,mi,mi,re,la,so,so,mi,so,so,do,
re,do,re,so,so,re,re,mi,so,so,mi,mi,mi,re,do,re,mi,mi,so,mi,re,la,so,so,so,la,so,so,la,so,re,re,re,re,mi,so,la,so,re,re,mi,mi,la,la,so,la
correct intervals: 0 correct intervals:
username:user5 first missed intervals: 9 incorrect intervals: la,so,la,so,so,so,do,do,la,so,la,so,la,la,re,do,so,mi
correct intervals: 0 correct intervals:
username:user7 first missed intervals: 9 incorrect intervals: re,mi,re,re,do,re,mi,mi,re,do,so,mi,re,mi,mi,mi,do,re
correct intervals: 0 correct intervals:
username:user10 second missed intervals: 16 incorrect intervals: re,re,so,la,so,la,so,so,so,la,mi,re,mi,mi,mi,mi,mi,mi,re,la,la,re,mi,
re,re,mi,so,re,re,do,do,mi correct intervals: 2 correct intervals: re,mi,so,so
username:user11 third missed intervals: 17 incorrect intervals: mi,so,mi,mi,mi,mi,la,so,la,so,do,do,do,re,re,mi,so,mi,mi,mi,do,do,
la,la,so,la,do,re,re,mi,mi,so,la,la correct intervals: 10 correct intervals: mi,re,do,re,do,re,re,mi,mi,re,so,so,la,so,la,so,mi,so,mi,re
username:user12 third missed intervals: 27 incorrect intervals: do,do,do,do,do,re,re,do,so,la,so,la,so,la,mi,so,so,la,so,mi,la,la,so,
la,la,so,re,do,mi,mi,re,re,mi,so,mi,mi,so,so,re,do,so,la,so,mi,do,do,so,so,re,do,re,mi,mi correct intervals: 0 correct intervals:
username:user14 first missed intervals: 8 incorrect intervals: mi,re,la,la,mi,mi,so,mi,re,re,mi,re,mi,do,re,do,do
correct intervals: 1 correct intervals: do,re
username:user15 third missed intervals: 24 incorrect intervals: so,la,so,so,do,do,re,do,la,la,re,re,re,re,so,mi,so,la,re,mi,do,do,so,
so,re,re,la,so,mi,so,so,mi,mi,so,do,re,so,mi,mi,mi,mi,mi,la,so,re,do,la,so correct intervals: 3 correct intervals: do,re,do,do,do,re
username:user17 first missed intervals: 5 incorrect intervals: mi,so,so,la,la,so,mi,so,la,la
correct intervals: 4 correct intervals: do,re,so,so,so,la,mi,mi
username:user19 first missed intervals: 5 incorrect intervals: la,la,re,mi,so,mi,mi,so,so,la
correct intervals: 4 correct intervals: do,re,mi,mi,re,mi,re,do
username:user20 third missed intervals: 24 incorrect intervals: do,do,so,so,so,la,re,re,re,do,la,so,re,mi,re,re,re,re,mi,mi,re,do,do,
do,re,re,do,re,re,re,do,so,mi,re,mi,so,mi,so,la,do,re,re,re,so,so,mi,mi correct intervals: 3 correct intervals: do,re,do,re,re,do

g.

Fig. 4. Pitch Matching Game: a. Login step 1; b. Login step 2; c. animation; d. demo; e. gameplay
interface; f. "Success!"; g. Recorded data (missed tones)

5   Testing Design

5.1   Pre-testing

The testers are hired undergraduate senior students from the department of the Digital Content Design. Before they can execute the formal testing in preschools, they have to pre-test the games, record all deficits, and hypothesize the possible problems. The game is revised and improved until it can be played by preschoolers. During this process, the testers were also familiarized with the subjects by attending their daily activities and playing with them to facilitate their work with the young preschoolers and a smoother testing experience later on.

5.2   Testing Process

The 21 subjects consist of 9 at age 4 and 12 at age 5 from a local private preschool. They are tested in classroom settings connected to another room separated by wooden screen doors. 2 video recorders are equipped to record the entire testing section. During the test, the child is offered a tablet running the android system and a headphone set to isolate him or her from outside noises. However, they do not really appreciate the headphone sets. Eventually the tests were executed in a normal classroom with no sound proofing. The testers follow a standard procedure to execute every testing and are also required to use succinct and accurate words that young children can easily understand. For each game, every child is asked to play for 10 minutes. If the child quit accidentally, he or she would be asked whether he or she wants to continue. If the child is not willing to quit, he or she would be gently asked to finish the last game when 10 minutes have passed.

5.3   Testing Results and Discussions

Though participation observation is based on the observer's personal interpretation of participant's behavior occurred in the testing process. It also reflects the observer's educational training, teaching experience, and personal decision making pertaining to this particular research. The following section presents examples of the observations.

Observation 1. Repetitive use is the essence of this programmed game. Children often play repeatedly until the content of the game is learnt and played fluently. Table 4 shows the collected data from the android tablets. The missed and complete numbers displayed in Table 4 show that they missed most of the games, but most of participants kept trying until the time was up. Their well-behaved manner and passive attitude can be seen from the recorded video clips.

Observation 2. Although research shows that before the age of 3, half of children can sense steady beats, this skill is obviously lacking in these preschoolers. There could be many internal and external factors. However, conversations with subjects sometimes expose how they solve problems. Subject 4 (age 4) and subject 5 (age 5) provide an interesting contrast.

Subject 4 would sit still and watch how the testers demonstrate. At first she did not respond to any questions or suggestions. After the testers showed her how to interact with the tablet, she grasped the idea in an instant. After several tries, she finished the game and watched the animation. She showed interest and continued to play for many times (26 times) and succeeded for 13 times. She saw all the feedback and talked about the expressions of the penguin. Then she laughed at the sliding penguin played in a short animation after finishing the game. For the entire section, she seemed to enjoy all details in this game.

Subject 5 stared at the screen while the testers tried to demonstrate. He agreed upon the question asking if he understood how to play the game. After several unsuccessful tries, he started to press hard on the screen. It seemed he did not notice the musical beats. Then, he wanted to change the instrument. He assumed that a different instrument might give him a better chance to succeed. He noticed, at least, there were many different instruments. The tester tried to ignore his request and explained to him that another instrumental sound would play the same game. He did not give up and asked again. The tester repeated the same explanation. He continued to play and did not quit. In the end, he said the tablet would do things automatically even if he did not press anything. He was very confused and did not learn how to interact with the game interface.

Observation 3. Subject 12 moved her hand between instrumental selections when asked by the tester. She began to tap by palm and accidentally quit the game. The young preschooler sometimes responded very slowly and made mistakes constantly because her physical movement might not have been mature enough for 5 year old activities. The hesitation and indecisive actions might explain her attitude and behavior to unfamiliar activities and the testers. When working with such children, the tester should demonstrate every step slowly, give clear directions, and affirm comprehension by asking questions. She definitely deserved more attention and opportunities to practice.

Observation 4. Subject 14 also reacted fast to direction and paid close attention to any movement or gesture from the tester. She used her left hand and changed to her right hand when she found the replay icon on the right hand bottom on the screen. She successfully completed 3 beats accidently while pressing hard and long. Later on, she realized it was not the main reason she succeeded so she changed strategy to try index and middle fingers, two index fingers, and tapped many times with both fingers. She worked on problems with both hands. Physically, she might be an ambidextrous person and probably depends on this ability to solve problems.

Observation 5. The game shows and replays any missed beats. Subject 21 was especially good at the first and second beat tapping. When the replay was shown, she would observe and expressed displeasure at missing beats. The testers were anxious to encourage her. Most of the time, she tapped right on 3 beats and missed all the fourth beats. She kept working on it for about 5 minutes. In the end she did not successfully finish any game. She was almost ready for steady beat counting.

Observation 6. In the test of pitch matching, the testers explain by using the rainbow ladder as an analogy for the C major scale of do, re, mi, fa, so, la, and ti (or si). When showing the first demonstration, every subject must point to each step of the rainbow ladder and sing note names along with the scale played by piano. The second demonstration displays how to match the pitches by tapping the steps of the ladder. Because the incorrect pitches would not sound, every child tried to match by tapping every step on the ladder. Eventually, every subject actually successfully finished at least one game (with 9 matches in a random manner). Those subjects who continued playing several games continued using the same strategy to accomplish each game. In gameplay, the subjects seemed to depend on the visual skills with carefully tapping gesture on every step of the rainbow ladder. The rising steps on the rainbow ladder parallel to the rising scale in music was slow to process in these young minds, but the gameplay engaged them and they were worked diligently on it.

Table 4. Tested Subjects Age Information and Collected Data

Subject	Age	Steady Beat Game (4 beat/recount at 3 missed) Missed beats/Accomplished	Pitch Matching Game (13 2-tone files/9 matching sub-games) Play x times/Missed matches/Accomplish ed matches	Experience times	Improvised tones/Experienc e times
1	5	9/0	3/24/ 3	2	5/2
2	4	3/0	1/ 5/ 4	2	5/2
3	5	1/0	1/ 9/ 0	2	$5/1^{st}(4/2^{nd})$
4	4	35/13	1/ 8/ 1	4	5/1
5	5	90/ 0	2/16/ 2	2	5/3
6	5	6/0	1/24/ 3	1	5/2
7	4	6/0	3/17/10	4	4/1
8	5	20/1	2/18/ 0	3	$1/1^{st}(5/2^{nd})$
9	4	10/0	2/18/ 0	1	5/3
10	5	54/ 0	3/26/ 1	1	5/9
11	5	35/ 0	1/ 5/ 4	1	5/1
12	4	2/ 0	1/ 9/ 0	1	5/1
13	4	2/ 0	1/ 7/ 2	4	5/3
14	5	62/ 0	4/36/ 0	3	5/3
15	4	68/ 0	3/ 27/ 0	6	5/1
16	5	3/ 0	1/ 8/ 1	4	$5/1^{st}(4/2^{nd})$
17	4	1/ 0	3/24/0	2	5/3
18	4	4/ 0	2/14/4	4	5/4
19	5	4/ 0	1/ 8/ 1	5	5/9
20	5	37/ 0	1/ 9/ 0	1	5/4
21	5	7/ 0	1/ 7/ 2	1	5/2

4   Conclusion

The goals of this study are not to emphasize the cognitive challenge or musical learning but provide well-programmed opportunities to experience music by playing games. Through review of related studies of cognitive theory and musical development, the researcher establishes a set of principles for designing serious games for young preschool children. These principles are not only applied in serious game design but also in experimental research tested in a local private preschool.

This research created 4 games to provide experience and challenge of steady beats, pitch making, up-down melodies, and improvisation. To provide age appropriate material integrated with cultural heritage, it uses pentatonic scale tones in different tone colors (different instrument sounds) for listening materials and auditory cues device. The researcher uses Finale to compose and export the thematic music and single tones in wave format. Unfortunately, in the process of transferring and compressing sound files to tablet PCs, the sound volume and quality are degraded greatly. To avoid such problems, the researcher has to use sound editors to regain the volume and quality of musical sounds.

To design the testing, additional programmed functions of collecting information progression record certain testing results. Video recording of the entire sections is setup for observing, comparing and contrasting the progress during testing and for later analyses.

Due to technical problems, the testers have to be replaced and retrained. The first recommendation here is that the standard procedure of testing has to be established and every tester has to abide the guidelines. In many cases, the subjects were often confused by the testers' verbal expressions. Working with young children, simple words and clear direction are most helpful. They pay more attention to hand movements of the testers and less to verbal instructions.

Considering the limitations of the situation and the cautious expressions from the subjects in reaction to impinged questions from the testers, the imperfect testing environment, and which may be interrupted by noise from outside, the subjects might feel more comfortable and safer under a more familiar learning circumstance such as a classroom setting.

In schooling, the start and the results of learned knowledge and skills are often more observed than the process. In other words, focus is on final outcomes as an assessment. Musical development can by no means be assessed with this concept. The data listed on Table 4 does not display the final outcome of testing, but only the beginning of much recorded gameplay and musical development to come. The second round of the same testing is being planned to collect more data for comparing and contrasting to the first half so that the progress can be observed. According to the methodology of this research, the unfinished part will assess qualitative validity. This step will be executed in the near future.

Acknowledgements. This research is funded and sponsored by the Ministry of Science and Technology in Taiwan, ROC.

References

1. Chung, S.-M., Wu, C.-T.: Intuitive Game Design for Early Learning in Music. In: Farag, A.A., Yang, J., Jiao, F. (eds.) Proceedings of the 3rd International Conference on Multimedia Technology (ICMT 2013). LNEE, vol. 278, pp. 395–406. Springer, Heidelberg (2013)

2. Egenfeldt-Nielsen, S., Meyer, B., Sørensen, B.H. (eds.): Serious Games in Education: A Global Perspective. Aarhus University Press, Aarhus (2011)
3. Gee, J.P.: What Video Games Have to Teach Us about Learning and Literacy? Palgrave Macmillan, Basingstoke (2003)
4. Prensky, M.: Digital Natives, Digital Immigrants Part 1. On the Horizon 9(5), 1–6 (2001)
5. Malone, T.W.: Toward a Theory of Intrinsically Motivating Instruction. Cognitive Science 5(4), 333–369 (1982)
6. Bowmann, R.F.: A Pac-Man Theory of Motivation. Tactical Implication for Classroom Instruction. Educational Technology 22(9), 14–17 (1982)
7. Provenzo, E.F.: Video Kids: Making Sense of Nintendo. Harvard University Press, Cambridge (1991)
8. Csikszentmihalyi, M.: Flow: the Psychology of Optimal Experience. Harper and Row, New York (1990)
9. Egenfeldt-Nielsen, S.: The Challenges to Diffusion of Educational Computer Games. In: The European Conference on Game-Based Learning, Copenhagen, Denmark (October 2010)
10. Piaget, J.: The Essential Piaget. In: Gruber, H.E., Vonèche, J.J. (eds.) Basic Books, New York (1977)
11. Swanwick, K.: Music, Mind, and Education. Routledge, London (1988)
12. Phillips Jr., J.L.: The Origins of Intellect: Piaget's Theory. W. H. Freeman, San Francisco (1969)
13. Sigel, I.E., Brodzinsky, D.M., Golinkoff, R.M.: New Directions in Piagetian Theory and Practice. Lawrence Erlbaum Associates, Hillsdale (1981)
14. Elliott, D.J.: Praxial Music Education: Reflections and Dialogues. Oxford University Press, New York (2004)
15. Bangert, M.W., Parlitz, D., Altenmüller, E.: Neuronal Correlates of the Pianist's "Innerear." In: Proceedings of the Conference on Musical Imagery, Olso (1999)
16. McLauglin, H.: Babies and Toddlers as Musicians. In: Respecting the Child in Early Childhood Learning: Proceedings of the Eighth International Seminar of the Early Childhood Commission of the International Society for Music Education. International Society for Music Education, Cape Town (1998)
17. Suzuki, S.: Nurtured by Love. Exposition Press, New York (1969)
18. Flohr, J.W., Woodward, S.C., Suthers, L.: Rhythm Performance in Early Childhood. In: Respecting the Child in Early Childhood Learning: Proceedings of the Eighth International Seminar of the Early Childhood Commission of the International Society for Music Education. International Society for Music Education, Cape Town (1998)
19. Buckton, R.: A comparison of the Effects of Vocal and Instrumental Instruction on the Development of Melodic and Vocal Abilities in Young Children. Psychology of Music 5(1), 36–47 (1977)
20. Wassum, S.: Elementary School Children's Vocal Range. Journal of Research in Music Education 27, 214–226 (1979)
21. Drexler, E.N.: A Study of the Development of the Ability to Carry a Melody at the Preschool Level. Child Development 9(2), 319–322 (1938)
22. Flowers, P.J., Dunne-Sousa, D.: Pitch-pattern Accuracy, Tonality, and Vocal Range in Preschool Children's Singing. Journal of Research in Music Education 38(2), 102–114 (1990)
23. Welch, G.F.: Vocal Range and Poor Pitch Singing. Psychology of Music 7(2), 13–21 (1979)
24. Choksy, L.: The Kodály Method: Comprehensive Music Education from Infant to Adult, 2nd edn. Prentice-Hall, Inc., Englewood Cliffs (1988)
25. Warner, B.: Orff-Schulwerk: Applications for the Classroom. Prentice-Hall, Inc., Englewood Cliffs (1991)

26. Jorgenson, L.B.: An Analysis of the Music Education Philosophy of Carl Orff. University of Wisconsin, La Crosse (2010)

27. Wheeler, L., Raebeck, L.: Orff and Kodály: Adapted from the Elementary School. Wm. C. Brown Company Publishers, Dubuque (1972)

28. Yuan, E.: Hakka Affairs Council: Demographics of Hakka People in Taiwan, 2010-2011. Government Census Report, Taipei, Taiwan (2012)

29. Shü, C.: Fu-Lau-Si-Ming- Ker (Holo folksongs). The Institute of Chinese Folk Art and Culture Center Taipei, Taiwan (1976)

30. Chung, S.-M.: A Music Program for Grade One Based on the New Music Curriculum Standards (1993) in Taiwan. Dissertation. Texas Tech University Press, Lubbock, Texas (2003)

31. Lincoln, Y.S., Guba, E.G.: Naturalistic Inquiry. Sage, New York (1985)

32. Lincoln, Y.S., Guba, E.G.: Criteria for Assessing Naturalistic Inquiries as Reports. Presented at the Annual Meeting of the American Research Association, New Orleans (1988)

33. Colwell, R. (ed.): MENC Handbook of Research Methodologies, p. 297. Oxford University Press, New York (2006)

Immersive Composition for Sensory Rehabilitation: 3D Visualisation, Surround Sound, and Synthesised Music to Provoke Catharsis and Healing

Jessica Argo[1], Minhua Ma[1], and Christoph Kayser[2]

[1] Digital Design Studio, Glasgow School of Art, UK
j.argo1@student.gsa.ac.uk, m.ma@gsa.ac.uk
[2] Centre for Cognitive Neuroimaging, University of Glasgow, UK
Christoph.Kayser@glasgow.ac.uk

Abstract. There is a wide range of sensory therapies using sound, music and visual stimuli. Some focus on soothing or distracting stimuli such as natural sounds or classical music as analgesic, while other approaches emphasize the active performance of producing music as therapy. This paper proposes an immersive multi-sensory Exposure Therapy for people suffering from anxiety disorders, based on a rich, detailed surround-soundscape. This soundscape is composed to include the users' own idiosyncratic anxiety triggers as a form of habituation, and to provoke psychological catharsis, as a non-verbal, visceral and enveloping exposure. To accurately pinpoint the most effective sounds and to optimally compose the soundscape we will monitor the participants' physiological responses such as electroencephalography, respiration, electromyography, and heart rate during exposure. We hypothesize that such physiologically optimized sensory landscapes will aid the development of future immersive therapies for various psychological conditions, Sound is a major trigger of anxiety, and auditory hypersensitivity is an extremely problematic symptom. Exposure to stress-inducing sounds can free anxiety sufferers from entrenched avoidance behaviors, teaching physiological coping strategies and encouraging resolution of the psychological issues agitated by the sound.

Keywords: Surround sound, Ambisonics, Anxiety, Physiological monitoring, Exposure therapy, desensitization, immersive virtual environment.

1 Introduction

Immersive Composition for Sensory Rehabilitation is an interdisciplinary research project based in the optimal audio-visual production suite of Glasgow School of Art's Digital Design Studio, in collaboration with the Centre for Cognitive Imaging, at the University of Glasgow's Institute of Neuroscience. In a collaboration between a sensory artist practicing in diverse socio-cultural contexts, a serious games specialist and a neuroscientist, high-quality, innovative sound works will be composed and psychophysically tested to quantify emotional and visceral affect. The compositions will incorporate personalized sound triggers identified through interviews with Anxiety,

M. Ma et al. (Eds.): SGDA 2014, LNCS 8778, pp. 134–149, 2014.

Depression and Trauma sufferers (rather than the common implementation of familiar music or natural sound). A key variable in the research is the effect of spatial immersion in a soundscape composed in 5.1 Surround Sound, along with Ambisonic and 3D Visualisation experiments, compared to existing psychophysical studies which focus on the arousal caused by specific isolated timbres or naturally occurring sounds, primarily using stereo sound through headphones.

2   Established Modes of Sensory Therapy

2.1   Music Therapy: Listening versus Active Participation

Music and Arts Therapies often prefer an active approach, encouraging clients to play instruments or sing to *express* their own emotions. Yet, the benefits of passive listening to the prescribed *mood induction* [1, 2] within existing music are widely acknowledged. An optimal compromise between passive listening exposure and expressive performance-based therapy could be giving the participant-receiver a degree of input. Previously, input could be as minimal as asking musicians performing cathartic hospital *recovery services* for diverse empathetic song requests, from the elegiac to flamboyant pop-rock [2]. True Aristotelian catharsis ("the cleansing of the soul through an emotional experience" [3]) was even provoked in terminal AIDS sufferers, by addictive listening to Arvo Part's *Tabula Rasa* [4]. Furthermore, participant input could become as incremental as a compositional decision: to include their own anxiety triggers or sounds associated with pleasant memories; to choose between rousing and soothing tempo, or major and minor chords [5].

Sound, movement or visualization provides non-verbal catalysts for catharsis: the sensation and stimulation during exposure can provoke unexpected feelings, a powerful discussion stimulus, as listeners primarily reflect on the intensely emotional session itself and then verbalise their more underlying emotions stirred. Hospital patients "sharing innermost feelings" bring myriad benefits: a patient-clinician dialogue aids a more personalised treatment; nausea can be reduced and musically triggered endorphins boost the immune system [2].

Music is known for its' powerful mood-inductive ability, capable of provoking *renewal ecstasies* [6] through peak musical experiences. Moments of viscerally felt *frisson* occur in traditional music at an instantaneous climax, or can appear in waves, with a build of texture or complexity. Gabrielson notes a biological mimicry to musical features, as an accelerando sets a pulse racing, shivers are provoked by deviation of anticipated harmony, and emotionally expressive melodies cause tears [6]. The overstated 'heart-rending and ghost-ridden' shock chord in Mahler's Tenth Symphony (where the whole orchestra suddenly roars in dissonant minor thirds) commonly triggered a *Strong Emotional Experience* among several participants. [6].

So music can provoke powerful sensations on even emotionally stable listeners; however the subjective experience of sound for those with neurological disorders can be remarkably heightened. Anxiety sufferers can experience hypersensitivity to any sonic intrusion, but especially to sounds imbued with connotative reminders of a traumatizing experience. Musical frisson, a sensation commonly perceived as pleasurable, can initially disturb a sensory therapy participant with anorexia, as it enforces a strong physiological reaction – clients are reminded they "have a body"[5]. Conversely, a symptom of repression of a traumatic experience is a defensive sensory switch-off, or emotional deadening. Detachment is problematic, rendering the traumatized sufferer's stability extremely fragile, as attempts to avoid conscious emotional realization will eventually be overwhelmed. If trauma sufferers' "spontaneous impulses become short-circuited by secondary inhibitive ones" [5], perhaps embodied music cognition may encourage a break from sensory-emotional avoidance. A pulsating rhythm that strongly invokes finger-tapping may surprise listeners into physical movement, as the non-verbal musical stimuli can bypass cognitive, linguistic modes of perception, with potential to be received kinesthetically. Even coma patients exposed to music in an Intensive Care Unit have shown a consequential reduction in blood pressure - the music can filter through their sympathetic nervous system, although they may not be cognitively interpreting it [2].

Mental disturbance caused by poorly recorded or considered audio, for use in rehabilitation, is often overlooked. Patients in physical pain and mental distress are soothed by natural organic, ordered smoothness, and can be irritated by digital distortion [7]. Soothing music and natural soundscapes reduce stress and anxiety in the post-operation patient, pregnant women, palliative care patients, and a virtual sensorial opposite (immersing a burns victim in a "snow-world scene") offers a distracting analgesic [8]. So, the sound composer must sensitively produce high quality audio and carefully consider the sonic events to feature in the soundscape. However, an analgesic stress reduction soundscape will doubtless need to be more delicate and soothing than sounds for sensory exposure therapy, which need to become more abrasive and challenging over time.

Another innovative use of auditory stimulation is found in *EASe* (Electronic Auditory Stimulation effect) Listening Therapy CDs [9], designed to habituate children with hypersensitivity disorders by means of sophisticated manipulation of sound frequencies (the Berard AIT modulation system). A low-pass filter is imposed on passages of music, with the high frequencies only emerging in 0.3-second intense volume-boosted bursts. The bursts are constructed to be too short to trigger the flight-or-flight response, so the child becomes familiar with the stimulation but is not frightened - encouraging tolerance of real-world sensory cacophony.

2.2   Exposure Therapy: Visual Virtual Reality versus Immersive Audio-Visual Composition

Using immersive soundscapes to reconstruct the frightening sensations of neurological disorder in a safe environment encourages trauma and anxiety sufferers to stop their life-restricting reliance on *safety behaviours* through training to endure, acknowledge and feel more at ease during stimulation. Current exposure therapies mostly rely on visual stimuli, such as the replication of fearful situations in virtual reality, with accompanying sound - but rarely with sound as the focus. However, using sound alone has great visceral potential, using non-verbal and non-literal imagery that could be used to enhance or complement exposure therapies. Using spatially pointed sonic cues can negate the need for a visual overload of information [10];

using sound alone can even encourage the user to close their eyes to induce immersion and block out external distractions. Visual-less games such as *Beowulf* show an innovative shift of focus onto the auditory imagination rather than dominating visual quality, arguing that prominent spatial cues in the game-soundscape can stimulate a richer, individualized internal mental imagery [11]. Roy et al. showed the amygdala's marked fear response became diminished as war veterans used visual Virtual Reality Exposure Therapy (VRET), where they re-enacted combat situations through a gaming environment [12]. However, creating soundscapes can provoke otherworldly, spiritual catharsis – through the established mood-inductive emotional triggering from musical structures, fused with real world sounds, and the unnatural timbre of digital synthesis. Perception of sound is a far more personalized, memory-triggering mode of reception than watching a visual VR: sound feels more directly applicable to our own memories and real life encounters - no matter how realistic or universal a visual image is, it is unlikely it will match our memories and experiences as precisely as replicable sound events do [11]. Moreover, using aversive sound stimuli is crucial in desensitization, since auditory hypersensitivity is the most common sensory-perceptual abnormality, more prevalent than visual and tactile hypersensitivity. Panksepp and Bernatzky [13] even deemed sound to have a more direct neurological affect (primarily in the subcortical emotional systems) than visuals. It has also been found that to enhance a subjective sense of presence within a mediated environment, spatial surround sound is not the key sonic augmentation - it is in fact the addition of Low Frequency Effects (bass) and a rise in volume that align with the vibratory tactility of everyday sound perception [14]. However 5.1 Surround Sound importantly does raise enjoyment, therefore engagement and likelihood to consistently attend a program of exposure therapy.

The opiate receptors are a crucial element of the emotions and physical sensations of bliss and shock triggered by music, the most influential neurochemical secretion being the release of dopamine linked to a momentary musical climax. Altenmuller [15] notes that when participants were monitored during listening to pleasant and unpleasant music, that serotonin levels rose substantially when they found the music pleasing. Our research will investigate the neurochemical and psychosomatic effect of a more continuous catharsis and evolved anticipatory system reaction to abstracted electroacoustic and found-sounds akin to Shaefferian *Music Concrète*. We hypothesize that unpleasant music may regulate the opioid secretion: an unpleasant but complex, sculpted soundscape could be intellectually intriguing, thus have more of a long-term reward than a fleeting pleasurable sensation. A gradual fade to a pleasing sound may even generate a more stable, healthy neurochemical response than a manic low-to-high jump.

Personalising VRET to individual perspectives is expensive and time consuming, but it has been shown that even one simulated situation (e.g., the 9/11 terrorist attack) can be effective for numerous survivors, as Goncalves et al. [16] find that only some stimuli depicted in the virtual environment are required to produce enough anxiety to activate the traumatic memory. The use of a partial sensory exposure focusing on one isolation of specific stimuli can be adequate to stimulate anxiety (shown from of public speaking to a VR simulated audience of disembodied eyes [17]), and may even be helpful as the user realizes it is not necessarily a whole situation that is feared, perhaps just one sensory hypersensitivity that can stimulate a panic attack. Whilst it is ideal to tailor soundscapes to include personalized sonic triggers, the commonality of psychophysical affect provoked by abrasive sounds and unfamiliar synthesized timbres mean that one soundscape may provide a rich, diverse array of sounds applicable to many unique sufferers. Indeed the ambiguity of reduced listening to sonic stimuli may even lend itself more readily to a wider range of disorders and circumstances than a specific situational narrative exposure. Additionally, humans' inherently selective perceptual processes (such as the *Cocktail Party Effect* which enables focus on one voice in a chatter-saturated environment) mean that each participant will internally amplify those sounds with most relevant resonance in their own memories.

Post Traumatic Stress Disorder (PTSD) sufferers are not merely sad, but have fragmented memory of the event and even struggle to process new memories. They are hypersensitive to stimuli, can be unable to focus, and can have indescribable feelings, particularly unable to find an outlet for their anger or open up to feel pleasure [18]. Primarily, these are symptoms of a larger dislocation of the past-traumatized body from the present-self, as hallucinatory horror-memories intrude upon their daily life. Hence, engaging trauma sufferers in a composition that seizes their attention, and lets them over-react, could be a useful outlet and exaggeration for their struggles to fully experience emotion in everyday life. Karen Callaghan, a movement therapist experienced with torture survivors, notes a frustration of conflicting emotions, as victims stifle their anger by deliberate seclusion or self-harm "for fear of being overwhelmed or destroying others with their rage" [19]. Stimulating, aversive compositions could trigger this overwhelmed sensation within a safe environment, increasing confidence that sufferers can survive it and experience can make them more resilient. The over-stimulation is only temporary, and real life is rarely going to be as phenomenologically assaulting as the sensorial exposure therapy. Moreover, music has the capacity to integrate two or more conflicting emotions or messages through melodic layering, directly emulating psychological confusion: for example, the left hand on a piano can play slow peaceful melancholy notes, while the right hand plays sharp, staccato spiky fractured movements.

3   Sound Production Techniques to Physiologically Optimize Exposure

3.1   Compositional Technique: Idiosyncratic Triggers, Digital Manipulation of Sounds, and Inaudible Frequencies

Idiosyncratic Sonic Triggers. An illustrative example of a particularly problematic anxiety trigger sound is found in a torture survivor's report:

"Reemtsma… became the victim of a hostage situation and realized afterward that his intrusive memories were triggered by hearing footsteps or a knocking sound… he had heard footsteps approaching the cellar before the kidnappers knocked at the door during his captivity." [20]

So Reemtsma has a strong, visceral aversion to the sound of footsteps, due to the fear-conditioned response learned throughout his captivity. This account exemplifies the necessity for catharsis and desensitization to the sonic trigger: it is an extremely problematic aversion, as Reemtsma would frequently encounter footsteps in everyday situations - to stick to a strategy of avoidance, he would have to live alone locked in a soundproof domicile, socially paralyzed. A soundscape designed for Reemtsma's exposure therapy could include footsteps which fade in and out of focus, gradually foregrounding the composition, and transform through a variety of filters and reverberation to fully explore the acoustic qualities of the sound, dislocating it from its' learned causal association. Footsteps could also work as a universal anxiety trigger, due to the ominous threat associated with an angry gait rushing towards the listener, in a directionally pointed sound array. Indeed, there is a multitude of clichéd shorthand to provoke fear in the listener, universally used in film (especially *stingers*, short stabbing anthropomorphized instrumentation most recognized in the shrieking violins of Hitchcock's *Psycho* (1960)) and video games (like gunfire and explosions in first-person shooter games such *Call of Duty*)[21]. These shorthands are sometimes created through inventive instrumentation, but are also sound effects including barking dogs, squeaking doors, cats screaming, ravens caw-ing, and lightning strikes. Whilst these sounds are acoustic symbols widely known to induce fear, the hypersensitivity of anxiety actually renders a wide array of causally inoffensive sounds frequenting everyday environments just as traumatic, if not more due to their chronic, ongoing nature. Initial searching for "sound triggers for anxiety" in online forums such as psychcentral.com, [22] revealed a plethora of individual sensitivities, which can then be categorized into several common sources: domestic, environmental, social and visceral. The domestic triggers seem to recur frequently, perhaps due to the invasive nature of the unwanted sound - the sounds of inconsiderate neighbors pervade what should be the anxiety sufferer's safe zone.

Table 1. Sonic triggers for anxiety shared by users on psychcentral.com

Domestic	Environment	Social	Visceral
vacuum cleaners	cars splashing water,	toddlers running &	cracking bones
"loud bass drum noise	coming & going, idling	screaming	(fingers, ankles,
when a neighbor has a	dogs barking	people talking	knees)
party"	lawnmowers	"people that talk loud	nail-picking "it
"floor shaking when air	leaf blowers	by nature"	makes me feel
conditioner is running"	power tools	people hollering	utterly sick to my
"the shower & toilet	high-pitched drill	whistling	stomach"
above me"	hammering	footsteps "especially	tinnitus
abruptly opening doors	revving motorbikes	women in high heels"	loud clapping
squeaky hinges on a	airplanes	crackling sounds of	snoring
door	siren	wrappers or chip bags	eating sounds "like
doors slamming	birds singing	tapping	Chomp, chomp,
"too much sensory input	"constant mechanical	"low repetitive beat of	slurp, sip, squish"
going on (TV, chat,	noise of printer wheels"	the big drum in a live	
radio, computer)"	hand-dryer	band"	
loud TV commercials			

Categorizing by Shaefferian *reduced listening,* that is distinguishing the acoustic property of the sound, provides further creative potential as we can use the acoustic property as a template to record or create different nuanced sound messages based on the aversive properties.

Table 2. Categorization of sonic triggers by quality using Shaefferian reduced listening

Mechanical	Loud, abrasive frequency	Vocal	Repulsive Visceral	Rhythmic irritation: Irregular - Repetitive
vacuum cleaners	cars splashing	toddlers running	cracking bones	cars idling outside
"floor shaking	water	& screaming	(fingers, an-	doors slamming
when air condi-	"the shower &	people talking	kles, knees)	abruptly opening
tioner or washing	toilet above	"people that talk	nail-picking,	doors
machine is run-	me"	loud by nature"	"it makes me	loud TV ads
ning"	crackling	people hollering	feel utterly sick	"loud bass drum when
lawnmowers	sounds of	whistling	to my sto-	neighbor has party"
leaf blowers	wrappers or	too much sen-	mach"	birds singing
power tools	chip bags	sory input going	tinnitus	dogs barking
high-pitched drill	cars coming &	on (TV, talking,	loud clapping	"low repetitive beat of
airplanes	going	radio, computer)	snoring	big drum in live band"
siren	revving motor-	football crowds	eating sounds	hammering
mechanical noise	bikes		"like Chomp,	footsteps "especially
of printer wheels	squeaky hinges		chomp, slurp,	women in high heels"
hand-dryer	on a door		sip, squish"	tapping

Digital Sound Manipulation. Recording in real world sites known for their striking acoustic properties, predicting the type of sound that would be made in the space makes for a solid base to start a soundscape composition. Using a *reduced listening* technique to select intriguing, sudden, or tonal sounds provides hundreds of short clips, which can be stitched together in looping musical sequences. These sounds can then be creatively skewed to reproduce the unsettling phenomenological distortion perceived during moments of panic, anxiety or depression, using digital filters, time stretching, delays or even altered equalization to sweep up from a natural sound to a distorted high frequency, or to strip a voice of its clarifying harmonics to abstract words or make it sound monstrous. These initial composition techniques are further enhanced by the mind-bending capabilities of surround-sound panning, used frequently in mass entertainment (mainly to aid suspension of disbelief and heighten immersion in cinema or to provoke fear in theme parks).

Researching the psychological aims of Fear Extinction and Exposure Therapy also provides a creative stimulus, as the techniques can be translated into concrete sonic ideas. Fear Extinction aims to desensitize (reduce the activation of the amygdala) through repetition of aversive stimuli, or through counterconditioning, to "establish a new stimulus–outcome association where the trauma reminder no longer signals danger" [20]. So a form of counterconditioning could be pairing an aversive auditory

Table 3. Recording sites chosen by Jessica Argo, their acoustic properties and sounds found

Recording Site	Acoustic Property	Sounds Found
Grand Central Terminal, New York	Ambience transitions from noisy to serene echo chambers transport of sounds in arches	Impromptu singing in *Whispering Gallery* Children singing, screaming, coughs High heels clacking on marble Buzzing of cleaning machines Coins rattling and dropping Trains screeching resembling bowed strings
Times Square, New York	chaotic cacophony of traffic road works bursts of music from shops, phones and cars	Tourists shouting, manic laughing "Grrrr!" Frustration at congestion Unfamiliar languages and dialects spoken Drills, buzzing, and hissing dissonant tone, ambiguous subway rumbling Grinding, squeaking, beeping, revving Tinny drumbeats as phone ringtone Cheesy pop music blaring from shops
Opera de Paris, Paris	hauntingly quiet empty auditorium balcony with heavy traffic packed with tourists marble floors in large atrium long reverberance	baby crying in auditorium, child singing stilettos clacking, floorboards creaking dragging footsteps French speech, gaspy breaths, coughs faint piano playing wavering alarms, camera shutters clicking
Search and Rescue Helicopter, Glasgow	Huge helicopter circling back and forth outside silent room	flitting between high frequency whipping blades and low frequencies of engine's roar

stimulus with a pleasant visual stimulus (e.g. the sound of a pneumatic drill played alongside a soothing visual animation). It can even emerge from a singular stimulus, a grating timbre that gradually transforms to pleasant, through semantic means (a baby crying gradually transforming to laughing) or purely through sonic structure (a high frequency gradually stepping down to more comforting lower frequency, or a baby crying at close range moving further away, drifting into a indistinct echo). Even classical music uses transformation to express and provoke psychological resolution, when distressed jerky bows of a violin in a Minor mode modulate to gentle calm strokes in a Major mode.

Reverberation is the naturally occurring reflection of sound waves after an initial source, idiosyncratic to each architectural space - a longer decay time indicates a larger room, and a glass-walled room produces a longer decay time than a foam-walled studio. Reverberation provides a sense of depth, enhances a mood, or reconstructs a natural or overemphasized decay time, with ability to sample real-world acoustics using an impulse response recorded on location. It can be used either to realistically match sounds to a visually depicted environment, or to create a hallucinatory inner-subjective viewpoint if there is no reverberation, to show the sound is not occurring in a real space but is merely imagined.

Equalization is either boosting or removing the low, middle or high frequencies from a natural sound (often a complex blend of several harmonics) or music, either to emphasize verbal clarity or to distort the voice beyond the point of recognition. Each sound quality has distinct connotations [23], often unconsciously associated, as shown across the frequency spectrum in Table 5.

Table 4. Psychoacoustic connotations of various frequencies boosted using equalization.

Frequency (Hz)	Low 20 Hz ———————————————————➤ High 20kHz		

Excess	boomy
	   muddy
		honky
		  nasal
			harsh
			sibilant

Connotative Association	power rumble ominous dizzied perception	natural unthreatening	definition loud edgy bright sparkly presence
Deficiency	Thin anaemic wimpy	dull too realistic	distant

Mood-induction sampling. Samples from film scores, created with a specific manipulation of mood, can attach false emotions to an abstract image or film. In *Ghosts* (Argo, 2013) the most prominent example is *Virtua Mima (Voice Version)* from Satoshi Kon's *Perfect Blue* (1997). This haunting, a-cappella theme has layered chromatic chanting, with stop-starts and demonic throaty sounds. The "mm-mm" taunts run in two tracks each floating past in opposite directions; a solitary choral voice is centered; one of the last "aaaas" floats from front to back. The voices are panned to burst through from the front and float away to the back as they end. The disembodied voices are activated to frighten the viewer and test the limits of the exit sign effect, making the viewer question their listening space, and waking them from the lull of the pleasant. As the listener is forced to listen to bombing sound effects with a visual absence of the cause, or haunting disembodied chanting vocals, their listening mode is changed, converting causal or semantic listening into a pure reduced appreciation of noise. If anything, the out-of-focus visual of people moving through galleries (being completely void of narrative and at times even of recognizable features) is anempathetic to emotionally charged music. They are merely spaces suggesting reverberation or ambience. Perhaps pairing these sounds with meaningless visuals creates a paradoxical middle ground of *unemotional physiological stirring*.

Spatial Panning. Jessica Argo's portfolio of surround-soundscapes, produced in the Digital Design Studio, provides diverse examples of mind-altering affects induced by spatially directed sounds. *The Anti-Cocktail-Party-Effect* (2013) [24] replicates the sudden manifestation of irrational panic attacks in social situations. When an anxiety sufferer sits in a crowded restaurant, they can become hyper-attentive and paranoid of passers-by or fellow diners' scrutiny - this perception is conveyed by the dizzying swirling panning, as the chatter originates in a normal static surround (in all channels), then slowly jumps from one isolated point to the next, then runs around the room, the crowd transforming into a terrorizing poltergeist. The chatter is manipulated using interactive wavering tremolo on MAX MSP - the chatter fractures, becomes compressed and overloaded, speeds up, evolving to monstrous pure digital warping, sweeping to a totally incomprehensible high pitch. This is the antithesis of our inherent perceptual ability to decipher language in a crowded room: the opposite of the psychoacoustic *Cocktail-Party-Effect*. Wine glasses clink with unnerving regularity blasting from various points in the room, in a lack of synchresis with the images of static glasses. The chatter and background music is at first familiar and amiable and then gradually the noise becomes overwhelming and the low-frequency effects channel is used liberally to physically shake the listener.

Encoding a sound composition into a phenomenologically engaging spatial array can be implemented through various panning styles. For example, *Blood Set in Motion* (2013) [25] is a simple hymnal synth harmonic progression with a simulation of mirror neural and circulatory responses, and corporeal imitation (imagined singing). Breathing, spatially pulsing movement of music replicates the idea of rhythm catalyzing the acceleration of heart rate. Sonic events include swooshes of a whipping stick, set in a rhythmic pulse, and the bubbling of a fountain to hyperbolize a rush of blood. *Trauma* (2013) [26] has an ominously quiet organ prelude, with an unsettling percussive arrhythm, suddenly launching into a cacophony of messy oscillating, searing chaos. Like a brain swarming with traumatic assaulting memories, random strikes burst through from all directions, and the piece ends in a blare of tinnitus. A listener, Marco Biagini, gave feedback that the timbres evoked "a digital machine gun"[27]. *Harmonising the Musical Present with the Musical Past* [28] emulates the notion of perceptual fusion of temporal events within a musical structure, as a familiar harmonic progression through G Major/E Minor, gradually morphs to a wide overlap of notes through the delayed piano and layering of timbre. The tension between F-sharp and G recurs again and again, but always harmonized slightly differently. Tape ghosts from re-recording are simulated, using occasional bursts of discordant synths, panned to emerge from the rear speakers. In 5.1 surround-sound, the illusion of appearing and disappearing ghosts is created by short bursts drifting past the listener from front to back.

Inaudible Frequencies. Steve Goodman's accounts of *Sonic Warfare* (e.g. the *Wandering Ghost* wailing voice blared to scare the Buddhist sensibilities of Vietnamese soldiers, and the nausea-inducing beating of ultrasonic frequencies from the *Squawk Box* used in Ireland [29]) exemplify the extremes of psychoacoustic manipulation, using sound as a weapon to mentally disturb or cause permanent physiological harm. However there is a therapeutic potential to use the *imperception* of *unsound,* the tactile and neurological sensations provoked by inaudible frequencies out-with the range of human hearing. *Infrasound* comprises of sound waves with low frequencies below 20 Hz and *Ultrasound* describes high frequencies above 20 kHz. The sub-bass felt resonating throughout the whole body (especially in the chest) with infrasound could have therapeutic benefits – the physiological stirring caused by the physical vibration and buzzing could be a more passive encouragement of mindfulness than physical exercise like yoga or dance. The depression or anxiety suffer may be unwilling to engage in a public movement class, known to promote ideals of awareness and enjoyment of bodily sensations and physical exertion, so offering a bodily stimulant through mere immersion in a sonic vibration can provide a passive somatic awakening. This would also be applicable to anxiety sufferers' *depersonalization* when they feel disconnected from their body [30], or a sensory numbness or fatigue felt by depression sufferers. Goodman also highlights "certain infrasonic frequencies plug straight into the algorithms of the brain and nervous system... frequencies of 7 hertz coincide with theta rhythms, thought to induce moods of fear and anger" [29]. So through carefully selecting specific frequencies we can actually alter a brainwave pattern, bypassing a cognitive or semantic reading of the sound - a synthetically generated 7 Hz tone will not even be heard by the participant, only felt directly. Oohashi et al. [31] also discovered a "hypersonic effect", as listeners showed a markedly increased alpha brainwave activity upon exposure to inaudible high frequencies over 22kHz placed in an auditory stimulus (compared to the EEG data recorded when the subject hears the stimulus missing the High Frequency Component). Alpha activity is linked to relaxation, found to emerge upon the closing of the eyes, attenuating when the eyes open or during mental exertion – so the marked change in brain state shows the affective role of the HFC as it bypasses the cognitive circuits of hearing but nevertheless elicits relaxation. The power of the alpha reading was lowered significantly when the HFC was removed with only Low Frequency Component remaining in the audio stimuli. However, the alpha-EEG reading would not increase when the HFC or LFC was played in isolation, so it appears the inaudible sounds are only effective when integrated into a larger sonic composition. Using Positron Emission Topography, Cerebral Blood Flow in the brain stem and left thalamus increased (along with the alpha-EEG reading in the occipital region) when the HFC and LFC were played together, compared to reception of the sound without the HFC. Qualitative feedback showed that the subjects "felt the sound containing an HFC to be more pleasant than the same sound lacking an HFC" [31]. So the affect triggered by inaudible high frequencies was notable, and we also learn that the subjects would find a sound lacking a complete frequency spectrum unpleasant, in addition to diminishing of the relaxed alpha state.

3.2   Physiological Monitoring to Inform Compositional Decision

We will collect audience-response data, ranging from quantitative physiological data (unconscious response) to qualitative verbal feedback (subjective response). The benefit of employing encephalography and portable physiological monitoring is that it enables regular testing in the optimal sensory environment of 5.1 and Ambisonics arrays at the Digital Design Studio. The physiological monitoring system will be four-fold, as signatures of acoustic processing are actually sometimes easier to see on the skin, than from measuring brain activity alone. Electromyography (EMG) will measure muscle contraction and tension induced by abrasive sounds, or sonic shocks activating the startle mechanism; electrical skin conductance will measure instantaneous sweat secretion and piloerection from fear or musical frisson; respiration and heart-rate will identify moments of shock or waves of relaxation; electroencephalography (EEG) will measure accurate real-time brainwave patterns to locate brain stimulation and identify if memories are being triggered or there is a purely sensory engagement. The EEG device measures raw brainwaves, distinguishing mental states across a broad spectrum, meaning that a listener's instantaneous moments of musical pleasure can be identified: from when the listener's state of engagement with the sensory environment (alpha brainwaves at 8-12 Hz), his/her expectation of changes in the sensory environment, e.g. due to stressed, anxious states (Beta brainwaves at 12-38 Hz), to the active processing of acoustic sensations (Gamma brainwaves 30-70 Hz). Thus, the sensory stimulation composition should be provoking the stressed Beta waves, which can then lead to a sensory-euphoric Gamma state, encouraging a leap through and out of a depressive state.

Serious Games are employed as enjoyable, interactive learning strategies. Exposure therapy serves as a catalyst for a dual learning: as psychoeducation about the physiology of anxiety; but also a deeper learning, as the user uncovers repressed events buried within their psyche. There is future potential to use real-time EEG and psychophysiological data as biofeedback game input during exposure to manipulate the playback of sound events to challenge the player. For example, the more relaxed the user becomes, the louder or faster the composition could sound, integrating more abrasive timbres or triggering a higher pitched distortion so the user will always be optimally challenged to their maximum coping capacity. As the soundscape becomes louder or higher pitched, the user will know that it is a direct cause of their physiological vital signs adapting to the exposure, thus their confidence can be boosted.

Biofeedback is often used to visualize or notify a tangible reward for a user's strengthened endurance of exposure, or an excited bio-signal can even transform the music featured in a game, to empathetically match the player's nervous state [32]. Ubisoft's O.zen uses a fingertip heart rate monitor (a photoplethysmograph) as an interface to play lighthearted racing or shooter games as part of a holistic bio-monitoring package recommending personalized breathing and cardiovascular exercise programs, as well as providing psychoeducation to understand the detriment to health of stress-inducing breathing [33]. A Serious Game to aid pediatric treatment for anxiety and depression, *The Journey to the Wild Divine* [34], implements biofeedback-controlled guided-imagery situations such as a bridge construction exercise, where any progress on the structure literally crumbles as the user becomes frustrated, only allowing completion upon sustained relaxation. So instead of merely accomplishing the fleeting feeling of being relaxed, the user achieves tangible outcomes. The game trains recognition of the physiological symptoms of anxiety and bolsters the user's faith in being able to control their own predicament through disciplined regulation of breathing states for concrete short-term rewards. Indeed, it is also beneficial for the therapist to log all recorded bio-data during exposures, to build concrete psychophysical results with which to review the user's habituation progress over several sessions.

In addition to the less invasive physiological monitoring, it may prove insightful to install a speaker array in a functional Magnetic-Resonance Imagery Scanner. Issues of sonic contamination from the excessively loud scanner will need to be addressed, by means of tailoring the soundscape to account for specific loud moments, or indeed incorporating the scanner's mechanistic timbre. Participants can also feel claustrophobic in the confined space, interfering with the emotional response.

The qualitative verbal feedback will primarily include pre- and post-exposure interview and questionnaires and at times choreographic feedback (gestural response in informal exposure environments). Real time objective physiological data is absolutely necessary: if questioned after exposure, test subjects forget certain nuances - we can notice when we feel chills, (Loui et al.'s study, *Effects of Voice on Emotional Arousal* allowed the participant to document their frisson using a joystick interface, which is problematic due to delay to allow for conscious realization [35]) but we need accurate pin-pointing of unconscious response to reveal which isolated sounds and images cause each emotion or physiological stirring. In addition to memory loss from delayed questioning, the subjective verbal response will also be subject to *social masking* [36], varying introspective ability, questionable validity of the questionnaire, and uncontrolled participant honesty; hence the necessity of real-time measure of unconscious, nervous response.

The effects of mere stereo listening will be compared to effects from immersion in spatial arrays of 5.1 surround sound and Ambisonics. The effects of sound alone, versus synchronized audio-vision, versus audio with asynchronous visual accompaniment will be compared, to quantify a higher level of engagement when the two modalities are merged, or discern if the visual is a cognitive distraction from the visceral audio, or if mismatching audio-visual causes discomfort. The difference in response to a more tangible musical melody will be compared with the response to more abstract, temporally extended use of sound in a non-musical manner. Importantly, difference in listener response between personalized soundscapes and non-relevant soundscapes will also be measured.

Table 5. Distinctions between physiological effects provoked by contrasting media outputs

Compare effects of...	stereo listening	→	surround-sound immersion
	sound alone	→	synchronized audio-visual
	synchronized audio-visual	→	asynchronous audio-visual
	tangible musical melody	...to effects of...	non-musical use of sound
	personalized soundscapes	→	non-relevant soundscapes
	real world natural sounds	→	digitally synthesized sounds
	real world video	→	abstract animation

Considerations for Response Monitoring. For EEG monitoring, an average response will need to be discerned, across repeated listens (to cancel out noise artifacts) as well as an average across subjects, to find correlations and distinct uniform responses, dispelling the subjective differences. However, repeated listens will be problematic as it may cancel the effects of musical novelty, diluting the initial shock factor of certain sounds, so these measures of repetition should be thoughtfully integrated into the composition as a whole. In fact, the method of *looping*, through isolating a sound event in a field recording and using it as a rhythmic musical structure, or continuous timbre enables this discern of an average response through repetition, or extension of sound.

3.3   Participants: Healthy Subjects or Neurological Disorder Patients

We acknowledge it will be a lengthy legislative process to invite participants diagnosed with a severe mental illness, possibly out-with the scope of a three-year project. The NHS stipulates that we need to test the compositions on healthy participants without adverse affect, before access to anxiety and depression sufferers is granted (to test the stimuli as an Exposure Therapy). Instead, we propose first to test on healthy people first with a view to testing on anxiety and depression sufferers after, with a preference for medically healthy people who feel stressed from time to time.

4   Conclusions

An ideal amalgamation of sensitive compositional aids from Music Therapy, with the theories behind psychiatric treatments such as Fear Extinction and Exposure Therapy along with painstakingly considered high-quality audio production would provide optimized sensory rehabilitation for hypersensitive anxiety sufferers. We aim to quantify the increase in affect provided by optimized presentation modes, such as surround sound and Ambisonics and abstract synthesized soundscapes, through rigorous psychophysical testing, corroborated by qualitative questioning of participants. Upon collation of the quantitative bio-data, we may uncover applications for the fluctuating electrophysiological signals (the notable affect) to be used as a Serious Game interface; indeed an integrated reactive playback system may be the optimal mode of engagement to soundscape exposures, to maximally challenge the user.

The resulting compositions compiled from real anxiety triggers could also spread the awareness of the physicality of mental illness by replicating sufferers' altered sense-perception (rather than attempts at verbal explanation) facilitating empathy from non-sufferers. This could reduce stigma of the less visibly understood mental disorders, and provide a sensorial avenue for psychological connection, between healthy audience members and the oft-alienated anxiety sufferer - to communicate a sensation that cannot be expressed in words.

References

1. Cohen, A.: Music as a Source of Emotion in Film. In: Juslin, P., Sloboda, J. (eds.) Handbook of Music and Emotion: Theory Research and Applications. Oxford University Press, Oxford (2001)
2. Greenman, D., Meulenberg, F., White, M.: The Power of Music. In: Bolton, G.: Dying, Bereavement and the Healing Arts. Jessica Kingsley, London (2008)
3. Have, I.: Background Music and Background Feelings - Background Music in Audio-Visual Media. The Journal of Music and Meaning 6 (Spring 2008)
4. Ross, A.: The Rest is Noise: Listening to the Twentieth Century. Harper Perennial, London (2007)
5. Austin, D.: Songs of the Self: Vocal Psychotherapy for Adults Traumatized as Children. In: Carey, L. (ed.) Expressive and Creative Arts Methods for Trauma Survivors. Jessica Kingsley, London (2006)
6. Gabrielsson, A.: Emotions in Strong Experiences in Music. In: Juslin, P., Sloboda, J.A. (eds.) Music and Emotion: Theory and Research. Oxford University Press, U.K. (2001)
7. Fassbender, E., Martyn Jones, C.: The importance and creation of high-quality sounds in healthcare applications. Awaiting Publication (2014)
8. Hoffman, H.G., Chambers, G.T., Meyer, W.J., et al.: Virtual Reality as an Adjunctive Non-pharmacologic Analgesic for Acute Burn Pain During Medical Procedures. The Society of Behavioral Medicine (41), 183–191 (2011)

 9. Mueller, W.: EASe Listening Therapy (1995), `http://www.easecd.com/EASe1.html`
10. Schnall, S., Hedge, C., Weaver, R.: The Immersive Virtual Environment of the digital full-dome: Considerations of relevant psychological processes. International Journal of Human Computer Studies 70(8) (2012)
11. Liljjedahl, M.: Sound for Fantasy and Freedom. In: Grimshaw (ed.) Game Sound Technology and Player Interaction: Concepts and Developments. Information Science Reference (2011)
12. Roy, M.J., Francis, J., Friedlander, J., Banks-Williams, L., Lande, R.G., et al.: Improvement in cerebral function with treatment of posttraumatic stress disorder. Annals of the New York Academy of Sciences 1208, 142–149 (2010)
13. Panksepp, J., Bernatzky, G.: Emotional sounds and the brain: the neuro-affective foundations of musical appreciation. Behavioral Processes (60), 133–155 (2001)
14. Freeman, J., Lessiter, J.: Here, There and Everywhere: The Effects of Multichannel Audio on Presence. In: Proceedings of the 2001 International Conference on Auditory Display (2001)
15. Altenmuller, E., Schlaug, G.: Neurologic music therapy: The beneficial effects of music making on neurorehabilitation. Acoustical Science & Technology 34(1), 5–12 (2013)
16. Goncalves, R., Pedrozo, A.L., Coutinho, E.S.F., Figueira, I., Ventura, P.: Efficacy of Virtual Reality Exposure Therapy in the Treatment of PTSD: A Systematic Review. Plos One 7(12) (December 2012)
17. Herbelin, B., et al.: Virtual Reality in Cognitive Behavioural Therapy: a Study on Social Anxiety Disorder (2002) (Unpublished)
18. Grillon, C., Franco-Chaves, J.A., Mateus, C.F., Ionescu, D.F., Zarate, C.A.: Major Depression is Not Associated with Blunting of Aversive Responses; Evidence for Enhanced Anxious Anticipation. Plos One 8(8) (August 2013)
19. Callaghan, K.: Torture – the body in conflict. The Role of Movement Psychotherapy. In: Liebmann, M.: Arts Approaches to Conflict. Jessica Kingsley, London (1997)
20. Wegerer, M., Blechert, J., Kerschbaum, H., Wilhelm, F.H.: Relationship between Fear Conditionability and Aversive Memories: Evidence from a Novel Conditioned-Intrusion Paradigm. Plos One 8(11) (November 2013)
21. Jönsson, A., Breslin, R., Ma, M.: The Ambience Table: A Serious Gaming Interface for Aiding Sound Design. In: Ma, M., Oliveira, M.F., Petersen, S., Hauge, J.B. (eds.) SGDA 2013. LNCS, vol. 8101, pp. 151–164. Springer, Heidelberg (2013)
22. Rhiannonsmoon, Sundog, Sabrina, BrokenNBeautiful, Boodles, BlueEyesToo, on Psych-Central, `http://forums.psychcentral.com/anxiety-panic-phobias/156400-noises-triggering-anxiety.html`
23. McGeoch, C.: Equalization lecture at Glasgow School of Art (2013)
24. Argo, J.: Anti-Cocktail-Party-Effect (2013), `http://www.youtube.com/watch?v=LmiEy9dqhqE`
25. Argo, J.: Blood Set in Motion (2013), `http://www.youtube.com/watch?v=3VzDMNfsrbg`
26. Argo, J.: Trauma (2013), `http://www.youtube.com/watch?v=YoHUeD_BvKs`
27. Argo, J.: From Phrase to Phase: Evolving Musical Affect by Transformative Visceral Catharsis. Masters Thesis, MDes Sound for Moving Image at Glasgow School of Art (2013)
28. Argo, J.: Present Past (2013), `http://www.youtube.com/watch?v=FaSKPuu_c84`
29. Goodman, S.: Sonic Warfare: Sound, Affect, and the Ecology of Fear. MIT Press, Massachusetts (2010)

30. Gerlach, A.L., Neudeck, P.: Interoceptive Exposure. In: Abramowitz, J.S., Deacon, B.J., Whiteside, S.P.H. (eds.) Exposure Therapy for Anxiety: Principles and Practice. The Guildford Press, New York (2011)
31. Oohashi, T., Nishina, E., Honda, M., et al.: Inaudible High Frequency Sounds Affect Brain Activity: Hypersonic Effect. Journal of Neurophysiology, The American Physiological Society 83, 3548–3558 (2000)
32. Champion, E.: Augmenting the Present with the Past. In: Playing with the Past. Human-Computer Interaction Series. Springer Verlag London Ltd. (2011)
33. Ubisoft, Introducing O.zen, a gamified stress management tool from Ubisoft (2013), http://www.youtube.com/watch?v=oUFiWYAXL0A
34. Knox, M., et al.: Game-based biofeedback for pediatric anxiety and depression. Mental Health and Family Medicine (8) (2011)
35. Loui, P., Bachorik, J.P., Li, H.C., Schlaug, G.: Effects of Voice on Emotional Arousal. Frontiers in Psychology 4, Article 675 (2013)
36. Kim, S., Andre, E.: Composing Affective Music with a Generate and Sense Approach. American Association for Artificial Intelligence (2004)

Gaming the Future of the Ocean: The Marine Spatial Planning Challenge 2050

Igor Mayer[1], Qiqi Zhou[1] [*], Xander Keijser[2], and Lodewijk Abspoel[2]

[1] Faculty of Technology Policy and Management, TU Delft, The Netherlands
{i.s.mayer,Qiqi.Zhou}@tudelft.nl
[2] Ministry of Infrastructure and the Environment, The Netherlands
Lodewijk.Abspoel@minienm.nl, xander.keijser@rws.nl

Abstract. The authors present and discuss the conceptual and technical design of the game Marine Spatial Planning (MSP) Challenge 2050, developed with and for the Netherlands' ministry of Infrastructure and Environment. The main question in this paper is: What constitutes the socio-technical complexity of marine areas and how can it be translated into a simulation model for serious game-play with marine spatial planners? MSP Challenge 2050 was launched in March 2014 in a two day session with twenty marine planners from six countries. It aims to initiate and support MSP in the various Atlantic regions by bringing policy-makers, stakeholders, scientists together in a 'playful' but realistic and meaningful environment. In the North Sea edition of the game, six countries make and implement plans for this sea basin over a period of 35 years, with cumulative effects of their sectoral and national decisions emerging. The authors conclude that the combined and iterative use of complexity modelling and gaming is effective from the perspectives of design (development of a MSP model), research (insight acquired on MSP) and policy (policy-oriented learning and analysis for MSP). Further development and global dissemination of MSP Challenge 2050, as well as research and data collection, is foreseen.

Keywords: Complexity, Global System Science, Integrated Planning, Marine Spatial Planning, Policy game, Simulation-game, Serious game, Design.

1   Policy Making in the Wake of Complexity

For most of history, man has had to fight nature to survive; in this century he is beginning to realize that, in order to survive, he must protect it. Jacques-Yves Cousteau, (French Explorer, 1910-1997).

1.1   Socio-Technical Complexity

There are many examples that can back the proposition that socio-technical complexity is at the forefront of public policymaking, and that managing socio-technological

---

[*] The sections on socio-technical complexity and Figures 1-4 are adapted from the second author's PhD thesis currently in print as: Zhou, Q. (2014). The Princess in the Castle: Challenging Serious Game Play for Integrated Policy Analysis and Planning. TU Delft.

M. Ma et al. (Eds.): SGDA 2014, LNCS 8778, pp. 150–162, 2014.

complexity is the common denominator among the *grand challenges* of modern-day society [1]. Climate change, the banking crisis, the flooding of urban areas, migration are just a few consequences (or manifestations) of socio-technical complexity. In short, socio-technical complexity (STC) means that the complexity residing within the *natural-technical-physical* (NTP) realm spirals the complexity residing in the *socio-political* (SP) realm and vice versa (see Figure 1).

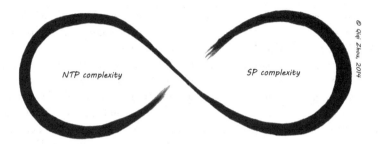

Fig. 1. Socio-technical complexity

Such spiralling complexity between NTP and SP complexity is prone to give the public policymakers involved persistent and recurrent headaches. That being the case, the diagnosis that grand challenges in society are both socially and technically complex, does not say very much about the 'patient's' condition or prospects, or about effective remedies (if there are any). So, the question should be asked what makes problems socio-technically complex and, even more important, how can we support public policymaking in the wake of socio-technical complexity?

1.2   Policy Response

Fortunately, there is growing awareness among scientists and politicians of the importance of understanding complexity and finding new ways to make policy in the wake of it. A connection with new media and computer technology is commonly made in these new forms of public policymaking, because things like big data analysis, visual analytics, citizen science, crowd sourcing, e-participation, and new forms of modelling, simulation and gaming (MSG) seem particularly suited to surround sophisticated analysis with extensive participation [2]. Many of such methodological innovations are – feel, look - *like game play* because they aim to let stakeholders play with (digital) models of complexity. The current EU initiative on *Global System Science* (DG Communications Networks, Content and Technology) calls for Global System Science ('FETPROACT-1-2014,' n.d.): 'Global challenges need fundamentally different policies, more *integrated* across sectors and stronger rooted in evidence and broad societal engagement. [...] GSS will provide scientific evidence highly *integrated* across different policy sectors [...]. Upfront stakeholder engagement in the process of gathering evidence is insufficient, e.g. in input to policies to reduce climate change impact. Collaborative ICT tools will facilitate *stakeholder engagement* in evidence gathering and thereby increase trust in *scientific evidence*.' ('Global Systems Science

- European Commission,' n.d.). This general perspective on Global System Science has significant consequences for the wider H2020 research agenda, among others in the work programme for *Blue Growth: Unlocking the potential of Seas and Ocean*s (H2020-BG-2014/2015).

1.3   Earth Systems

Earth systems (forests, rivers and oceans, etc.) are an obvious target of global system science because they are under pressure from climate change and economic growth, and full of uncertainties and controversies about causes, consequences and coping strategies. Here, the dual nature of STC manifests itself clearly. In the realm of NTP complexity, earth systems are governed by the laws of nature, although we face severe limitations in how much we know about them (i.e. the hand of God). Scientists can be confused or err, but what we do know is stored and analysed in databases, GIS systems and simulation models that can simulate complexity through cause–effect and feedback relations. These may give us a glimpse of the future [5]. However, if we decide to negotiate out 'truth' for the sake of 'politics', reality will strike back sooner or later. At the other end of STC – the realm of socio-political complexity – there are enormous interests at stake in the way we, for instance, arrange our future energy provision. Because in the world of politics, truth is largely constructed, we can 'negotiate out' political problems by making compromises and deals. We can, for instance, decide to manipulate, ignore, buy off or compensate those who suffer the effects of shale gas drilling. Furthermore, data and knowledge systems are scattered among an almost infinite number of proprietary institutions. Large-scale trends associated with climate change, such as sea-level rise and weather extremes, affect numerous other issues at various geographical and spatial levels and in such sectorial domains as transport, health, housing and water. In *'big problems'*, everything is connected to everything [6].

1.4   Fragmentation

In order to reduce the complexity of 'big problems', system boundaries need to be drawn; but this gives rise to further fragmentation and compartmentalization into numerous 'silos' of governance and research. To some extent, this silo'ing is unavoidable – it is pragmatic, efficient and legitimate. But it is also a reductionist approach: when the problem becomes too big to handle, we simply break it up into manageable pieces [7]. Unfortunately, 'big problems' do not stay within the arbitrary boundaries of governance departments and research disciplines. So, the question is, how and when the various fragments of a 'big problem' can be put back together again. This in a nutshell explains the call for global system science, integrated (holistic) science and integrated policy analysis. Let us give an example from one of the most important earth systems: the ocean. What constitutes the socio-technical complexity of marine areas, and how can we understand and manage it in an integrated manner? And can we game the complexity of the ocean to achieve more integration in planning?

2   The Socio-technical Complexity of Marine Spatial Planning

2.1   The Rising Importance of Marine Spatial Planning

In 2008, the European commission published its 'Roadmap for maritime spatial planning: Achieving Common Principles in the EU' [8], followed by a 2010 Communication 'Maritime Spatial Planning in the EU — Achievements and Future Development' [9], which paved the way for a Framework Directive for Maritime Spatial Planning [10]. Under the EU marine strategy framework directive (MSFD), member states are required to make an initial ecological assessment of their waters in respect of each marine region or sub region and then define measures, including MSP, to achieve 'good environmental status' (GES). In March 2014, agreement on the directive was reached, and it now needs to be confirmed by the Council and the European Parliament. According to the responsible EU commissioners, 'the directive will help Member States cooperate more closely over cross-border sea areas, enabling them to take full account of land-sea interactions when developing their Maritime Spatial Planning. (...) Maritime Spatial Planning is a cornerstone of the Commission's Blue Growth (BG) strategy and of Integrated Maritime Policy. (...) It should (...) help establish coherent networks of Marine Protected Areas, for which cooperation on planning across borders is essential, and ensure the participation of all stakeholders in planning processes.' ('Maritim Affairs and Fisheries Newsroom,' n.d.).

2.2   Modelling STC of Marine Areas

The 'big' problem of MSP is that marine ecosystems around the globe are increasingly being affected by human activities such as fisheries, shipping, offshore petroleum developments, wind farms, recreation, tourism and more. These can be visualized as the 'pressures' that human activities have upon marine eco- and geo systems (see Figure 2). The data and knowledge about how ecosystems are affected human activities by human activities are visualized as stressors (see Figure 2).

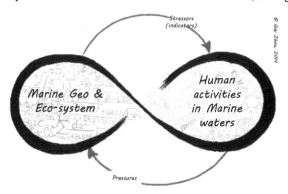

Fig. 2. Pressures and stressors

The simple scheme in Figure 2 gives us a first understanding of how NTP complexity and SP complexity spiral into STC complexity of marine areas and can be further elaborated as follows (see Figure 3):

1. *NTP-complexity:* This is represented by the feedback loop and delay symbols in the left part of Figure 3. Geo-system and eco-system of marine areas by themselves are of staggering complexity, full of non-linear behaviour, feedback relations, delays, and interaction rules. There is no saying how much we know about the complexity of marine ecosystems, but is fair to say that there is more that we do not know, than know. Scientists for instance model the build-up of pollutants in the ecosystem, and the effect it has on sea life [12]. Yet, it may take some time before the interaction effects within geo and ecosystems become apparent. In terms of scales and levels - from deep below sea floor to high above sea level - there is enormous heterogeneity of elements. Boundaries of subsystems are almost arbitrary: when it comes of seas and oceans, everything is connected to everything. Therefore we break up our knowledge into disciplines, theories and methods. Parts of what we know are captured in *geographical information systems* (GIS). Data about wind speed, currents, sea depth, sea levels, geological layers and minerals are stored in numerous data bases and models. Marine biologist, ecologist, and others have become quite advanced in modelling eco-systems, for instance with models and simulations like Eco Path (a food chain model) [13]. Some of this can be publically accessed but many data-systems and simulation-models are proprietary; and there is so much scattered information that searching and finding it, is almost impossible. The coupling of more data and more simulation-models is proposed to find more integrative knowledge about the complexity of the marine geo- and ecosystem.

2. *SP-complexity:* This is represented by the feedback loop and delay symbols in the right part of Figure 3. Human activities at sea are wide ranged and profound: from recreational sailing, diving and fishing, to mineral exploitation and wind farming. Many of the human activities at sea are linked to other complex systems, such the global energy or innovation system. One human activity at sea – for instance off shore wind farms or oil platforms - may cause or hinder other human activities, such as the redirection of shipping routes, the flying of helicopters, or the ban of fishing. A human activity today may prevent other human activities in the future. Furthermore, there are multiple interactions among all socio-political actors who have divergent beliefs, stakes, interests, actions, claims etc. with regard to the marine area.

3. *STC:* The interactions between the NTP and the SP complexity spiral into an even higher level of complexity, e.g., flaring stakeholder disputes on the cumulative impact of several human activities in a marine area. Despite the trend to more data, better models and more integrative simulations, there is an awful lot that scientists do not know about the marine geo- and ecosystem. There are cumulative effects of many human activities upon the marine ecosystem, but these are largely unknown and/or disputed. Indicators to monitor the stress of human activities put on the geo- and ecosystem are insufficient, inadequate or disputed. Trans-boundary issues spiral the complexity of MSP: e.g., human activities or policy measures in/by one country can be the problem of another country, and so on.

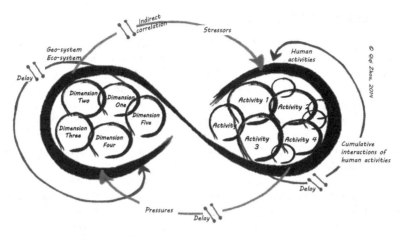

Fig. 3. A STC model of MSP

2.3 The Science-Policy Interface

The 'big problem' of managing the human pressures upon the marine ecosystem, needs to be resolved in the nexus or interface of science and policy. This explains the culmination of proposals and methods for an integrated, eco-system based approach to MSP. Calls from scientists for integrated science and modelling usually entail the incorporation of more data about the impact of more economic sectors upon more dimensions of the eco- and geo system. Politicians and stakeholders on the other hand will commonly urge for more stakeholder consultation in the consideration of interests (see Figure 4). In this fashion, the demand for integrated analysis and stakeholder participation, is driving marine spatial planning. The fusion of the two in integrated, participatory analysis, makes it 'like game-play'.

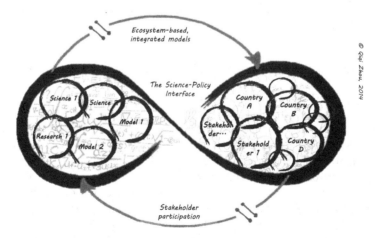

Fig. 4. Worlds of Science and Politics in marine spatial planning

2.4   Marine Spatial Planning

In most simple terms, MSP is 'spatial planning at sea', thereby dealing with human use of sea space. In many cases (especially in Europe) two or more countries share the same sea basin or marine space, as in The Sound, the Kattegat and the Skagerrak, the Gulf of Finland, the Baltic Sea and the North Sea. The cumulative effect of all human maritime activities and all sectoral planning decisions in one or more countries in a marine basin can impact the entire basin as an ecological and economic system. In other words, marine ecosystems are not bounded by administrative borders (see Figure 4 at right side). Consequently, there is a need for transnational co-operation in MSP to ensure that these pressures and effects are adequately managed and planned, and also that opportunities are identified and realized. Given the fact that MSP is about competing spatial claims, assessing the potential impact of human activities is bound to lead to controversy [14]. Societal or stakeholder discussions are likely to flare up about the potentially negative impact of, say, constructing wind farms [15], [16] or offshore drilling for gas on sea birds and mammals. Or, as during the Brent Spar controversy, scientific claims may be used to win a strategic game [17], [18]. In cases of uncertainty and controversy, planning professionals and stakeholders commonly turn to science for answers – that is, for facts and proof – and arbitration. Although we know a lot about marine ecosystems, there is even more that we do not know, especially when marine ecosystems are influenced by the cumulative activities from socio-political systems. One major uncertainty, for instance, concerns the amount of stress that specific human activities put on the marine ecosystems and how then marine ecosystems respond in the short, medium or long term. This becomes even more problematic when we consider the cumulative effects of so-called stressors, i.e. the negative impact of the marine eco-system such as reef degradation and habitat destruction. Actually, dealing with cumulative impacts is one of the big challenges for MSP. GIS technology allows us to overlay various activity, pressure and impact maps and at the first glance to determine the sum of those impacts, but the effects may actually be much more complicated and subtle than simply adding together impacts.

3   Gaming the Complexity of Marine Spatial Planning

3.1   Gaming

STC complexity needs to come to some kind of synthesis at the Science-Policy Interface. Precisely this argument was put forward, in slightly different words, by Dick Duke in Gaming: the Future's Language [19], where he argued for gaming as a holistic language of complexity. 'The interweaving of problems in this era has forced attention to wider and more complex fields by each decision maker and by staff or research efforts set to aid him. The mode of understanding is one of gestalt appreciation rather than explicit knowledge of bits of data.' [19, p. 43] [...] The citizen, policy researcher or other decision-maker must first comprehend the whole – the entirety, the system, the gestalt – before the particulars can be dealt with.' [19, p. 10] Let's see how the STC of MSP can be turned into a complexity model that can be played.

3.2   First Experiences with MSP Challenge 2011

MSP Challenge 2050 is a follow up on an earlier version of a similar game that we refer to as MSP Challenge 2011. To understand the 2050 edition, it is necessary to

Table 1. Comparison between 2011 and 2050 editions

MSP Challenge 2011	MSP Challenge 2050
Development in 2011	Development between 2012-2014
Played in Lisbon 2011 & Reykjavik 2013	Launched in Delft, February 2014
Four countries	Flexible number of countries: 4 - 8
Sea of Colours	Sea of Colours
Based upon Kattegat but changed	Based on accurate data of North Sea
60-80 players in one session	18-40 players in one session
Minimum of 8 hours play	Four to forty (discontinuous) hours of play
Planner roles with eight stakeholder groups per country	All players in a country are planners
Simplified data	Realistic data and maps
Digital drawing tool	Simulation, foodweb calculations
60 layers of map information	Flexible number of layers of map information
2D	2D to 3D zoom in
Individual lap tops, not networked	3 lap tops per country, networked
Learning, training, collaboration	citizen and stakeholder participation, learning, training, policy exploration, design and scenario development, etc.
Limited performance indicators	Performance indicators, dashboard, analytics
Limitations:	*Limitations*
Great event effort; large facilitation effort	No stakeholder interaction
No simulation;	*Future:*
Not networked;	Interconnection with GIS;
No underlying performance model;	Customization and changing maps
Case not changeable	Train the trainer; dissemination (website, licensing, trailer).

know a little about the first edition. In 2011, the Netherlands Ministry of Infrastructure and the Environment (I&E) commissioned and financed the design and facilitation of the simulation game on behalf of an international planning group led by the International Council for the Exploration of the Sea (ICES). Actual design of this edition of the game took place between August and November 2011, and it was played at two occasions, in 2011 (Lisbon) and 2013 (Reykjavik) with around sixty international marine planners in each session. Results of the Lisbon session have been published in [20]. In November 2013, policy makers from the Nordic countries played the MSP Challenge game in Reykjavik, Iceland. The one-day game-play was part of a two day workshop commissioned by 'Havgruppen' (transl., marine group) under The Nordic Council of Ministers (Nordic Council of Ministers, n.d.). The aim was to establish a common understanding of the ecosystem approach and the application and administration of the Nordic seas. Both sessions were considered a success and the Netherland's ministry saw potential for a new edition of the game, with advanced features but easier to disseminate and organize. The end vision is a digital aquarium where multiple users in different countries can playfully make marine spatial plans on the basis of real and accurate data. Table 1 compares the 2011 and 2050 editions.

MSP Challenge 2050 initiates and supports integrated MSP planning processes in the various Atlantic regions by bringing policy-makers, stakeholders, scientists and citizens together in a 'playful' but realistic and meaningful environments. The game has three potential uses that can be combined:

1. Enlightenment (e.g. awareness, general education)
2. Planning support (exploration, consultation, design)
3. Research and analysis (data collection, meta-analysis of results, evidence based recommendations).

The game is designed to make maximum use of participants' general and expert knowledge about the region. The game is not well-suited for, or interesting to players who lack affinity for its content and context. The format of game-play is flexible, it can be played in a national or international workshop or meeting, be part of a conference, it can be integrated into a curriculum, or demonstrated in a science museum. It can even be distributed (online). The exploration with MSP Challenge can be quick and shallow (e.g., for demonstration purposes), or be longer and profound (e.g. in a planning process). The game-play can be paused periodically for facilitated discussions among participants and /or lectures that go in-depth on certain issues, like cumulative effects or safety zones in shipping routes. It is also possible to spread out the game-play over a longer period of time, like three days of a conference, a week of training or several weeks of a curriculum. The objective of MSP Challenge 2050 is to contribute to international learning processes with regard to ecosystem-based, integrated and participatory MSP (as described above), with a particular focus on the following aspects:

1. The underlying socio-technical complexities of MSP
2. The underlying regulatory principles and institutional frameworks of MSP, and how they might vary from country to country

3. The joint development of best practices for MSP amongst stakeholders and countries
4. The use of science, knowledge, data, methods and tools in MSP

3.3   The 2050 Edition

MSP Challenge 2050 is a multi-player, computer-supported game involving considerable social interaction between planners. A trailer of the game can be viewed at www.mspchallenge2050.com. The game is built around a flexible number of countries (e.g. four to eight) represented by a flexible number of players per country (e.g., three to six) that share a sea basin (e.g. the North Sea, the Baltic, the North Atlantic). For reasons of simplicity and abstraction the real sea basin, is renamed into 'Sea of Colours'. At present we have a North Sea edition of the game, and the real countries are indicated as colours: Orange (the Netherlands), Blue (Belgium), Green (Norway), Yellow (Germany), Red (Denmark), Purple, (the UK), Indigo (Scotland).

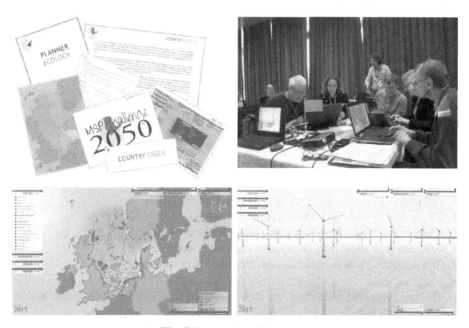

Fig. 5. Impression of the game

Three to six players form a group of country planners with different sectoral authorities, thus requiring a total of 18 to 36 players with knowledge and expertise in the field. The players are briefed and receive general information on paper about the geographical, ecological, political and other characteristics of the countries concerned. Each country and player is provided with a specific profile containing goals and objectives to achieve during the game. The players' goal is to plan and manage the development in their EEZ from 2015 until 2050 as well as they can. The planners' task is difficult, as they handle the content and substance of the planning, as well as the consultation and coordination process with other countries. There are several additions to the game that make it interactive and engaging, such as a news blog called the Puffington post. Players can send Puffins (a kind of local twitter) from their mobile or tablets. A Game Overall Director (G.O.D) has the authority to intervene by taking up a role at the boundary of the game, such as European Commission (EC) or minister of a country.

3.4   Simulating Complexity in the Game

An interactive digital planning tool, partly designed in the Unity game engine, plays a crucial role in the game. The tool is designed to be highly interactive, robust and stable, in addition to being attractive for gameplay. It allows 2D to 3D zooming to view the marine world. The complexity model that drives the simulation consists of the following components:

1. Human Activities (A)
2. Factors in the Geo system (G)
3. Factors in the Ecosystem (E)
4. Pressures (P)
5. Indicators (I)

The interaction effects among the components (positive/negative, strong/weak, or quantified when possible etc.) are identified in a number of matrices:

1. A/A matrix to show the cumulative impact of Activities upon other Activities
2. G/A Matrix to show what Activities can be performed under what conditions in the Geosystem
3. A/P matrix to show what Pressures come out of Activities
4. P/G matrix to show how Pressures influence the Geo system
5. P/E matrix to show how Pressures influence the Ecosystem
6. G/A matrix to show how Geosystem changes affect Activities
7. E/A matrix to show how Ecosystem changes affect Activities.

The pressures and indicators are then attributed to countries in the game and/or stakeholder interests (e.g., fishery, conservationists, green energy sector):

1. Country model to assign weight of Pressures and Indicators to specific countries
2. Stakeholder model to assign weight of Pressures and Indicators to specific stakeholders

Fifty-five layers with geo and eco information present sufficient detail and richness without becoming overwhelming. Examples of map layers include oil and gas infrastructure (platforms); commercial fishing; energy; sea cables and pipelines, and marine protected areas. A layer can contain one or a few similar objects (wind farms, birds, wind speed) in the form of points (power grid connector), lines (e.g., shipping routes) or shapes (e.g., marine protected area). Some layers like sea depth, and wind speed are static and cannot be changed. Proposition layers such as for wind farming can be changed by the players to propose or make a plan. It basically works like a standard digital drawing tool. The simulator continuously runs in the background of the game. It manages the cause-effect matrices and works on three levels. First, when planning human activities, the simulator checks potential conflicts with other activities or the environment in the Activity/Activity and Environment/Activity matrices. When confirming a plan, the activity starts up and the simulator uses the Activity/Pressure matrix to apply the pressures caused by the activity, and potential effects of the activity on other activities in the Activity/Activity matrix. Second, the internal ecosystem (modelled with an Ecopath food chain model) continuously adapts itself to pressures and changes through a feedback loop based on Pressure/Ecology and Ecology/Ecology rules. When players approve a plan, the simulator will start updating a layer. The impact of the simulation is fed back to the players in a visual way by changes in the 2D and 3D world. Furthermore, the effects are summarized in a dashboard with dynamic indicators.

4   Conclusion

In this paper, we have presented a model to understand the socio-technical complexity of marine areas and demonstrated how it can be translated into a simulation model for serious game-play with marine spatial planners. The combined and iterative use of complexity modelling and gaming proved effective from the perspectives of design (development of a MSP model), research (insight acquired on MSP) and policy (policy-oriented learning and analysis for MSP). At the time of writing, the MSP Challenge 2050 has only just been launched. One of the key results was the confirmation that over a period of decades, there is insufficient space on the North Sea to meet all sectorial spatial claims and that the cumulative pressure on the eco-system will rise to an unsustainable level. No data have been collected yet. Further development and large scale global dissemination of MSP Challenge 2050, as well as systematic research and data collection, is foreseen.

Acknowledgements. The game-architecture, models and simulator as well as the design and user interfaces were designed and built by Signature Games.nl, and we wish to acknowledge the significant contributions of Bas van Nuland, Joel van Neerbos and Linda van Veen. The underlying food chain calculations were modelled by researchers from Deltares. We wish to thank all other people that have contributed to the game in the form of financing, providing information, play-testing and promotion.

References

1. Byrne, D.: Complexity Theory and the Social Sciences: An Introduction. Routledge, London (2001)

2. Misuraca, G., Broster, D., Centeno, C.: Digital Europe 2030: Designing Scenarios for ICT in Future Governance and Policy Making. Gov. Inf. Q. (2012)

3. FETPROACT-1-2014, http://ec.europa.eu/research/participants/portal/desktop/en/opportunities/h2020/topics/2074 -fetproact-1-2014.html (accessed: April 04, 2014)

4. Global Systems Science - European Commission, http://ec.europa.eu/dgs/ connect/en/content/global-systems-science (accessed: April 04, 2014)

5. Pahl-Wostl, C., Schlumpf, C., Bussenschutt, M., Schonborn, A., Burse, J.: Models at the interface between science and society: impacts and options. Integr. Assess. 1, 267–280 (2000)

6. Head, B.W.B.: Wicked Problems in Public Policy. Public Policy 3(2), 18 (2008)

7. Nowotny, H.: The Increase of Complexity and its Reduction: Emergent Interfaces between the Natural Sciences, Humanities and Social Sciences. Theory, Cult. Soc. 22(5), 15–31 (2005)

8. Commission of the European Community, Roadmap for Maritime Spatial Planning: Achieving Common Principles in the EU, European Commission, Brussels, Belgium (2008)

9. Commission of the European Community, Maritime Spatial Planning in the EU – Achievements and Future Development, Luxembourg, COM (2010) 771 (2011)

10. Commission of the European Community, Proposal for a directive of the European Parliament and of the council, establishing a framework for maritime spatial planning and integrated coastal management, vol. 0074 (2013)

11. Maritim Affairs and Fisheries Newsroom, http://ec.europa.eu/information_society/newsroom/cf/ mare/itemdetail.cfm?item_id=15072&subweb=342&lang=en (accessed: April 08, 2014)

12. Halpern, B.S., Kappel, C.V., Selkoe, K.A., Micheli, F., Ebert, C.M., Kontgis, C., Crain, C.M., Martone, R.G., Shearer, C., Teck, S.J.: Mapping cumulative human impacts to California Current marine ecosystems. Conserv. Lett. 2(3), 138–148 (2009)

13. Christensen, V., Walters, C.J.: Ecopath with Ecosim: Methods, Capabilities and Limitations. Ecol. Modell. 172(2-4), 109–139 (2004)

14. Voyer, M., Gladstone, W., Goodall, H.: Methods of social assessment in Marine Protected Area planning: Is public participation enough? Mar. Policy 36(2), 432–439 (2012)

15. Jay, S., Street, H., Sheffield, S.: Spatial Planning and the Development of Offshore Wind Farms in the United Kingdom 1. Renew. Energy, 1–10 (2007)

16. Kannen, A., Burkhard, B.: Integrated Assessment of Coastal and Marine Changes Using the Example of Offshore Wind Farms: the Coastal Futures Approach. GAIA - Ecol. Perspect. Sci. Soc. 18(3), 229–238 (2009)

17. Huxham, M., Sumner, D., Park, M.: Emotion, Science and Rationality: The Case of the Brent Spar. Environ. Values 8(3), 349–368 (1999)

18. Side, J.: The Future of North Sea Oil Industry Abandonment in the Light of the Brent Spar Decision. Mar. Policy 21(1), 45–52 (1997)

19. Duke, R.D.: Gaming: the Future's Language. SAGE Publications (1974)

20. Mayer, I.S., Zhou, Q., Lo, J., Abspoel, L., Keijser, X., Olsen, E., Nixon, E., Kannen, A.: Integrated, Ecosystem-based Marine Spatial Planning: Design and Results of a Game-based Quasi-Experiment. Ocean Coast. Manag. 82, 7–26 (2013)

Off the Beaten Track! The Infinite Scotland Serious Game Design Approach

John Truesdale, Neil Suttie, Sandy Louchart, and Ruth Aylett

MACS, Heriot-Watt University, Riccarton, Edinburgh, EH10 4AS, UK
{jtt5,ns251,s.louchart,r.s.aylett}@hw.ac.uk

Abstract. In this article, we discuss the development of the Infinite Scotland Facebook serious game. The Infinite Scotland serious game was supported by the Scottish National Heritage, Creative Scotland and Creative Services Scotland in order to promote the links between biological and cultural diversity in Scotland. To engage a younger demographic, Infinite Scotland developed a knowledge-based, puzzle-centric serious game for a social media platform (Facebook); projecting the links between biodiversity and cultural diversity via player exploration and competitive gameplay. In this article, we describe our motivations for conducting the work, discuss the game design in detail, and finally speak about the implementation and development of Infinite Scotland.

Keywords: Serious Game, Cultural Heritage, Infinite Scotland, Reinforcement Learning, Social Media.

1 Overview (Motivation)

Scotland is a rich and varied country, which benefits greatly from tourism and its associated economic activities. The Infinite Scotland (IS) serious game described in this article is a collaboration between the Scottish National Heritage [1], Creative Scotland [2], Creative Services Scotland [3] and the Digital StoryLab [4] at Heriot-Watt University in Scotland. Serious game development has come a very long way in recent years and as such, is diverse and varies in its approach. Serious games can be designed to implicitly and indirectly allow players to assist in solving complex problems or aid in the learning and retention of specific knowledge; evaluating the analytical and logistical outcomes of player's playthrough cases for success.

IS is the latter: a Facebook-orientated serious game aiming to highlight the biological and cultural diversity of Scotland. The IS serious game aimed to attract an adolescent and young adult demographic to the *"Infinite Scotland"* material. IS is a knowledge-based, puzzle-centric, interactive serious game which allows players to both develop and enhance their knowledge of Scotland; in particular it aims to highlight the biological and cultural diversity that represents a modern, yet historic Scotland.

The design methodology, specifically the design pattern, was originally developed to first **introduce** players to the six ecosystem types of Scotland, then

M. Ma et al. (Eds.): SGDA 2014, LNCS 8778, pp. 163–175, 2014.

deepen their knowledge of these unique and diverse aspects, and finally **reinforce** this knowledge through competitive gameplay via Facebook. By completing a jigsaw puzzle via player exploration around Scottish sites, the player develops the links between biodiversity and cultural diversity through active engagement; resulting in a greatly more enjoyable retention method over that of a more passive presentation model.

IS was developed so that it could be deployed via social media, specifically Facebook, and additionally via Scottish Schools, in order to make it accessible to a wider demographic. The IS serious game content used the Infinite Scotland multi-media materials already assembled, of which were collected by Creative Services Scotland. IS's game design and production was completed on a £5k budget funded by Interface (Scottish Funding Council). In this article, we first focus our attention on the motivations and game design (section 2), followed by discussing the technical development and the implementation from a system's architecture perspective (section 3), before briefly addressing the current state of the IS serious game and projected future work (section 4).

2   Game Design (Theory)

2.1   The Serious Game Remit

IS is an exploration of Scotland's DNA - one strand is its biodiversity, the living and inert elements it is made of: rocks, insects, animals, plants, soil and fish - the other strand is the culture of the human beings that live in it: the way they celebrate, express themselves, live, play and describe their environment. [10] At its core, IS implores this fundamental exploratory approach to learning, gifting the player the ability to determine what information they would like first to digest.

Yet the process of breaking down an entire country into concise and coherent segments of information was no small task. When an ecologist has this problem they take a sample at random by throwing a quadrat - a small wooden square - and count the number of species in its boundaries. IS is built upon such an approach, although the metaphorical quadrat will be constructed of the most well known six ecosystem types rather than a few metres. The six ecosystem types are: *"Badenoch and Beyond"*, *"Trossachs and Stirling"*, *"Small Isles"*, *"Orkney"*, *"Edinburgh and the Lothians"*, *"Dumfries and Inner Solway."* (Fig 1). Via this method the player is aided in clustering the learning material into appropriate sub-locations that compose Scotland, allowing them to identify where information is specific to, yet still leaves the scope of the information vast.

The purpose of IS lies in how the two DNA strands are connected and it would suggest that the true personality of Scotland is better appreciated by both. Yet, IS is only an introduction and not an encyclopedia or a definitive guide to Scotland's flora, fauna and culture. It aims to provide a comprehensive taster of some of the most distinctive aspects of each, and that it whets your appetite to find out more, and perhaps to add your own thoughts, images and knowledge. In order to further assist the player in taking in this data, information

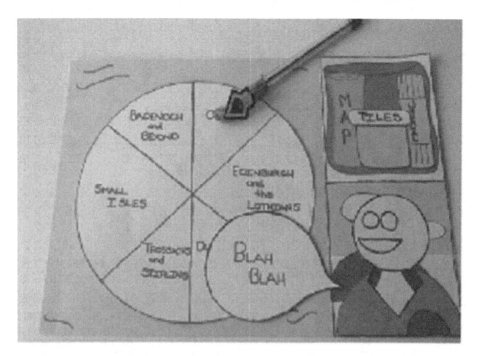

Fig. 1. Early paper prototype demonstrating the basic interface design

is subsequently further broken down and placed into one of four classification types so that relationships can be formed between entities.

The four classifications are: *"Wildlife, Environment, Culture and Connections."* Firstly, wildlife represents the biodiversity of Scotland with respect to the 90,000 species that inhabit it. Secondly, environment consists of the mosaic of habitats and scenery that make up the complex and varied landscape. Thirdly, culture is composed of folklore, myth, religion and custom, including the two indigenous languages. Lastly, connections describes the quirky, the little known, the weird and strange of Scotland. With information now specific to particular classifications, in conjunction with locational attributions, players now have the ability to absorb a vast array of information in a logical manner. The introduction of knowledge has now been completed.

2.2   The Infinite Scotland Gameplay

With both the goal and scope of information laid out, the process in which a player gains access to this information is key. The gateway to this introductory, yet now meta-constructed, surplus of information is represented graphically through the use of an ecosystem-orientated, top-down map of Scotland (Fig 2). Yet the player's ability, and innate desire, to freely explore at will may lead to a dysfunctional and highly unproductive learning session; in turn leading to

Welcome to Infinite Scotland traveller. I'll be your tour guide on your journey around Scotland.

NEXT

Fig. 2. Final top-down map illustrating the six ecosystems and navigational guide component

confusion or frustration at a lack of progress, or overwhelming absorption of information.

Thus a navigational guide has been implemented to assist the player by providing preliminary instructions with the aim of developing the user experience in a structured manner, providing an indirect, implicit goal to data gathering. This is achieved through the use of a highly primitive, intuitively implicit narrative structure that frames the information as a series of checkpoints in a backpacking trip around Scotland. Through player exploration of Scotland, a player has the ability to visit any of the six ecosystem types on their visit, upon which the map will then zoom in to show the ecosystem type in full with all of the available classification data entries. It must be noted that classification entries are constant, and not random, to their specific ecosystem types in order for the player to attribute knowledge at a classification level to an ecosystem type level - of which will be used for player reference and later reinforcement.

Yet in order to provide this catalog of information in a manner not similar to the direct, overextended data-push, there exists an additional goal, discussed later, which requires not only learning the information, but applying it in a competitive manner. As suggested by our design pattern, both learning depth and reinforcement must be exercised. Thus the information for any classification

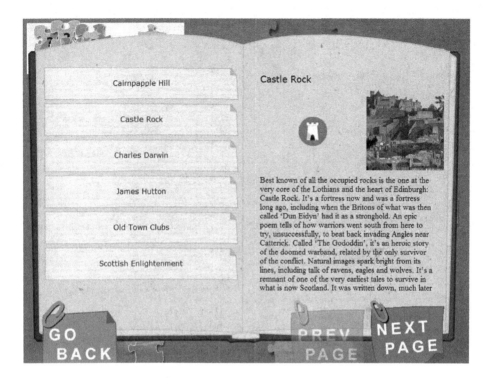

Fig. 3. The IS game diary detailing an ecosystem's classification entry

within any ecosystem type will be presented as only a brief overview of the information itself. The full text, along with complementary assets, appears within the complementary, comprehensive diary (Fig 3). The diary was developed for a number of reasons: to encase the full text of any classification for further information, enable the player to readdress relevant information for competitive advantage, and to allow the player to gauge their progress on their trip in full. Through the use of this mechanic, it aims to allow the player to get the gist of the essential information at a glance, whilst providing the player access to additional information that can develop further but at the player's own pace; disregarding the requirement for the player to read all of the information in one sitting and risk becoming disillusioned or agitated. The deepening of knowledge has now been completed.

Yet the introduction and deepening of information on its own is not serious game compliant if there exists no way in which to reinforce, thus test, the player's knowledge gained. Subsequently a direct, yet optional, goal for the player to undertake whilst obtaining information is to complete an interactive puzzle, specifically one in the form of a jigsaw (Fig 4). The reinforcement mechanic employed is a reactive one, working in parallel with the learning mechanic, as the player is required to make use of the data gathering in order to partake in

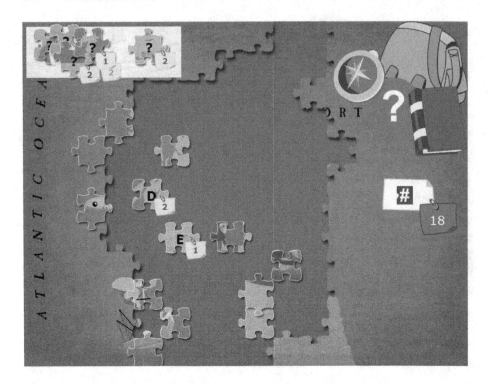

Fig. 4. The IS jigsaw game mechanic illustrating a mid-journey breakdown

the jigsaw, yet this remains optional and can be undertaken at the players's own pace and discretion.

The jigsaw is composed of three parts: the first is collecting pieces, the second is fitting pieces into the jigsaw outline, of which when completed, is a map of Scotland, and the third is of a competitive nature. Although a number of additional parameters are used, the premise is that random jigsaw pieces are awarded by visiting classification entities. Each awarded jigsaw piece is the same standard shape yet is composed of a unique overlay image, representing the map in some way.

The base mechanic implores the player to use the visual cue to attempt to place the jigsaw piece into the correct position, yet such a primitive approach does not attempt to reinforce the player to make use of information relevant to what they had learned about Scotland, in particular the data within its ecosystem and classification types. Thus, each jigsaw piece has an additional clue in the form of a random snippet of information, presented in a similar manner to the classification data entries, which allow the player to recalibrate a jigsaw piece's hypothetical location based on an ecosystem type rather than purely on visual, making the jigsaw both sensory and logistical in form.

The enhanced mechanic would now implore that if the player knows the location of a jigsaw piece's information, then the player now has a hypothetical one in six better chance of being correct. Yet it must be noted the provided information is random and thus a player may or may not have visited that classification site as of yet, thus not having the knowledge to make use of it. The overall challenge for the player lies in recognizing and making use of information to assist in placing a jigsaw piece relevant to both its image and location in order to complete the jigsaw. The reinforcement of knowledge has now been completed.

2.3 The Game Design Construction

Once a serious game has laid out its proposal, decided its approach in terms of learning outcomes, and justified the implementation of its design pattern, the application of game design theory is now needed in order to develop the application further. The IS serious game has so far employed two base mechanics in order to achieve its desired design pattern: learning and reinforcement. The latter of which is more relevant to game theory as it includes the use of a traditional game mechanic; in the form of the jigsaw puzzle. A strict balance must be adhered to in order for a player to enjoy the serious game whilst at the same time providing some degree of feedback, in this case, the continued interest level of a player. In order to accomplish this goal, a number of additional mechanics were employed with relation to the main jigsaw mechanic.

But with a quick consideration for the meta-design methodology, there always existed the desired prospect of IS appealing to a variety of user play styles or 'player types'; such that IS would be both presentable and enjoyable to the target, and to a considerable degree, a wider demographic. Thus the high level design decision to incorporate a variety, and not purely a single game mechanic or play element, was stipulated for the jigsaw mechanic. In that IS would deliver both a competitive achievement subsystems whilst addressing social and exploratory prospects. Such a tactic designates the design address theory just as much as an iterative design process to deliver a substantiated play experience for all hypothetical players involved. Yet with the inclusion of a target demographic, certain priorities must be maintained in order to address that target group, and the subsequent prospected play styles, as priority.

The core design consideration for IS was that it would be integrated on Facebook under the concept of a *"one minute game"*. The notion of *"jump-in, jump-out"* gameplay was developed through the use of a move counter feature; such that each classification would spawn a random jigsaw piece of the same classification, of a select color, and award a move for that classification move counter. Specifically this meant that in order to attempt and place a jigsaw piece of color red, the player must first visit the red classification type(s) in order to be awarded the jigsaw piece in the first place, and use the awarded subsequent red moves to attempt it.

Additionally the spawn location of the jigsaw pieces was limited, and employed a tower stack effect such that the player would not be able to unlock everything and then attempt the puzzle - as lower jigsaw pieces would be piled beneath the highest. Lastly, was the mechanic of locational suggestive feedback or the *"hot or cold"* effect, where after placing a jigsaw piece on the board it would feedback an appropriate grade based on the distance the player was incorrect. Thus an A+ would mean the piece was correct and would snap into place versus an F which meant the player was nowhere near correct, and all the variance in between.

These control constraints allow the gameplay to remain consistent and coherent over the course of the journey through Scotland. Additional features and mechanics which aim to control the puzzle mechanic in such a way to allow it to remain rewarding over the course of multiple attempts were developed. First were the additions of *"powerups"* which rewarded the player for such things as using the journal to source information, to slotting a jigsaw piece correctly the first attempt. Such instances of power-ups, include free automatic slotting to a higher snap grid for the next placed jigsaw piece. These were pivotal in continually rewarding the player over the course of many visits to IS for completing constructive events. In effect, even though visiting the journal to recap information in order to get a lower move multiplier might come as innate nature, the prospect is that the player learned additional information than was not originally present in order to achieve their goal.

The other mechanic developed to encourage both a higher level of difficulty and substantial solo-play prospects was the *"rotten jigsaw piece"* feature. This in effect meant that if the player left a jigsaw piece on the board too long without moving it, it would start to decay and begin a countdown timer. If the player did not move the jigsaw piece again before the timer reached zero, then the jigsaw piece would be returned to the box and a negative effect would be applied to the board; such as hiding the grade score of all jigsaw pieces on the board to removing an already slotted jigsaw. These additional mechanics were developed through the use of iterative development of design theory and user feedback.

As stated previously, in order to avoid the pitfalls of the traditional data-push approach, IS will incorporate a competitive or oppositional configuration with regards to the jigsaw puzzle mechanic, in particular a *"best"* play or high score system. This approach will be accomplished via a number of global parameters that will be visible to other players via the Facebook completion screen in order to incite competitive tendencies - such as map percentage complete and total moves taken. The highlighted count of the number of moves one player has taken to achieve a particular completion percentage is used as a competitive incentive to keep both the player in question, and any other social users, coming back to play.

The integration of IS within Facebook was deemed pivotal as it would allow both the scope and magnitude of the information to be accessed further via social ties, thus allowing for such competitive aspects to be formatted. Yet due to the nature of competitive play the notion of fairness was addressed with all players getting random pieces irrelevant of their previous knowledge of Scotland. The inclusion of Facebook additionally offered the prospect of Creative Scotland to collect analytical information on such keys items as the most visited ecosystem type to the highest number of views for all journal entries in order to better develop the material and tailor it towards the player in the future.

3   Game Implementation (Application)

3.1   The Architecture

While primarily designed with social media integration in mind, the IS game required both a fully featured online version and an offline version to be run in environments where internet and social media access may be limited (e.g. schools and universities). For this reason we made the design decision to develop and produce IS with Adobe Flash. Whilst a serious game developed in HTML5 and Javascript may have allowed for greater integration through a wider range of web-enabled devices, packaging the game through Adobe Air [5] provided us with a mature technology for deployment to both web and desktop platforms - with the same code base. Furthermore, by building IS atop the open-source Starling Cross Platform Game Engine for Flash [6] we would be able to in the future to extend our deployment to both the Apple and Android App stores with minimal development costs.

The core of the IS game architecture (Fig 5) was built upon the open source Starling Game Engine developed by Gamua [6]. The IS game consists of three main layers: the Game Layer (built with the Starling Game Engine Framework [7]), the Storage Layer (integrating the game with a Flox server back-end [8]), and a Social Media Layer (a JavaScript Layer that implements the social media provider APIs). The Game Layer encapsulates the game logic and controls communication between the layers through generic events (e.g. save game, login, login failure, post status). The Storage Layer allows us to save game locally when no internet access is available and to save the data to the cloud when it becomes available again. The Social Media Layer controls access to the social media functions and handles account access, log in, progress posting, etc. The separation of these layers allows us to maintain a workable version of the game even when web-based features are not available.

3.2   The Game Layer

The Game Layer contains all the game specific logic as well as controlling access to the various embedded assets (sprites, sounds, information and dialogue), input devices (mouse, keyboard, touch screen, etc.), as well as controlling sounds, screen transitions and the Graphical User Interface (GUI). IS was developed as a primarily event driven game and takes advantage of the event management system within AS3 and the Starling Framework to handle messages within the Game Layer. When an event is triggered an event 'bubbles up' the display list hierarchy to the Game Core. The GUI employed a similar layered technique as seen in (Fig 6).

The Game Core then decides to handle the message itself or to pass it back down a branch of the display hierarchy to the correct event handler. For example, when the player correctly places a puzzle piece on the tile screen, a gameplay event will be triggered. This event will then 'bubble up' the flash display list from the tile object to its parent screen and finally to the Game Core. Both

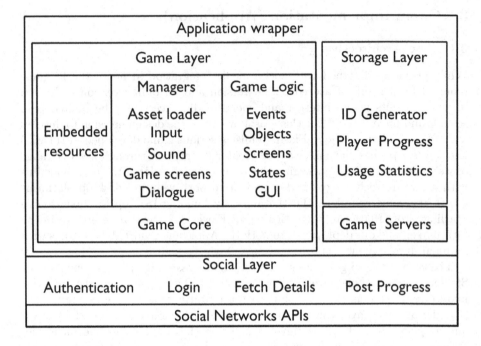

Fig. 5. The IS game architecture detailing the various levels of system design

the Storage Layer and the Social Layer will be subscribed to this particular event. In this case the Storage Layer will update the player's progress and save if appropriate. While the Social Layer will - provided a successful log in attempt has been made - request to post the player's progress to their Facebook wall.

The asset loader stores a list of game assets by name and serves to abstract the location and type of the asset from the core game logic. This allows us to load assets without needing to know whether they are stored locally or are being pulled from the web on application start-up. This allows for a potential extension of the game to include assets pulled from user-generated content on the Infinite Scotland website.

3.3   The Storage Layer

Since the IS game was developed as a social media game, we had to take into consideration the possibility that our players would be accessing the IS game across a number of different devices, platforms and use conditions. We chose the Flox game back-end as it met all our necessary requirements at minimal development cost. Flow allows us to save locally, or to the cloud and access the data from any devices using a unique user ID. This ID is generated by the Storage Layer based on the user's Facebook ID, email address (when Facebook access is denied), or as a random value tied to the current device. While the third option

Fig. 6. The IS GUI broken down

does not allow for users accessing data across multiple devices, it still allows for cloud storage for the current device and provides a unique identification for the storage and analysis of usage statistics.

3.4   The Social Media Layer

For the web version of the game, IS was deployed as a hybrid JavaScript/AS3 application. Social media integration was implemented via JavaScript within the application's HTML wrapper [9]. This allows us to directly utilize the JavaScript API's provided by social media service providers without having to implement third party libraries within the game logic core (Fig 7). This allows us to stay up to date with the latest implementation features through generic calls to this layer triggered from within the Game Layer (e.g. login, log out, post status) without altering our game code itself.

The current implementation of the IS game has been successfully deployed and tested in both its web-based version and offline version in both Windows and Mac environments. The Social Media Layer currently only implements functionality for accessing Facebook accounts. Future work may include expanding the Social Media Layer to cover a wider range of Social Media services (i.e. Twitter) and better integration with Facebook features such as game achievements and friend lists. Fully porting the IS game for deployment to Apple and Android

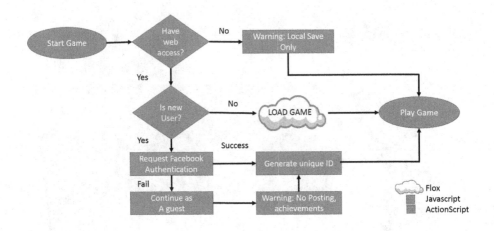

Fig. 7. Facebook JavaScript API [9]

devices would require implementing a Social Media Layer within the Game application. Thus, modifying graphic libraries for a number of different devices and a number of interface enhancements within the Game Layer to ensure readability of interface elements across the wide spectrum of display sizes available in these marketplaces.

Analysis of usage statistics on a wider scale after the IS serious game is fully launched to the public on the Facebook game store. Further potential future work would include integrating the IS serious game with the rest of the Infinite Scotland ecosystem (website and apps). Thus, user generated web/app content could be integrated into the gameplay experience.

4 Proposed Game Evaluation

The evaluation for IS is currently underway, and whilst it cannot be fully detailed here at this time, both the method behind the evaluation method of choice and an overview for the desired outcomes can now be discussed. The purpose of evaluation within a serious game is to justify the design decisions, and specifically for IS, with two parameters in mind: did IS achieve its serious game remit and did IS achieve its user remit?

Specifically for the serious game aspect of IS, Creative Scotland wishes to know a variety of analytical data in order to ascertain on how to proceed with IS in terms of data and future content. Such data could include what ecosystems users enjoyed the most (visited percentage) to what classifications users retained the best (correction percentage). With such preliminary data, Creative Scotland would then have the prospect to include further classification entries with regards to their user group in order to better associate IS to its target demographic. With regards to the IS design pedagogy and methodology, this analytical data could then in turn evaluate whether or not the user learned from the material or not.

More specifically, both if a user was introduced to new material and if they could retain and use it could be evaluated.

The second form of evaluation is more user centric and would follow traditional game design evaluation. It would consider such factors such as if the game is worth playing to the player or as to whether or not it is considered fun. This could in turn adjust the difficulty of the puzzle by looking at the desired time of completion in comparison to actual time of completion. Such evaluation could then adjust the game to make it more susceptible to the target demographic and additionally allow IS to deliver more analytical data back to Creative Scotland.

5 Conclusion

IS is a knowledge-based, puzzle-centric, interactive serious game which allows players to both develop and enhance their knowledge of Scotland; in particular it aims to highlight the biological and cultural diversity that represents a modern, yet historic Scotland. The IS serious game developed a unique design pattern and adjusted game mechanic to address the transfer of knowledge of a highly scoped catalog of Scottish information. It accomplished this feat through structured exploration and the introduction of ecosystem types and classification entities, deepened that knowledge through enhanced journal entries, and enhanced that further through application in a motivational, yet traditional, game mechanic.

Acknowledgment. The authors would like to thank the Scottish Funding Council and the Interface Innovation Voucher scheme for funding this project.

References

1. Scottish National Heritage, http://www.snh.gov.uk/
2. Creative Scotland, http://www.creativescotland.com/
3. Creative Services Scotland, http://www.creativeservicesscotland.co.uk/
4. Heriot-Watt University, MACS Digital Storylab,
   http://www.macs.hw.ac.uk/cs/digitalstorylab/
5. Adobe Air, http://www.adobe.com/products/air.html
6. Gamua, http://gamua.com/
7. Starling, http://gamua.com/starling/
8. Flox, http://gamua.com/flox/
9. Facebook JavaScript API, https://developers.facebook.com/docs/javascript
10. Infinite Scotland, http://infinite-scotland.com/

Measuring the Commercial Outcomes of Serious Games in Companies – A Review

Johann C.K.H. Riedel[1], Yanan Feng[1], Aida Azadegan[2], Margarida Romero[3],
Mireia Usart[4], and Jannicke Baalsrud Hauge[5]

[1] Nottingham University Business School, Nottingham, UK
[2] School of Computer Science, University of the West of Scotland, Paisley, UK
[3] Université Laval, Québec, QC G1V 0A6, Canada; [4] ESADE Law & Business School, 60-62
Avenue Pedralbes, Barcelona, Spain, [5] BIBA, Hochschulring 20, D-28359, Bremen, Germany
{Johann.Riedel,Y.Feng}@Nottingham.ac.uk,
Aida.Azadegan@uws.ac.uk, margarida.romero@gmail.com,
mireia.usart@esade.edu, baa@biba.uni-bremen.de

Abstract. The objective of this paper is to review the work on the measurement of the commercial outcomes of serious games in companies and to provide a framework for their measurement in companies. The literature on the evaluation of training and in particular serious games is presented. A systematic literature review of studies of the impacts of business games in companies was undertaken. The paper summarises the existing studies on measuring the effectiveness of serious games in companies. A search of the grey literature was also conducted to establish what kinds of commercial outcomes have been measured and how. Finally, the paper presents some examples of measuring the commercial outcomes. It also provides some advice on how to measure commercial outcomes.

Keywords: Serious games, commercial outcomes, evaluation framework, evidence, literature review.

1   Introduction

The objective of this paper is to review the work on the measurement of the commercial outcomes, that is, organizational impacts, of serious games in companies and non-educational organizations. The concept of serious Games (SG) effectiveness in the field of business is described. We start by introducing Kirkpatrick's model of learning assessment. Then the concept of SG effectiveness in companies is presented along with an evaluation timeframe framework for measuring the commercial outcomes of SGs.

The paper summarises the existing literature on measuring the effectiveness of serious games in companies, along with some example studies. A systematic literature review of studies of the commercial impacts of SGs in companies was conducted. The literature suffers from a dearth of studies; and the few studies that have been conducted have many weaknesses. The few studies identified are summarised. This

M. Ma et al. (Eds.): SGDA 2014, LNCS 8778, pp. 176–191, 2014.

literature review was complemented by a search of the grey literature on the internet to establish what kinds of commercial outcomes have been measured and how. Finally, the paper presents some examples of measuring commercial outcomes. It also provides some advice on how to measure commercial outcomes.

1.1   Kirkpatrick's Framework for Training Effectiveness

Kirkpatrick devised his framework for training evaluation in the late 1950s (1959). Although Kirkpatrick's four levels of evaluation are known in professional contexts and management education, his model has not been recognized by the community of researchers in the field of psychology or the learning sciences. The model, shown in Table 1, is composed of four levels: reaction, learning, behaviour and results (1994).

Table 1. Kirkpatrick's Four Levels of Training Effectiveness

Kirkpatrick's 4 levels	
Level 1: Reaction	To what degree participants react favourably to the training
Level 2: Learning	To what degree participants acquire the intended knowledge, skills, attitudes, confidence and commitment based on their participation in a training event
Level 3: Behaviour	To what degree participants apply what they learned during training when they are back on the job
Level 4: Results	To what degree targeted outcomes occur as a result of the training event and subsequent reinforcement

A fifth level, ROI (return On Investment) has been added by Phillips (2007). See Bartel (2000) for a review of this approach. TrainingZone (a web resource on training) make the point that although training professionals are adept at designing and delivering training, they are not so good at ensuring participants actually apply what was learned in their job (TrainingZone). In order for this to occur participants have to apply the behaviours they learnt in the training to their daily job – only then will it result in commercial outcomes. These outcomes could be both financial in terms of costs saved or increased sales, but they can also be improved processes, improved customer service, etc. This diversity of potential outcomes presents a challenge to trainers and others who wish to determine the commercial effectiveness of SGs.

The use of the Kirkpatrick model in Game Based Learning (GBL) in general, and in Serious Games (SG) in particular has been limited, and mostly conducted during the last 10 years. Most of the uses of the Kirkpatrick's model in GBL and SG research are related to the use of SG in professional contexts. Johnson and Wu (2008) used the serious game Iraqi™ in the context of Marine Corps training, and analyse the impact of the SG Iraqi™, using the level 3 and 4 of the Kirkpatrick model: "tactical Iraqi™ training led to improved on-the-job performance (a Kirkpatrick level 3 result) and this in turn contributed to improved organizational outcomes (a Kirkpatrick level 4 result)" p. 521. In a review of SGs' learning outcomes, O'Neil et al. (2005) found "only two studies involved Level 3 (on-the-job changes due to training), and one study involved Level 4 (benefits to the employer, for example: cost effectiveness)." Martínez-Durá and colleagues (2011) studied effectiveness in safety training SGs. Different games were discussed by the authors, divided into three different domains: health and safety in construction, public safety and pedestrian safety. In these contexts, two types of games were identified: interactive games, where the player must undertake different tasks in order to win the game, and "observation-based" games, concerning safety regulations. Following the Kirkpatrick model, the authors focused on level 3 as the most important for safety training. They argue that the transfer level aims to evaluate to what extent the knowledge and skills acquired through the game are used by the learner. Level 4 (results), are important: a reduction in the number of work related accidents.

2   Serious Games' Evaluation Framework

As mentioned above the learning effectiveness of serious games has been widely studied in the educational context. A systematic framework for evaluating serious games has been produced by Mayer et al. (2013). Mayer and colleagues aimed to understand to what extent, and which factors, of SGs contribute to advanced learning, and if the lessons learnt can be transferred to the real world. In their study, focused on the requirements and design principles for a comprehensive social scientific methodology for the evaluation of SGs, they focus on 12 different SG experiences in formal and informal learning environments, for different ages and contexts. The key factors they identified include: organizational commitment, organizational characteristics (structure, culture, process), participant characteristics (position, expertise, personality, learning style), participant socio-demographics, and participant motivation. After their review, the authors highlight the lack of studies providing high-quality evaluation frameworks for SGs. Referring to Kirkpatrick's four levels for evaluating training they admit (p. 9) that "this model is difficult to use for exploratory or explanatory hypothesis generation and testing." Furthermore, there are even fewer evaluation frameworks of game-based learning in higher education, let alone professional, in-company training, or group and organizational learning.

The standard evaluation technique has been the quasi-experimental design with pre- and post gaming tests (Mayer et al. 2013; Bellotti et al., 2013; Baalsrud Hauge et al., 2014). For the case of evaluating commercial outcomes this model needs to be refined, see Fig 1 below.

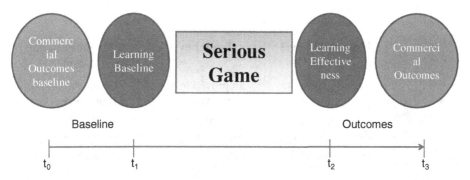

Fig. 1. Evaluation Timeframe Model

The above SG evaluation timeframe model shows that before the impact of a serious game can be determined, it is necessary to determine the baseline level of knowledge (learning) of the participants and the baseline level of the targeted commercial outcomes. These have to be measured at different times and places/contexts: the commercial baseline needs to be measured in context at the workplace and this has to be done some time before the serious game (t_0). This measurement may have to be done some months before the serious game (due to difficulties of measurement or other constraints). The learning baseline is typically measured in the training room immediately prior to participation in the serious game (t_1), and typically involves the use of questionnaires (Mayer et al, 2012). The learning outcomes are also typically measured immediately after the serious game (t_2), again using questionnaires. However, the commercial outcomes need to be measured in context at the workplace and the measurement needs to be delayed until the SG's impacts have had chance to take effect (t_3) – this again could take some months. It is also advisable to make the same measurements of a control group who are not subjected to the SG, so as to show that the SG produced the observed outcomes.

There is an issue with determining the commercial outcomes of a serious game. This is an SG specific factor – if managers have a means to measure the impact of the serious game, particularly its commercial impact, they would be more willing to adopt. However, in practice it can be difficult to identify the outcome. There is a further difficulty in that some of the outcomes, eg. cultural change, change of mindset, soft-skills development and change of behavior are hard to quantify and therefore hard to measure. For example, observation of behavior can be used; however, unless an experienced researcher carries it out, the results may be unreliable. It would be better to use objective, or factual, outcomes in the measurement. Hence, further research is needed to identify what the commercial impacts of serious games are and how they can be measured. The following table illustrates some of the behaviours and accompanying outcomes that can result from serious games. Behavioural change can occur at the individual, team and organizational levels.

Table 2. Classification of Training Outcomes

	Individual Level	Team Level	Organisational Level
Level 3: Behavior	Change in attitudes Change in individual behavior Improved skills	Improved team-working Improved decision-making Improved problem solving	Change in organisational processes/ practice Cultural change Strategic change Reduction in resistance to change
	Non-Financial Outcomes	*Metrics*	**Financial Outcomes**
Level 4: Results	Reduced time Improved productivity	*Financial*	Increased sales Reduced costs
	Improved quality Fewer adverse events Improved Customer service Improved health outcomes	*Non-financial*	Reduced warranty, insurance/ compensation claims Increased sales

The above table shows that even non-financial outcomes, such as reduced time to complete work and improved productivity can be measured with financial metrics. Other non-financial outcomes cannot be easily measured in financial terms – such as improvements in quality, in customer service and health outcomes. The next section reviews the existing studies in the academic literature.

3   Evidence of the Effectiveness of SGs in Companies

In the field of medical education, SGs are relatively new. de Wit-Zuurendonk and Oei (2011) made a literature review on the effectiveness of SGs as a training method for future doctors. They argue that simulations have long been considered as effective in the medical field, and that games could also be effective because learning takes place within contexts that are meaningful to the student. Nevertheless, results of their study show that SGs effectiveness has not been conclusively demonstrated in this particular area, when compared with military training.

When measuring the training effectiveness of SGs, Oprins and Korteling (2012) used a control group receiving conventional on-the-job training. They measured both performance and competence by observation and self-assessment. Results showed that both variables were higher for the group playing a SG.

In order to clarify the question a systematic literature review was conducted in order to identify the evidence of the effectiveness of serious games used in companies. We want to find studies, or evaluations, of serious games that have been carried out in companies, or at the very least with employees. Thus we ruled out papers which were simply descriptions of business related games or reflections on the potential of serious games. We also excluded from consideration games for business which have been evaluated in an educational context or with student participants – as we are looking for evidence of the impact of serious games on companies. According to Mulrow (1994), systematic literature review has been found to provide the high quality and most efficient method for identifying and evaluating extensive literatures. The current theoretical and empirical literature is evaluated in order to provide recommendations for future research directions for scholars in serious games, training and development, human resource management, computer science and social psychology.

The first step in the literature review is to define the set of keywords to use for searching the databases. The process of identifying the search terms and keywords was an iterative process, several meetings were held within the review team to decide on the search strings that are most appropriate for the review. After discussions, five search terms were selected: 'company', 'evaluation', 'study', and 'business game' or 'business simulation'. During the search, we excluded 'game theory' because a large number of articles using game theory as theory or experimental studies were found which are irrelevant to the current research. These five key search terms were selected because we were interested in the evaluation of business games used in companies, and these five key search terms can best reflect the parameters of this review. In order to ensure the comprehensive coverage of the literature search, we did not refine the type of game, such as serious game, video game etc., but rather, we included any business relevant game which has been used or evaluated in companies.

We focused on peer-reviewed full-text English-language scholarly journal articles when conducting the literature search. According to Armstrong and Wilkinson (2007), journal articles are likely to have the highest impact on the field and can be considered validated knowledge. We also included conference proceedings, given that serious games is an emerging field so there might be relevant conference papers which have not yet been published in journals. There is also a tendency for computer science related research to be published in conference proceedings rather than journals (eg. ACM's HCI conference – CHI).

We began with a keyword search using several electronic databases, including Science Direct, ProQuest/ABI, ACM Digital Library (DL), IEEE XExplore Digital Library and the Academy of Management database. These databases were selected to cover the following disciplines: social science, business and management, computer science in order to max-imise the chances of finding relevant articles. The specific reason for selecting Science Direct is that this is a leading scientific database in both science and social science areas. More than 2,500 journals and almost 20,000 books can be found from Science Direct. ProQuest/ABI is one of the most comprehensive business databases. It includes in-depth coverage for over 3,730 publications, with more than 2,670 available in full text. We also selected the ACM and IEEE XExplore digital libraries, since they have extensive coverage of the databases in computer science and information technology. The ACM Digital Library is the most compre-hensive collection of full-text articles and bibliographic records covering the fields of computing and information technology, it also indexes the Springer collection. The full-text data-base currently consists of more than 44 high impact Journals as well as more than 275 Conference Proceedings. The IEEE XExplore digital library database provides full text access to more than 140 technical journals and approximately 900 annual conference proceedings published by the Institute of Electrical and Electronics Engineers (IEEE) and the Institution of Engineering and Technology (formerly the Institution of Electrical Engineers). We also included the database of the Academy of Management, since it publishes leading journals in the business and management field and provides the highest quality papers. The reason for us to include this database is to identify if there are papers on serious games so that we can learn from their best research practice. The Academy publishes five journals: articles published in

Table 3. Summary of the database search results, showing the number of articles found

Key search terms	Business game + company + evaluation	Business game + company + study	Business simulation + company + evaluation	Business simulation + company + study
Science Direct	3	15	10	53
ProQuest/ABI In-form	4	14	5	12
ACM digital library (includes Springer publications)	5	0	0	0
IEEE XExplore digital library	1	3	0	0
Key search terms	Game + company		Business simulation	
Academy of Man-agement	5		5	

the Academy of Management Journal (AMJ) empirically examine theory-based knowledge; the Academy of Management Review (AMR) provides a forum to explicate theoretical insights and developments; The Academy of Management Learning and Education (AMLE) provides a forum to examine learning processes and management education; the Academy of Management Perspectives (AMP) publishes accessible articles about important issues concerning management and business; and the Academy of Management Annals provides up-to-date, comprehensive examinations of the latest advances in various management fields. Each volume features critical research reviews written by leading management scholars.

After the literature search of the databases, a total of 137 articles were found (see Table 3 above). Following the rigorous methodology used by Tranfield, Denyer & Smart (2003), the reviewer reviewed all the 137 articles in-depth, articles that met all the inclusion criteria and which manifested none of the exclusion criteria were selected. For example, to be included in the review, an article had to address games/simulations used for education, training or learning purposes in companies. Other studies, for example, on simulations (especially with equations) which are used for modelling real organisational processes and games that are used for student education purposes (except executive education) were not included. This resulted in a total of 29 articles. As the decision regarding inclusion and exclusion remain relatively subjective (Tranfield, Denyer & Smart, 2003), after the first selection process, a number of discussions were held within the review team to further discuss the criteria for selecting articles. Finally a total number of six articles were identified. A summary of the studies is in Table 4.

As can be seen in Table 4, serious games have been found to be an effective teaching tool, as, for example, it has increased learners' participation and interest in the study of insurance company operations (Trifschmann, 1976). The findings of Ben-Zvi (2007) demonstrated the potential for using business games as an educational tool for teaching management information systems (MIS) and Decision Support Systems (DSS). In Pourabdollahian, Taisch & Kerga's (2012) study, a high level of engagement among learners was exhibited during game play based on the evaluation framework adopted. In addition, Wolfe (1975) found that management games could reward rational policy and decision making practices. Seven broad groupings' of performance behaviours were also identified in Wolfe's (1975) research.

Of these six studies, four studies used executive education students, one study used a combination of both students and company employees and only one study was carried out with engineers and project managers in a company in Italy. The type of game used ranged from an insurance game, a management game, a concurrent engineering (new product development) game and other business games. The application domain, therefore, included insurance, HRM, business policy and decision making, engineering and information systems. The levels of analysis/operation in the games included the individual, team and firm levels. The evaluation methods employed included experiments, for example, Cook (1967), which simulated the operations of a multi-firm, one-product industry and Wolfe and Luethge (2003), who conducted quasi-experiments with senior managers in companies and made comparisons between the engaged firms and unengaged firms in terms of their returns on equity and assets and earnings per share. Four studies used questionnaires, to measure participants' attitudes (Cook, 1967), the level of engagement among learners (Pourabdollahian, Taisch, & Kerga, 2012) and the use and contribution of information systems (Ben-Zvi, 2007).

The limited number of evaluation studies found in the literature may be due to several reasons. First, the fact that companies who adopt serious games would not wish to disseminate the evaluation information to their competitors, so it remains confidential and hence difficult for scholars to access. In addition, it seems difficult to develop appropriate measures for the learning outcomes, especially for measuring soft skills outcomes (for example, interpersonal skills, leadership and negotiation). Management and HR researchers need to develop validated measures for these so that they can be applied in a standard way to evaluate serious games. There is also the lack of evaluation opportunity problem – serious games can be developed and deployed without evaluations being performed due to the lack of evaluation experts/researchers being there at the time to evaluate the impact. For the studies identified in the literature, although they provide interesting evidence for the use of serious games in companies, a number of methodological issues have been found as well. For example, the performance measures used in Wolfe and Luethge (2003) seem to be weakly formulated. They used in-game indicators, i.e. the return on equity and assets and earnings to evaluate participants' game performance. The use of in-game measures is problematic because we need to be sure that the game generates the correct measures – that is the fidelity and validity of the game's algorithms needs to be high. Separate studies of this validity of the game would need to be carried out, without learning outcome indicators; however, it is difficult to identify the learning effects from the game. Other methodological problems were present in the studies too, in Trifschmann's (1976) research, no sample size was reported and it is thus difficult to evaluate the validity of study.

This systematic literature review has found very limited empirical evidence for the effectiveness of SGs in companies. The next section reviews examples of evaluations of SGs in companies located on the internet. These studies have not been published in peer reviewed journals and so cannot be relied upon as being rigorously conducted, or having confidence in the findings

Table 4. Summary of the evaluation studies of serious games used in companies

Game	Authors	Methodology		Outcomes measured	Findings	Individual/Team Game	Application domain
		Evaluation method	Sample size				
The UCLA Executive game	Cook (1967)	Phase I: Experiment, which simulates the operations of a multi-firm, one-product industry	Phase I: 120 students from a university	Attitude, Frequency of feedback,	Attitudes of participants and performance results are directly related to the frequency of feedback on performance,	Team	HRM
		Phase II: Questionnaire	Phase II: 134 managers from 59 companies	Job performance			
An insurance game	Trifschmann (1976)	Experiment (This is inferred from the text, as there is no explicit mention of methodology)	No mention of sample size. Also no mention if they are executive students or not.	Game performance and their oral and written reports	The game was found to be an effective teaching tool, as it increased student participation and interest in the study of insurance company operations.	Team	Insurance
A management game	Wolfe (1975)	Interview	254 students from five sections of a senior-level business policy course	Effective performance behaviours	7 broad groupings of performance behaviours were identified; management games rewarded rational policy and decision making practices; and chance played no consistent part in company success.	Team	Business policy and decision making

Table 4. (*continued*)

The global business game	Wolfe & Luethge (2003)	Quasi-experiments	Senior managers in companies, MBAs No mention of sample size	Average quarterly earnings	The engaged firms who participated in the game obtained superior results; while the uninvolved firms fared the worst. The player-led companies beat the copycats and the uninvolved firms on their return on equity and assets, and earnings per share.	Team	Organisational Behaviour, corporate governance
The Set Based Concurrent Engineering (SBCE) Game	Pourabdollahian, Taisch, & Kerga (2012)	Questionnaire	36 engineers and project managers in the Carel Company in Italy	The level of engagement was measured	The results showed that a high level of engagement among learners is exhibited based on the evaluation framework adopted.	Team	New product development, engineering design.
A business game	Ben-Zvi (2007)	Questionnaire	18 companies, consisting of 90 graduating MBA students.	A number of relevant variables: use of systems, contribution of systems, association with systems and user satisfaction.	The findings demonstrated the potential for using business games as an educational tool for teaching management information systems (MIS) and decision support systems (DSS).	Team	Information systems

4   Examples of Commercial Outcomes of Serious Games

This section of the paper presents case studies of SG commercial effectiveness from three different companies Deloitte, Samsung and IBM (two cases) and examples of gamification effectiveness.

4.1   Samsung Electronics

Electronics firm, Samsung, planned to create more user-generated content and traffic for its global website – which often go hand-in-hand from an essential search engine optimization perspective for online marketing. Samsung created a social media-based loyalty program utilizing serious game principles.

Samsung, mixed frivolity with serious business initiatives and used gamification platform of Badgeville to fuel competition among visitors of the website and affect their online behaviour. Badgeville serious gaming platform, can track users' performance data to motivate behaviour, reward top performers, and create real-time notifications to engage inactive users. The Badgeville game let users level up, unlock badges, and gain subsequent rewards and recognition. Samsung, in return, saw 66 percent more users submitting 447 percent more product answers on its global Web site. Even more impressive, the user-generated content prompted 34 percent of users to put 224 percent more items in shopping carts."

http://www.designingdigitally.com/blog/2014/03/ibm-samsung-allstate   see-high-roi-through-serious-games#axzz31RcNKCXD

http://www.thegamifiers.com/customers-list/case-studies/123/samsung/

4.2   IBM – Innov8 Case Study

IBM's Innov8 is a serious games used for marketing purposes that explain business process management to college students and city planning processes to CEOs, presidents, COOs and other leaders.

Innov8, a serious game created on the Vicious engine, was rolled out as an IBM academic initiative to explain Business Process Management (BPM) to students. This means IBM has a foot in the door with rising generations. Students going through college and learning about BPM learn it through an IBM product with IBM branding attached to it. This game gives IBM a presence in schools, making an impression on the future leaders of the world and future potential customers. Moreover, Innov8 became the top brand for IBM within a few days of it going live in 2009.

http://www.designingdigitally.com/blog/2014/03/ibm-samsung-allstate-see-high-roi-through-serious-games#ixzz31VNIwbhq

Innov8: CityOne is now IBM's top lead generator. The pitch of the game is to "Level-up your skills and discover how to make our Planet smarter, revolutionize industries and solve real-world business, environmental and logistical problems." CEOs, Presidents, COOs and other top executives across the globe embraced the game. The ROI for *Innov8: CityOne* revealed that in five months, the game resulted in 100x the investment put into it. Tracking the people who played and who bought resulted in tremendous sales for IBM. *Innov8: CityOne* is free to play but registration is required to make it possible to track the results. Moreover, *Innov8: CityOne* now serves as a sales tool for IBM salespeople. The game can be customized for sales representatives based on the needs of clients. Creating a platform where sales representatives can cater to client's pain points proved to be an incredibly useful feature of *Innov8: City One*.

http://www.ignitesocialmedia.com/games/serious-games-the-new-frontier-of-online-marketing/

4.3   Deloitte Business Simulation Game

The Deloitte Business Simulation game is designed to train employees in corporate responsibility and sustainability. The game enables players to experiment with a realistic model of their company and its potential future scenarios. During the game, the players go through various scenarios and are confronted with the consequences of their decisions just as in the real world. This hands-on experiential learning helps to sharpen management skills through practice and feedback.

CoCo Sim, developed by Front Square, is a game based in a fictional New York-based chocolate store, where the player must manage cash flow and stock levels in order to achieve a high customer satisfaction level while also remaining profitable. The game integrates modules on business process, problem solving and basic accounting. Players' knowledge and skills are applied to the game in order to improve the score. Players' skills are tested with regular questions and the combined game and question scores are then posted on a leader board to help drive competition and engagement. Line managers and HR managers have access to the learning analytics to see who is doing well and who needs performance intervention.

4.4   Gamification Cases

Interest and application of gamification has been increasing in recent years. Business can apply gamification to improve both external and internal interactions and engagement. In terms of *External or Customer Engagement* gamification enables businesses to drive high-value customer behaviour. While it cannot add value to a product or service, its value can be made more visible if applied in the right way – keeping in mind the overall organizational goals, user experience, measurement and analytics needs, design of incentives, and information technology considerations.

- Companies like Verizon have leveraged gamification to increase the time spent by users on their website by 30%, with a 15% increase in page views.
- Nike used gamified feedback to drive over 5,000,000 users to beat their personal fitness goals.
- Another example is the gamification strategy used by the company Marketo. Marketo wanted to increase the adoption of, and accelerate customers to maturity with their software even more quickly by identifying and rewarding high-value behaviours - like asking questions, submitting and voting on ideas, watching videos,

etc. Through this gamification they produced an impressive increase in the daily activities that deliver healthy, active, engaged communities. The company layered Badgeville (the provider company) games on their community, resulting in 67% more engagement, 51% more active members and 10% more engagements per member (Pattabhiram, 2013).

In terms of *Internal or Employee Engagement* businesses stand to benefit from gamification in the workplace by improving employee motivation and hence driving better results. Companies like Badgeville, Achievers and Bunchball currently provide applications that capture and analyze behavioral and other user data of employees to facilitate rewards and recognition.

- LiveOps was able to witness an 8-10% increase in sales by providing timely performance feedback to its call center agents as part of a gamification initiative.
- Deloitte was able to reduce the time taken for training programs by 50% through the use of gamification, while increasing student involvement.
- Extraco Bank and Lawley Insurance were able to increase customer acquisition by 700% and sales activity by 15 times, respectively.

The Deloitte Leadership Academy, a digital executive training programme for more than 10,000 senior executives in over 150 companies around the world, partnered with Badgeville to add game mechanics to its leadership training programme to drive desired behaviours and increase engagement. The programme is delivered to senior executives via an online portal or mobile devices. As players contribute, share knowledge and complete learning programmes, they receive badges, rewards and can share these accomplishments on sites such as LinkedIn, improving their reputation in their field of expertise. After three months of use the results were impressive in terms of improved engagement and module completion (Donovan, 2012): a 46.6% increase in the number of users that return to the site daily; a 36.3% increase in the number of users that return to the site weekly; an average of three badges per active user. One user has earned the Leadership Academy Graduate badge which was expected to take 12 months to achieve.

http://www.mu-sigma.com/analytics/thought_leadership/decision-sciences-gamification.html

5   Conclusion

This paper has reviewed the work on the measurement of commercial outcomes of serious games in companies. The literature on the approach to the evaluation of serious games was summarized. A framework for evaluating commercial outcomes of serious games was presented, along with some examples and guidance on how to conduct evaluations. A systematic literature review was conducted to identify research studies carried out in companies, or with company participants. In summary, although serious games have been used for the purpose of training for a long time, limited empirical evidence was found for the effectiveness of serious games in companies. Serious games have two main effects in companies – learning outcomes and commercial outcomes. The few studies found suffered from several weaknesses – poor methodology and measures. An internet search revealed a selection of companies using serious games and reporting commercial outcomes. SGs were used for both internal engagement with employees (either in training or the gamification of corporate platforms) or with customers (as advertising or gamification of customer education). In both these types of use significant increases in participation/engagement were seen.

Future research is desperately needed to evaluate the effectiveness of serious games in companies. Development of more appropriate evaluation methods is also important in order to more accurately assess the effectiveness of using games in companies. Measures of the learning effects need to be developed, drawing on the many evaluation studies conducted in the educational context. Secondly, measures of the commercial impacts of serious games need to be developed – only if we can show that companies can gain commercial benefits will they be convinced to invest in serious games. There needs to be proper research on the benefits of gamification in companies. Gamification has drawbacks – promoting badge collection/ competition at the expense of learning/ behavior improvement. Has this been seen in companies and what do they do to counter it? A further recommendation is that serious games developers and evaluation researchers need to build strong relationships, so that the developed games can be evaluated with rigor and at low cost. Once we have good quality evidence from rigorous studies it will enhance the acceptance of adopting serious games in industry.

Acknowledgements. The research reported in this paper has been partially supported by the European Union, particularly through the project GaLA: The European Network of Excellence on Serious Games (FP7-ICT- 2009.4.2-258169) www.galanoe.eu, www.seriousgamessociety.org

References

1. Baalsrud Hauge, J., Boyle, E., Mayer, I., Nadolski, R., Riedel, J.C.K.H., Moreno-Ger, P., Bellotti, F., Lim, T., Ritchie, J.M.: Study design and data gathering guide for serious games' evaluation. In: Connolly, T.M., Hainey, T., Boyle, E., Baxter, G., Moreno-Ger, P. (eds.) Psychology, Pedagogy, and Assessment in Serious Games, pp. 394–419. IGI Global (2014), doi:10.4018/978-1-4666-4773-2.ch018
2. Bartel, A.P.: Measuring the Employer's Return on Investments in Training: Evidence from the Literature. Industrial Relations 39(3), 502–524 (2000)
3. Bellotti, F., Kapralos, B., Lee, K., Moreno-Ger, P., Berta, R.: Assessment in and of Serious Games: An Overview. Advances in Human-Computer Interaction 2013, Article ID 136864, 11 pages (2013), doi:10.1155/2013/136864
4. Ben-Zvi, T.: Using business games in teaching DSS. Journal of Information Systems Education 18(1), 113 (2007)
5. Cook, D.M.: The effect of frequency of feedback on attitudes and performance. Journal of Accounting Research 5, 213–224 (1967)

6. Connolly, T.M., Boyle, E.A., MacArthur, E., Hainey, T., Boyle, J.M.: A systematic litera-ture review of empirical evidence on computer games and serious games. Computers & Education 59, 661–686 (2012)
7. de Wit-Zuurendonk, L.D., Oei, S.G.: Serious gaming in women's health care. BJOG: An International Journal of Obstetrics & Gynaecology 118(s3), 17–21 (2011)
8. Donovan, L.: The Use of Serious Games in the Corporate Sector. A State of the Art Report. Learnovate Centre (December 2012)
9. Johnson, W.L., Wu, S.: Assessing aptitude for learning with a serious game for foreign language and culture. In: Woolf, B.P., Aïmeur, E., Nkambou, R., Lajoie, S. (eds.) ITS 2008. LNCS, vol. 5091, pp. 520–529. Springer, Heidelberg (2008)
10. Kirkpatrick, D.L.: Techniques for evaluating training programs. Journal of American Society of Training Directors 13(3), 21–26 (1959)
11. Kirkpatrick, D.L.: Evaluating Training Programs: The Four Levels. Berrett-Koehler Publishers, San Francisco (1994)
12. Martínez-Durá, M., Arevalillo-Herráez, M., García-Fernández, I., Gamón-Giménez, M.A., Rodríguez-Cerro, A.: Serious Games for Health and Safety Training. In: Prensky, M. (ed.) Digital Game-Based Learning. McGraw-Hill, New York (2001)
13. Mayer, I., Bekebrede, G., Harteveld, C., Warmelink, H., Zhou, Q., van Ruijven, T., Lo, J., Kortmann, R., Wenzler, I.: The research and evaluation of serious games: Toward a com-prehensive methodology. British Journal of Educational Technology (2013), doi:10.1111/bjet.12067
14. Mulrow, C.D.: Systematic reviews: Rationale for systematic reviews. British Medical Journal 309(6954), 597–599 (1994)
15. O'Neil, H.F., Wainess, R., Baker, E.: Classification of learning outcomes: evidence from the computer games literature. The Curriculum Journal 16(4), 455–474 (2005)
16. Oprins, E., Korteling, H.: Transfer of gaming: effectiveness of a Cashier Trainer. (2012), http://www.just.nl/en/files/2012/11/ TNO-paper-CASA-2012-Singapore.pdf
17. Pattabhiram, C.: Expanding and Engaging Marketo's "Marketing Nation" (May 17, 2013), http://blog.badgeville.com/2013/05/17/ engaging-marketos-marketing-nation/ (retrieved)
18. Phillips, J.J.: Measuring ROI – Fact, Fad, or Fantasy, ASTD White Paper (April 2007)
19. Pourabdollahian, B., Taisch, M., Kerga, E.: Serious games in manufacturing education: Evaluation of learners' engagement. Procedia Computer Science 15, 256–265 (2012)
20. Tranfield, D., Denyer, D., Smart, P.: Towards a methodology for developing evidence-informed management knowledge by means of systematic review. British Journal of Management 14(3), 207–222 (2003)
21. TrainingZone, http://www.trainingzone.co.uk/topic/kirkpatrick-new-world-level-3/155784
22. Trifschmann, J.S.: Teaching insurance with an insurance management computer game. Journal of Risk and Insurance 43(1), 43 (1976)
23. Wolfe, J.: Effective performance behaviors in a simulated policy and decision making environment. Management Science 21(8) (1975)
24. Wolfe, J., Luethge, D.J.: The impact of involvement on performance in business simula-tions: An examination of Goosen's 'know little' decision making thesis. Journal of Educa-tion for Business 79(2), 69 (2003)

Designing and Testing a Racing Car Serious Game Module

Babatunde Adejumobi, Nathan Franck, and Michael Janzen

The King's University, Edmonton, AB, T6B 2H3, Canada
{badejumobi,nathanfrank1}@gmail.com, Michael.Janzen@kingsu.ca

Abstract. We present a serious game module to insert into an entertainment video game and examine if knowledge and skills gained from the module can transfer into real life usage. The module consists of a map of a post secondary educational institute based on the real life layout. 21 people participated in a physical scavenger hunt around the institute (3 participants in a pilot study and 18 in a second study), where some played the video game prior to the scavenger hunt. The pilot study shows a large decrease in the time required to complete the scavenger hunt by those who first played the video game. A second study showed no statistically significant difference in the average time to complete the scavenger hunt by those who first played the video game; the results suggest an effect but are limited by large variation in the individual completion times in the scavenger hunt. The limitations of the study are discussed.

Keywords: serious game modules, virtual skills transfer, racing game.

1   Introduction

A premise of serious games is that games are useful for purposes other than entertainment and recreation; for example, video games can teach skills and knowledge. We are interested if skills or knowledge gained from a game created to be entertaining can transfer into real world skills and knowledge. Children don't seem to require external motivation to play video games as an average American youth (ages 8 to 18) plays 13.2 hours of video games a week, with boys playing an average of 16.4 hours a week [5]. In our prior work we encouraged the use of Serious Game Modules to add an educational component to existing commercial video games [3]. The game module models forest growth more accurately than growth found in turn based strategy games. Measuring the knowledge gained, however, is difficult as the serious game module is only one part of a large game. Consequently, we designed a racing car video game intended to teach the layout of a post-secondary institution to its players. The layout learned in the game should be testable through a scavenger hunt in the corresponding real world building. A goal of the racing car game is to be fun as it represents a video game sold as entertainment. Previous research notes that motivational features of video games are often lost in the process of making a serious game [6]. Consequently, the goal of the racing car game is to be entertaining and the goal of the map

M. Ma et al. (Eds.): SGDA 2014, LNCS 8778, pp. 192–198, 2014.
© Springer International Publishing Switzerland 2014

module is to teach a map layout without detracting from the entertainment aspect of the video game.

The sequence of discussion in the paper is as follows. We first describe some prior serious games intended to teach skills and knowledge useful in the real world (Section 2) before presenting our racing car game and module (Section 3). We then present our experimental method to measure the skills transferred from the game to the real world (Section 3.2) and results (Section 4). Finally, we discuss our results and future work (Section 5).

2 Related Work

Previous papers describe the use of a virtual environment or video game intended to teach skills and knowledge for use in the real world. They typically do not, however, focus on the application of a serious game module that could be used in an entertainment game, but rather a whole game as the learning component. For example, Fery and Ponserre examine if skills gained from a virtual golf game translate into golf skills in real life, in particular putting force control [4]. In both the virtual and real world participants putted a golf ball as close as possible to the hole while trying to avoid the ball falling into the hole. Participants were divided into an enjoyment control group and learning group. Participants in each group had 10 real-life putting trials in a pre-test and post-test, and 20 virtual trials in the video game between the real-life trials. The experimenters determined that both groups improved their performance, but the control group improved to a lesser extent than the group that was instructed to try to learn.

Cook *et al.* developed a simulation game, called PULSE, for teaching Intermediate Life Support for the nursing profession [2]. Five levels in a 3D game teach knowledge, skills, and techniques including crash trolley usage, defibrillator techniques, patient monitoring, and patient resuscitation. 34 participants participated in a study showing that the group using PULSE performed better than the control group in six of eight skills tested, however, three showed only borderline statistical significance.

Our previous work follows Bellotti *et al.* in describing a serious game module [1] [3]. Our prior work describes a forest simulator module that could be inserted into a commercial game designed for entertainment. The module models forest growth scenarios more accurately than mechanics found in games, such as natural growth and an invasive species scenario. We encountered difficulty, however, in developing an experiment to test if knowledge learned from the forest simulator in the virtual environment transfers to the real world.

3 Method

3.1 Racing Car Game

We created a racing car game using the Unity engine with loadable game modules in the form of game maps. One map models the layout of The King's University in Edmonton, Alberta, Canada. The player uses their keyboard to control a small car with the goal of maximizing points. With sufficient points they achieve unlocks, such as a rocket booster or the ability for the virtual car to jump. To score points, players go to predetermined locations within a set time. This is shown in the last screen capture of Figure 1 asking the player to go to the Sac (Student Activity Center). Depending on the time taken, players are awarded a gold, silver, or bronze score resulting in a high, medium, or low number of points. To aid in finding the next location the players are provided with a direction and distance to their target. As shown in Figure 1 the game makes simplifications from the real world such as excluding furniture and modelling windows as lit, white rectangles. The virtual world tiles all floors whereas the real world has a variety of floor covering. The virtual world models hallways and common spaces but does not permit the user to enter classrooms, offices, or washrooms. The geometry of hallways, locations of common spaces, and locations of targets correspond to the real world.

3.2   Experimental Method

To determine whether playing the racing car game results in transfer of knowledge to the real world, players participated in a scavenger hunt with locations in the scavenger hunt corresponding to virtual locations given as targets in the racing car game. Participants were randomly assigned to either play the racing car game or not. Two studies were conducted, a small pilot study involving three participants and a second study involving 18 participants. In the second study participants were randomly divided into three groups of six participants: those who did not play the video game (control group), those who played for 20 to 30 minutes (short play group), and those that played for 30 to 60 minutes (long play group).[1] Collectively we will call participants in the short play group and long play group the video game group. Participants in the pilot study were between 16 to 19 years of age with one male and two females. The second study included 15 participants under the age of 15, one participant was between 16 and 19, and two participants greater than 25 years of age. Nine males and nine females participated in the second study. All participants were selected to have a low prior familiarity with the post secondary educational institute. Chiefly, we did not use students who attend or attended the university. Upon commencing the physical scavenger hunt participants were given a physical map of the building and the first of six locations to find. Each of the six locations contained a letter for the participant to record and the next location to find. The scavenger hunt was confined to one floor to avoid complications of using stairs and elevators. We recorded the length of time for each participant to complete the hunt as well as the time they played the video game. Participants in the video game group completed the scavenger hunt immediately after playing the video game.

---

[1] We had shorter and longer playing times to consider, if the length of time playing the game directly correlates with time to complete the scavenger hunt. The difference in video game playing time, however, was not considered in the results when the overall result ended up being not statistically significant.

Fig. 1. Real World Scenes (left) and Corresponding Virtual World Counterparts (right)

3.3   Ethical Approval

This study was conducted in accordance with the ethical standards set at The King's University in Alberta, Canada. Participants signed an informed consent form describing the study and were informed they could withdraw consent at any time during the study. Participants under the age of 18 provided a parent or guardian signature on the informed consent form. The study did not involve deception.

4   Results

The pilot study showed a large decrease in the time to complete the scavenger hunt with a 5 minute time from the participant in the video game group versus 11 minute times for the control group participants. The second study results show no statistically significant improvement, but with large uncertainties. The video game group had an average time to complete the scavenger hunt of 12.92 minutes versus 13 minutes and a standard deviation of 2.3 minutes and 1.5 minutes respectively. The t-value comparing the six control group participants with the six long play group participants is $t = 0.33$, which indicates no significant difference. The margin of error for the difference, at 95% confidence, was ± 2.1 minutes. The data are shown in Table 1 and graphically in Figure 2.

One participant in the short play group mentioned a difficulty where a door was closed resulting in approximately four minutes of additional time required to complete the scavenger hunt. Hence the comparison of only the control group and

Table 1. Average scavenger hunt times

	Scavenger Hunt Time for Video Game Players (minutes)	Scavenger Hunt Time for Non-Players (minutes)
Pilot Study (3 participants)	5	11
Second Study (18 participants)	12.9 ± 2.3	13.0 ± 1.5

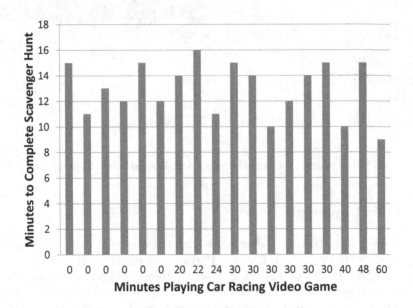

Fig. 2. Time Playing Video Game versus Time to Complete Scavenger Hunt

the long play group for the t-test. When this time is deducted from participants in the short play group the average time for all video game group participants decreased to 10.92 minutes with a standard deviation of 2.8 minutes. After deducting four minutes from the short play group, a one sided t-test comparing control group participants with the video game group yielded a difference of 2.08 minutes with values of $t = 1.94$, and $p = 0.036$.[2]

5   Conclusion and Future Work

We have presented a serious game module, chiefly a map added to a racing car game designed to be entertaining, and our experiment intended to measure the skills learned by participants playing the video game with the serious game module. While a goal of the video game is to be entertaining we did not measure how entertaining it was. Participants playing the game appeared to be amused and two participants asked if they could have a copy for home use, suggesting the game is entertaining. If the experiment is repeated in the future we will add a question on the exit survey to measure the participants' enjoyment of the game.

While the pilot study showed a large decrease in the time to complete the scavenger hunt for video game group participants, the difference in times on the scavenger hunt from the second study shows only a slight improvement for participants in the video game group. One item to note is no participants in the second study completed the scavenger hunt in 5 minutes or less[3], which was the time from the pilot study. The second study showed no statistically significant difference in times between the control group and the others. The individual times varied greatly between participants, however, resulting in a large margin of error. A one sided t-test has a p-value as low as 0.036, which is statistically significant. We, however, consider this result unreliable as it is only just significant, and uses the data where four minutes are deducted from the short play group. Repeating the experiment may confirm this result.

A number of factors and sources of error may contribute to the marginal difference in times between groups. First, since the number of participants is low it may be that a statistically significant result couldn't be detected. A ± 2.1 minute margin of error at 95% confidence would indicate that a larger group of participants may yield a statistically significant result. In terms of sources of error, it may be that participants in the scavenger hunt relied more on the map provided at the start of the physical scavenger hunt than their memory from the video game. This could be countered by conducting the experiment without providing any map to players. This approach, however, would be more difficult to implement in the current study format as it may require exclusive access to the building since participants could require a long search time. A second factor may be that the majority of time required for the scavenger hunt was for travel

---

[2] While $p = 0.036$ is statistically significant a two sided t-test has $p = 0.07$, which is not considered statistically significant.

[3] One participant came close at 6 minutes after four minutes are deducted to account for a closed door.

between locations. A solution may be to select nearby locations as checkpoints, however, the checkpoints should not be visible from each other as that would negate the need for knowledge of the building layout. Another possibility is that the length of time playing the video game was insufficient to learn the building layout. This could be countered by making tasks in the video game more engaging so as to maintain interest longer resulting in longer game play. In this study we did not determine if the accuracy of the 3D representation is sufficiently high enough to transfer to the real world experience. Some participants, but not all, expressed a familiarity in the physical world after playing the video game[4]. It may be that some participants navigate using objects present in the real world that were not rendered in the video game. It is also not clear if some of the participants have a higher natural or learned navigational ability when using a 3D rendering or physical map. If the study is repeated with a larger number of participants results may be grouped to compare participants of similar navigational abilities. These are factors we intend to address in a future study.

Acknowledgements. We would like to thank Andy Tu for his help with finding background information in Serious Games, and Diana Kyle and Chris Ulriksen with help in recruiting study participants. Thanks to Rob MacDonald for his assistance in improving the statistical analysis and an anonymous reviewer for their comments used to improve this paper.

References

1. Bellotti, F., Berta, R., De Gloria, A., Primavera, L.: Enhancing the educational value of video games. Computers in Entertainment (CIE) - SPECIAL ISSUE: Media Arts and Games (Part II) 7(2), 23:1–23:18 (2009)
2. Cook, N.F., McAloon, T., O'Neill, P., Beggs, R.: Impact of a web based interactive simulation game (PULSE) on nursing students' experience and performance in life support training – A pilot study. Nurse Education Today 32(6), 594–602 (2009)
3. Eymundson, D., Janzen, M.: Serious Game Modules for Entertainment Games. In: Ma, M., Oliveira, M.F., Petersen, S., Hauge, J.B. (eds.) SGDA 2013. LNCS, vol. 8101, pp. 206–211. Springer, Heidelberg (2013)
4. Fery, Y.A., Ponserre, S.: Enhancing the control of force in putting by video game training. Ergonomics 44(23), 1025–1037 (2001)
5. Gentile, D.A.: Pathological video-game use among youth ages 8–18: a national study. Psychol Sci. 20(5), 594–602 (2009)
6. Kuipers, D.A., Wartena, B.O., Dijkstra, A., Prins, J.T., Pierie, J.-P.E.N.: Design for Transfer: Meaningful Play through Metaphorical Recontextualisation. In: Ma, M., Oliveira, M.F., Petersen, S., Hauge, J.B. (eds.) SGDA 2013. LNCS, vol. 8101, pp. 239–246. Springer, Heidelberg (2013)

---

[4] There was one location, the lower part of the atrium, where players' cars frequently got stuck. A couple players mentioned the area afterwards indicating the area felt somewhat familiar. This area was not one of the locations to find in the scavenger hunt.

The Construction of Serious Games Supporting Creativity in Student Labs

Heiko Duin and Klaus-Dieter Thoben

BIBA – Bremer Institut für Produktion und Logistik GmbH
at the University of Bremen,
Hochschulring 20, D-28359 Bremen, Germany
du@biba.uni-bremen.de

Abstract. Solving challenges and complexities of today's businesses, organizational members need to come up with creative solutions that arise from joint ideation which harnesses the combined knowledge and abilities of people with different perspectives. Integrated to the creativity process is the act of play. Playing is considered as a powerful mechanism to support creativity, encourage exploration, inspire thinking out of the box and support cooperation and collaboration. Creativity is also the cornerstone of innovation and new product development generating a flow of new ideas ensuring not to stay behind of competitors in today's economic world characterized by high volatility and increasingly complex, fast-paced change.

In a lecture given at the University of Bremen master degree students of industrial engineering and management were introduced to diverse creativity supporting techniques with the goal to extract creativity inspiring elements of the various techniques to be used in Serious Games constructed by those students using a given online multiplayer engine. This paper reports on the outcomes and discusses approach and results.

Keywords: creativity methods, serious games for creativity, game based learning, game development, student lab.

1   Introduction

The success of the European economy is mainly depending on the ability of European businesses to be able to develop new and innovative products and services. Innovation is perceived to be Europe's key to economic success in the current market environment characterised by strong competition from both the established and the emerging Asian economies. While the conventional view on creativity has mostly focused on the individual person as the source of new ideas, recent findings have concluded that most innovations were a result of the social dimension of creativity gained through interactions with others, joint problem solving, and shared struggles [1].

An analysis of how innovations do "arise" shows that the process is mainly carried out in small discrete steps with or without a given timeframe. Most of the product innovations in Europe are not based on radical but on incremental product innova-

M. Ma et al. (Eds.): SGDA 2014, LNCS 8778, pp. 199–212, 2014.

tions. The success or failure of the innovation process is beside the ability to meet the market requirement also dependent on the time-to-market. Therefore, it is necessary to look on those processes being especially critical or time consuming for the outcome and most of them are cooperative or collaborative process steps [2].

The authors presented on the SGDA 2013 a student lab at the University of Bremen applying "traditional" creativity techniques and Serious Games to support creativity [3]. The games used were considered to be hard to get on board. Many students claimed that they don't know what to do when the game started. They said that a better introduction or demo round would help to better understand the game play and the story behind. They also claimed that the communication needed to be better. The two games supported communication through chat. Student's said that this kind of communication is not sufficient for exchanging and discussing ideas. Direct personal communication like in a brainstorming session is considered to be more inspiring as chatting via a web site [3]. This led to the idea to have students constructing their own creativity fostering Serious Game based on elements known from the "traditional" creativity techniques.

After a motivating discussion of the usage of Serious Gaming to foster creativity a course concept of the University of Bremen is introduced. The objective of the course is to introduce students to the concepts of creativity, creativity techniques and Serious Gaming and to develop an own concept of a creativity stimulating Serious Game. The results of the execution of the course in summer semester 2013 are presented and discussed.

2   Why to Use Serious Games to Support Creativity?

Integrated to the creativity process is the act of play. Playing is considered as a powerful mechanism to support creativity, encourage exploration, inspire thinking out of the box and support cooperation and collaboration. Creativity is also the cornerstone of innovation and new product development generating a flow of new ideas ensuring not to stay behind of competitors in today's economic world characterized by high volatility and increasingly complex, fast-paced change [4].

In Serious Gaming the player immerses in an immersive experiential experience struggling through exploration, trial and error and even failure in order to progress to the promise of a win. The competitive or collaborative aspects of Serious Games also lead to immersion, engagement, and triggers creative sparks.

Craft [5] emphasizes the growth of gaming and social networking as having a strong effect on the creative possibilities of young learners. The application of these technologies leads to a "possibility thinking" as the central element of the digital experience of a playful exploration of what might be. The learner in a creative space expands a question about what something is to include what might can be done with this? This extension of thought is leads to the development of imagination and the nurturing of creativity.

Connected to gaming is the possibility of failure. Games offer a risk-free environment in which the player can act and find and explore problems. Failure is part of the game and makes the game becoming challenging and compelling. However, the spirit of exploration does not, in itself, foster creativity. But, by providing such a safe space to enter into venues without knowing where they lead, we are beginning to move closer to environments more conductive to creative thinking. Any creative process is active rather than passive. Games and virtual worlds offer the ability to experience, to take control, to make decisions and to do rather than just to observe [6].

Luccini and Cheak provide two examples of games: World Without Oil (WWO) and FoldIt [4]:

- The game World Without Oil (http://worldwithoutoil.org/) represents an alternative reality collaborative problem solving game. It introduces a particular scenario and invites players – individually or collaboratively – to solve some specific challenges. The goal of the game is to use the collective intelligence of bloggers and gamers in order to create a bottom-up map of the scenario to live through a massive oil shortage in the US. Throughout playing the game participants acquire factual knowledge about the challenge itself and skills around creative thinking, collaboration and leadership. More than 1900 people signed up as players of WWO, generating over 1500 stories from inside the virtual "global oil crisis of 2007." The outcome created a rich, complex, and plausible collective imagination of the "what-if situation" oil crisis and stimulated a range of creative responses regarding how to such a crisis could be responded.
- The game FoldIt (http://fold.it/portal/) is an educational game developed in 2008 by researchers at the University of Washington. The game allows the public to play by modelling the genetic makeup of proteins. At the end of a three-week competition in 2010, top-scoring players had generated phase estimates that allowed researchers to identify a rapid solution of the crystal structure for a monkey virus related to AIDS. This structure had eluded researchers for more than 10 years. However, the nonlinear, cooperative, and creative problem-solving techniques used by these gamers seemed to be the skills needed to finally solve this problem.

Games represent a powerful technique to immerse users in an exploratory, hands-on experiential, collaborative environment, where they can solve problems collaboratively in a safe environment, which allows trial and failure, and which provides feedback and motivation. Such gaming environments are conducive to a creative process and boost creative outputs. Scenario-based problem solving games such as World Without Oil and online collaborative educational games such as FoldIt represent a step bridging the commercial and education world, by integrating many of the key features of the games such as convincing and meaningful context, feedback, goal-driven, conflict and challenge, autonomy and collaboration [4].

3   Design of the Student Lab

3.1   General Design of the Course

The course is named *Application and Comparison of Creativity Techniques* and design as laboratory, i.e. learning content is mediated by a mixture of theoretical and practical sessions.

The course is designed to mediate knowledge about intuitive, discursive and combined creativity methods in comparison to new approaches based on Serious Gaming. For this purpose some creativity techniques are applied to incremental and radical innovation problems.

Before the actual use of selected methods, a comparison framework is developed to be applied after the practical application of each method for evaluating the pros and cons. Results of the evaluation will be prepared and presented and serve as the basis for defining own game scenarios for two different types of innovation problems. Furthermore, the course contains:

- Introduction to the early phase of innovation projects (ideation phase)
- Introduction to creativity and creativity stimulating methods
- Development of practical innovation problems (case studies)
- Application of creativity techniques to practical innovation problems
- Application of Serious Gaming to practical innovation problems
- Comparative evaluation of the methods according to certain criteria (number of generated ideas, originality of ideas, etc.)
- Presentation of evaluation results
- Development of own game scenarios based on elements of creativity techniques
- Documentation and reporting of results of practical sessions

The main learning objectives of the course are:

- Processes in the early phase of innovation projects (ideation phase)
- Creativity techniques, their application areas, strenghts and weaknesses
- Intuitive Creativity Techniques (Brain Storming, 6-3-5-Method)
- Discursive Creativity Techniques (e.g. morphological Analysis)
- Combined Creativity Techniques (e.g DeBono's six Thinking Hats)
- Serious Gaming as a Creativity Technique
- Collaborative group work and exchange of knowledge for ideation
- Presentation and critical discussion of results and ideas

Students are divided into three (or four) member working groups. Ideally for a full-staffed course there are eight working groups with three members each. The execution of the course is planned in seven sessions lasting for four to six hours conducting the following steps:

- After getting an introduction to creativity and creativity techniques, students prepare presentations of different creativity techniques
- Presentations of different creativity techniques
- Students develop a comparison framework for comparison of the applied techniques (traditional methods and games)
- Students invent own innovation case studies for other students
- The working groups select creativity methods to work on the case studies (practical approach)

- Students play the two games. It is important that the students have not worked on the cases represented by the games.
- Students develop a common catalogue of 'creativity elements' which are the driving forces for each of the considered creativity techniques
- Students develop own game scenarios for be.mog gaming engine applying 'creativity elements' from the catalogue
- Presentation of evaluation results and discussion of draft game scenarios

3.2   Execution of the Course in 2013

The Student Lab "Application and Comparison of Creativity Techniques" has been conducted during the summer semester 2013 with 14 master degree students of the industrial engineering faculty of the University of Bremen.

The course was divided into seven blocks (sessions) with a duration of 4-6 hours each. All the sessions were executed between April and July 2013:

- Introduction. The first block is used for introducing the topic of creativity and creativity supporting methods in product development and innovation processes. Some models concerning the fuzzy front end to the product development process have been introduced together with underlying theory. Theoretical considerations of creativity have also been introduced including De Bono's concept of lateral thinking [7] and Csikszentmihalyi's concept of flow [8]. A rough overview on and a classification of creativity supporting methods has also been provided. At the end students were divided into four working groups (two groups with three participants and two groups with four participants). Each group selected a specific creativity method to be presented in the next meeting.
- Presentations. Students held presentations of the creativity methods (1) De Bono's Thinking Hats, (2) Provocation Techniques, (3) Osborn Check lists and SCAMPER, and (4) brain writing and variants, and (5) Mind Mapping.
- Evaluation framework. The method of stop and go brainstorming has been introduced and applied by two different teams of seven students which consisted of two joined working groups. After that the method of morphological analysis has been introduced and used to construct six case studies to be solved by the students.
- Practical application. Six different case studies have been developed and practically applied with the creativity techniques morphological analysis, mind mapping, the six thinking hats and provocation technique. An example for a case study is: A start-up enterprise in the service sector is looking for new ideas for providing mobility by cars to families with low income.
- Serious Gaming. During the serious gaming session two games have been played, i.e. *refQuest* and *theTakeover*, which have been described in [3].
- Introduction to be.mog and brainstorming of creativity elements. Be.mog is the BIBA Engine for Multiplayer Online Games and has been briefly described in [9]. Students were introduced to using a swim-lane diagram for planning the process and a set of tables helping the definition of the various game objects (organization, department, player, process steps, documents, actions, etc.) has been supplied. Finally, a brain storming session to identify creativity elements has been performed during this session.

- Final Presentation. Students prepared in each working group their evaluation and a new game scenario based on be.mog. At the final meeting each working gave a presentation and the results were discussed.

Finally, each of the four working groups had to prepare a report on the lab with a description of the procedure of the course, the practical applications they have executed and its results, a comparative evaluation of the applied methods including the serious games, and a justified design of a new serious game scenario based on selected creativity elements. It was expected from the students to add their initial presentation, the documentation of results concerning the practical application and the gaming, and the slides of their final presentation.

4   Results during the Student Lab

The results produced by the students during the execution of the course are an evaluation framework and an evaluation, a list of creativity elements and finally four concepts for games to support creativity.

4.1   Evaluation Framework and Results

The students developed a questionnaire to capture important information during the practical application of the various creativity techniques. The questionnaire contained 28 questions, an excerpt is given in Fig. 1.

The first group analysed the techniques of morphological analysis, the six thinking hats, the provocation technique and the two serious games *refQuest* and *theTakeover*. They analysed the pros and cons as well as the features of each method and came to the following conclusion: the technique with the best approach to structure ideation are the six thinking hats and *refQuest*. The method with the highest complexity is De Bono's thinking hats and except that one all methods have a high "fun factor". De Bono's methods of thinking hats and provocation are considered as the most flexible. The morphological analysis has the highest evaluation efforts, but provides the best process quality and maturity of generated ideas.

The second group analysed the techniques of mind mapping, the six thinking hats, the provocation technique and the two serious games *refQuest* and *theTakeover*. They defined three key performance indictors which are fun, usability and benefits. Behind each of these indicators is a formula to calculate a value on a scale between zero and five, where zero represents "very bad" and five represents "very good". The method they had most fun with it was the provocation method. The methods with the highest usability are the thinking hats and mind mapping, and the highest benefits are gained from the two Serious Games.

Common Questions		
01 Date		
02 Technique		
Preparation Phase		
03 What is the application area of the session?		
04 Which means have been used during the session?		
05 Is prior knowledge expected for using this technique?	☐ Yes	☐ No
06 Is prior knowledge expected for solving the topic of the session?	☐ Yes	☐ No
07 What are the expected costs for this session?		

Fig. 1. Excerpt from the evaluation questionnaire developed by the students of the course

The third group also analysed the techniques of mind mapping, the six thinking hats, the provocation technique and the two serious games *refQuest* and *theTakeover*. Their main focus of the evaluation was on productivity, quality of outcome and "other factors". Like the second group they defined key performance indicators and a weighting scheme which allowed them to come up with a final ranking of the methods under consideration: (1) mind mapping, (2) *theTakeover*, (3) provocation technique, (4) thinking hats, and (5) *refQuest*.

The third group also analysed the techniques of morphological analysis, the six thinking hats, the provocation technique and the two serious games *refQuest* and *theTakeover*. The defined and quantified seven criteria to evaluate the methods, i.e. structured approach, complexity of method, fun, combinability with other methods, flexibility of method, evaluation efforts, and maturity of output. Again their final statement was a ranking of the methods: (1) morphological analysis, (2-3) *theTakeover* and provocation technique, (4) *refQuest*, and (5) the thinking hats.

4.2   Creativity Elements

Before the students started to design own game scenarios to support creativity a brainstorming for the identification of creativity elements has been performed with the whole group. The portfolio of creativity techniques with theoretical and some practical experience was at this stage:

- Brainstorming, and some variants
- Brainwriting, and some variants (e.g. 6-3-5 method)

- Mind-Mapping
- Checklists like Osborn and SCAMPER
- Provocation Techniques
- De Bono's Thinking Hats
- Morphological analysis
- Serious games *refQuest* and *theTakeover*

The question for the brainstorming was: What are the main features or attributes of the creativity techniques which stimulate idea generation? The result of this brainstorming session included the following elements:

- Inspiration through the ideas of others
- Pressure of time
- Thinking beside the usual paths
- Common prioritization
- Checklists with predefined questions
- Combining dimensions and characteristics
- Varying of ideas
- Avoid early evaluation
- Changes in perspectives and/or roles
- Advancement of ideas
- Expert knowledge
- Supporting tools (hats, whiteboard) (moderator)
- Quantity vs. quality
- Structured process
- Exchange on ideas (discussion)
- Structured representation of ideas (e.g. clustering)
- Combination of ideas
- Incremental vs. radikal
- Documentation / storing of ideas
- Premise
- Anonymity
- Include „calm" persons
- Single vs. group work
- Thought-provoking impulses, e.g. by random words, reversion, exaggeration/understatement, surprise, external stimuli (audio, video), sudden change of topics, restrictions

4.3   Creativity Supporting Serious Games

The first group of students designed a game called "Skyfall". The use case is about the development of new safety systems for airplanes in an inter-corporate set-up. They combined two methods: brain writing with the 6-3-5-method and morphological analysis. But they also included elements from the six thinking hats by assigning different roles (perspectives) to the players.

Within the game scenario two organizations and three departments have been defined. In a first step employees of both companies are asked to generate new ideas. After that the best ideas are selected by the group. After both "camps" do a ranking of their ideas, an event takes place, which is an industrial spy of one of the two companies is detected. In the course of this event, each party gets information about an idea of the opposing group, and at the same time it is pointed out that they were also spied, but it remains unclear to what extent. The staff are first informed about this incident and now asked to reconsider their ideas among the new findings. Finally, they do again a ranking of the best ideas.

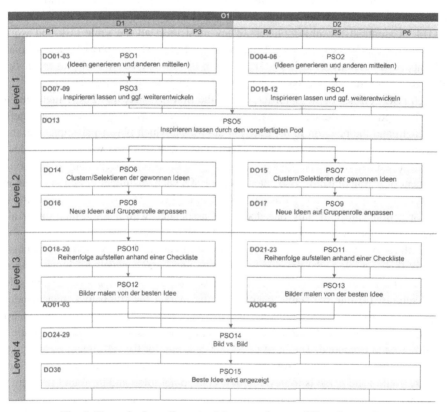

Fig. 2. The swim-lane diagram of the second group ("Four Seasons")

The second group designed a game scenario called "Four Seasons" and its swim-lane diagram is presented in Fig. 2. The four levels represent "ideation", "selection and adaptation", "visualization", and "selection".

The starting point is the organization (O1) which is the company itself. The organization includes various creative teams D1 and D2, where D stands for the department. Each team consists of three players, these are labeled "P1" - "P6". A total of six players can participate in the game. The right margin in the swim-lane diagram is intended to show the temporal occurrence of events. A total of two events (E1 and E2) are taking place that provide the player with new challenges. The middle panel of the swim-lane diagram includes all process steps displayed in chronological order from top to bottom, and the related documents (DO) and action objects (AO), which complete the game.

All in all, the game consists of 15 PSOs that can be divided basically into two variants. In the first variant, for example, the process steps PSO1 and PSO2, they are identical each for their own team. That each of the three players in each team has the same PSO and must therefore fulfill the same task. The other variant of the PSO, e.g. PSO14, is identical for all six players. They must meet all the same task and work together in the process. The main difference between these versions is that only participants of D1 are involved in PSO1, while in the second version all players of the game are involved. The process steps PSO1 - PSO15 have an identical structure.

Each PSO consists of an identifier, e.g. in the first instance, it is PSO1 including a short description and the necessary documents to process the respective process step. The length and the position in the diagram describes, which player participates in the respective PSO and to what level this occurs. The red designation within a PSO identifies the document or action objects that belong to the process step. If more than one document or action object is associated with a PSO, each document or action object is available for one player only. Basically, only that player can edit and use the document or action object. If only one document associated with a PSO, then either all players have equal access to it or just a specific one.

The third group came up with a game scenario called "Bike & Sons". The challenge of this scenario is the development of new ideas and concepts for bicycle innovations. The fictitious company "Bike & Sons Ltd." is the nation's leading bicycle manufacturer. Despite the stable position on the market the company's management thinks of the future of the company and the industry. Accordingly, the leadership should not only be maintained over the long term, but the distance to the competition should be even expanded. The most important criterion for the fulfillment of that goal is the development of innovative and trendsetting bicycle solutions. Therefore, the primary goal of the game is to develop new conceptual ideas and profound revolutionary improvements in order to change the bicycle market changed significantly.

The organization is divided into three departments: (1) research and development with two players, (2) marketing and sales with tree players, and (3) production with six players. Each of the players is randomly assigned one of twelve pre-defined roles (perspectives) which are combinations of one of De Bono's thinking hats and additional character descriptions.

Table 1. Overview on the four game scenarios developed in the student lab

Game	Topic	#Player	Creativity Elements
Skyfall	Development of new safety systems for airplanes	18	• Pressure of Time • Combining dimensions and characteristics • Changes in perspectives • Thought-provoking through surprise
Four Seasons	Generic, for organisations with teams (departments)	6	• Exaggeration • Inspiration through others • Common prioritization • Checklists • Thought-provoking impulse through surprise • Exchange of ideas • Change of perspective • Restriction • Visualization
Bike & Sons	Development of new ideas and concepts for bicycle innovation	12	• Change of role and perspective • Thought-provoking impulse through random words • Inspiration through the ideas of others • Common prioritization • Advancement of ideas
Television	Development of a new television	24	• Inspiration through the ideas of others • Changes in perspectives • Pressure of time • Common prioritization

First, a direction of ideation is identified through an action. These directions can be green production, reduction of costs, and technological excellence. The decision is communicated via the integrated chat. Afterwards each player gets a randomly drawn word acting as a provocation which should stimulate creativity. Each player generates three ideas. After that all ideas are rated by all players and the twelve best ideas are distributed randomly among the players to further advance the ideas within five minutes. The advancement of ideas under time pressure is performed in a second and a third round by distributing the ideas randomly again. Afterwards, each player summarizes one of the ideas including the advancements to a short concept, and finally the department leaders select the three best concepts.

The fourth group designed a game scenario around a television manufacturer. The company is structured into four departments: design, operations, usability and additional applications. The design department should work on a new design with the help of the morphological analysis. The operations department is responsible for operational buttons on the TV and its remote control. It must find alternatives for buttons and remote control by applying the method of the brain writing pool. Thus, the participants should support each other creatively. The third department deals with the menu of the television. There are plans to be made, how the menus of the TV should look like. The method of brainstorming is to be used here. The last department deals with special functions. They should develop new applications that extend the functionality of the TV, e.g. an application to display videos from the Internet. For this the Walt Disney method should be used.

The first round is scheduled for about 30 minutes. Thereafter, the departments are sequentially exchanged. Thus, members of the design department now deal in the second round with the operation and use for the brain writing pool. A total of four of these rounds are completed. All ideas of all groups are collected for each task area. In the next round, the participants should find from this pool of ideas using the 6-3-5 method a solution. It should be regenerated any ideas, but only the ideas from the pool to be used for this purpose. After 30 minutes, there are in every department 6 solutions. Then the best solution is selected per department. From these four solutions a new television can be developed.

An overview on the four game scenarios is given in Table 1 giving the name of the game scenario, the topic (innovation case), the number of players for the scenario, and a list of creativity elements used tin the design of the scenario.

5   Discussion

The learning objectives as outlined in section 3.1 have been reached by all students. They were introduced to different kind of creativity techniques (intuitive, discursive, combined methods) and Serious Gaming as mean to stimulate creativity and their application in the early phase of innovation projects. Furthermore, they experienced collaborative group work and prepared astonishing good presentations and final reports. Additionally, all of the students seemed to have a lot of fun especially during the practical application of selected methods even when the session has extended into the early evening. Also, the developed evaluation frameworks and the identified elements of creativity methods show that the students developed a deep understanding of the topic.

The differences in the evaluation of the various creativity methods can be explained by the case study method combinations, which were – except for the Serious Games – different among working groups.

De Bono's method of the six thinking hats has been considered ambiguously, on the one hand most students had problems to slip into and to change the roles during practical application, on the other hand most of them think that taking restricted perspectives is worthy element in creativity techniques. The change of perspective has been used by all working groups as an element incorporated to their game scenario design. The element of provoking thoughts has also been used by three of the four groups. The provocation is different: provocation was either caused by a random term or by a surprising event occurring during the gameplay.

When analysing the game scenarios developed by students one might notice that not all of the students had the same understanding of the mechanics of the game engine be.mog. But, this is considered less important because of the rich outcome of game scenario designs and the creative construction of new game scenarios incorporating important elements from creativity techniques.

During the evaluation of the Serious Games *refQuest* and *theTakeover* students claimed that the on-boarding is difficult and often players do not know what to do and others get bored because they cannot continue before specific tasks have been completed. Nonetheless, the newly developed game scenarios seem to have the same weaknesses – it might be a problem of the underlying model of the engine be.mog.

6   Conclusions

Creative thinking, especially when performed collaboratively, is an engaging activity that fosters participation, discussion and deep reflection about real-world problems. Creative thinking is thus one of the competencies expected from tomorrow's knowledge workers. These are all highly desirable characteristics in any learning process, and represent the core of the rapidly increasing academic effort towards using serious games to engage students in situated deep learning activities. This article presented the results of course conducted at the University of Bremen, where concepts of four Serious Games were designed for stimulating the creative thinking process.

A course designed as a student lab with hands-on practical applications of selected creativity methods is a good approach to mediate knowledge about and experiences in creativity stimulating techniques and methods. Students enjoy the practical sessions and learn by doing, e.g. the evaluation questionnaire, the case studies, and the list of creativity supporting elements have also been derived by applying creativity techniques (brain storming and morphological analysis).

The execution of that course also provided valuable results to be used as inputs for further research. There are promising game scenarios (e.g. the named "Four Seasons"), which should be implemented, tested and evaluated. Such games have the potential to be applied for a wide range of innovation problems. Furthermore, the development of a proven taxonomy of creativity stimulating elements is a challenging task. The result would be helpful for inventing new creativity techniques and games stimulating the creative thinking process.

This course has been conducted for the first time. It is mandatory to collect more empirical knowledge during upcoming courses to get a deeper understanding of how the decomposition of creativity techniques can be transformed into gaming elements to support creativity. The same course is scheduled for summer semester 2014 and we are looking forward to see new and exciting game scenrios.

Acknowledgement. The research reported in this paper has been undertaken within the GALA project, which is funded by the European Community under the Seventh Framework Programme (Grant Agreement FP7-ICT-258169). We the authors of the paper wish to acknowledge the Commission for their support. Furthermore, we wish to thank all the other members of the GALA consortium for their valuable work and contributions to this paper.

References

1. Fischer, G., Giaccardi, E., Eden, H., Sugimoto, M., Ye, Y.: Beyond binary choices: Integrating individual and social creativity. International Journal of Human-Computer Studies 63, 482–512 (2005)
2. Hesmer, A., Hribernik, K., Baalsrud Hauge, J., Thoben, K.-D.: Supporting the Ideation Process by a Collaborative Online-based Toolset. International Journal of Technology Management 55, 218–225 (2011)
3. Hauge, J.B., Duin, H., Thoben, K.-D.: The Evaluation of Serious Games Supporting Creativity through Student Labs. In: Ma, M., Oliveira, M.F., Petersen, S., Hauge, J.B. (eds.) SGDA 2013. LNCS, vol. 8101, pp. 188–199. Springer, Heidelberg (2013)
4. Luccini, A.M., Cheak, A.: Creativity and Games, http://www.galanoe.eu/index.php/home/665-creativity-and-games
5. Craft, A.: Creativity in Schools. Tensions and Dilemmas. In: Jackson, N., Oliver, M., Shaw, M., Wisdom, J. (eds.) Developing Creativity in Higher Education: An Imaginative Curriculum, pp. 19–28. Routledge-Falmer, London (2006)
6. Playfoot, J., Hall, R.: The Serious Business of Play: How Gaming can Unlock Creativity and Foster Entrepreneurship. In: 15th UNESCO-APEID International Conference (2011)
7. De Bono, E.: Serious Creativity: Using the Power of Lateral Thinking to Create New Ideas. Harper Business (1992)
8. Csikszentmihalyi, M.: Flow. The psychology of Optimal Experience. Harper and Row (1990)
9. Duin, H., Baalsrud Hauge, J., Thoben, K.-D.: An Ideation Game Conception Based on the Synectics Method. On the Horizon 17, 286–295 (2009)

The Choice of Serious Games and Gamification

A Case Study to Illustrate Key Differences

Manuel Oliveira and Sobah Petersen

Sintef, Technology and Society, S.P. Andersensv. 5, NO-7465 Trondheim, Norway
{manuel.oliveira,sobah.petersen}@sintef.no

Abstract. When analyzing past and existing trends, gamification has unarguably invaded the mainstream media in a more pervasive way than serious games. In the literature, there has been a wide range of meanings for gamification, some detractors abhorring the term to others stating it encompasses everything to do with games and entertainment. This inconsistent nomenclature and undefined scope has led to the erroneous belief that gamification and serious games are synonymous. The aim of this paper is to present the distinct differences supported by case study of the use of both gamification and serious games within the same project aimed at social innovation within the neighbourhoods.

Keywords: Serious Games, Gamification.

1 Introduction

Games as a means of influencing behaviour and promoting learning has been accepted for some time [1], giving rise to the research area of Serious Games and emphasizing attention to the relations between games, entertainment and learning [2]. While the uses of serious games may be considered to have limitations, the potential of achieving user engagement by leveraging ideas from games and careful game design remains attractive, and the approach was to reduce the scope to focus on ensuring user engagement of a process by means of considerate game design. As a result the term gamification was coined and the continued surging interest is captured in the trends analysis in the Gartner Hype Curve for Emerging Technologies 2013 [3]. The term Gamification had been defined and described by several people in the community, such as the following:

- The process of using game thinking and mechanics to engage audiences and solve problems [4].
- Using game techniques to make activities more engaging and fun [5].
- The broad trend of employing game techniques to non-game environments such as innovation, marketing, training, employee performance, health and social change [6].
- Gamification is using game-based mechanics, aesthetics and game thinking to engage people, motivate action, promote learning, and solve problems [7].

M. Ma et al. (Eds.): SGDA 2014, LNCS 8778, pp. 213–223, 2014.

In a few cases, some have tried to delve deeper into the meaning of gamification and what it implies, as in the case of [8] where the authors propose "gameful design" as an alternative of gamification when considering scientific debate. The authors present a structured framework based on two dimensions (whole/parts and gaming/playing) to counter the subjectivity associated to gamification and facilitate the task of distinguishing the differences between a gamified application and an actual serious game.

In this paper, a more pratical approach is taken by presenting the case study of MyNeighbourhood project where both gamification and serious game were used, thus illustrating the lessons learnt.

2   MyNeighbourhood Project

The United Nations [9] identifies the growing trend of mega-cities and estimates that in 2030, more than 80% of the world population will reside in urban areas. In addition, governments realize the unsustainability of central governance, requiring to tap into the civil responsibility of individuals within society. This is the key idea driving the "Big Society" policy flagship of the current liberal-conservative government [10], which has been described by many as a radical grounds-up approach to governance. However, the evidence has yet to demonstrate that such an approach works, as citizens have lost the necessary social cohesiveness for such policy to succeed. As a result, the MyNeighbourhood project [11] aims at using 'smart' ICT services and citizen/neighbourhood generated data to help recreate the social mechanisms which, in the past, ensured that urban neighbourhoods coincided with a social system of connected and trusted communities, where the quality of life was very high and people felt safe and happy with a true sense of belonging.

The MyNeighbourhood concept revolves around three main components:

- **Urban Living Labs (ULL).** ULL are considered open innovation environments grounded in the urban context of a city where the different stakeholders (non-governmental organisations (NGOs), municipalities, business partners, and citizens) come together to share their concerns and co-create together solutions.
- **Neighbourhood.** The neighbourhood is what the project considers as the minimum socio-spatial dimension for stakeholders, namely citizens, to share a common identity that ignites their capacity to become drivers of change.
- **Sustainability.** At the heart of any solution is the need for sustainability, although this does not imply that all business models are pivoted on cost/profit alone. In fact, in combination with the other dimensions of the MyNeighbourhood concept model, alternative forms of sustainability are feasible, some of which unconventional but accepted by the local communities.

To support the concept model, the project developed a toolkit of methods and tools to facilitate the implementation of ULL within a neighbourhood for sustainable change. In addition to the toolkit, the project developed a social network platform for the neighbourhood and with the visual language of the concepts supporting the ULL.

A key challenge was in attracting citizens to start using the platform and to interact with their neighbours through the platform as well as in the real world. Ideas from playful interactions can be used to support this and the gamification process by creating opportunities for people to start interacting either with the platform or with one another. However, there was also the need to convey the concepts to the different stakeholders, which would require a serious game to raise the awareness and facilitate learning.

3   Gamification in MyNeighbourhood

In the MyNeighbourhood project, we have defined gamification as :

> *"the process of employing game mechanics and dynamics to create an engaging user experience that leads to behaviour change"*

Anchoring to the key concepts of MyNeighbourhood such as ULL and co-design of services for social innovation, there was a need for supporting gamification that would also be appropriate in such neighbourhood contexts, where the citizens could engage in gamifying their activities and services for the good of the neighbourhood as a whole. This is a move away from common gamified services such as the bonus programs to encourage more usage practiced by some businesses such as airline companies, where the focus is on increased engagement of an individual customer. Another challenge is the need to support the design of the gamified services by the citizens themselves.

Emerging approaches for gamification did not provide sufficient support for non-experts to carry out gamification of existing processes, as in the case of Francisco et al.'s method that is based on four steps without much detail beyond the selection of an objective and initial scoping [12]. There exists gamification methodologies based on the use of cards, such as playgen's [13] and SCVNGR's [14]. However, these solutions require significant gamification experience from the facilitators, which makes it inappropriate for the use in the MyNeighbourhood pilots where the expertise of gamification is close to non-existent. In addition, the cards of these decks are tailored for more general application domains and do not address the particularities of user engagement of communities. Therefore, a new set of cards focused on overcoming the challenges mentioned earlier were created along with a methodology for supporting the gamification of services, where the citizens worked with the cards, in a co-design process, with the help of a facilitator

3.1   MyG Methodology

The MyNeighbourhood Gamification Methodology (MyG methodology) [15] consists of a workshop that is divided into three main parts:

- **Setting the context.** The MyG methodology makes the assumption that the workshop participants know little or nothing about gamification. Consequently, it is necessary to provide some context with regards to what gamification is along with some examples of gamified solutions. This provides the foundation for describing the MyG process.

- **MyG Process.** The MyG process is an iterative process that supports gamestorming of ideas and concepts towards a gamified solution. Depending on the time constraints of the workshop, the MyG process can be executed one or more times. This process is facilitated by someone familiar with the concepts of gamification the gamification cards are used to support creative co-design of gamified processes.
- **Crowning of best gamified solution.** The workshop participants are organized into teams of users that compete with each other for the best gamified solution, thus giving them incentive to excel at their gamestorming. The participants themselves vote and rank for the best gamified solution.

The set of gamification cards includes seven different types of cards; bringing together the underlying theoretical aspects from psychology, behavioural sciences, learning and gaming. The different types of cards are described below:

- **User Archetype.** These are the yellow cards in the deck and they identify the user archetype based on what their personality and how it affects their behaviour and decision making. These cards are best used to scope the solution space. An example of a user archetype is a Socialiser.
- **User Experience.** These are the black cards in the deck and they characterize the level of experience of the user. Similar to the User Archetype, these cards help scope the solution space. An example of this type is a Novice.
- **Goal.** These are green cards in the deck and they indicate the type of goal(s) to be achieved and that will shape the gamification process. An example of a goal is to bring a friend.
- **Motivation.** These are the red cards in the deck and they represent the intrinsic motivation of a user that will influence and shape their decisions. An example of motivation is a power.
- **Social Mechanic.** These are the orange cards in the deck and they capture the social drivers that influence the behaviour of an individual user. An example of a social mechanic is barter.
- **Game Mechanic.** These are the dark blue cards in the deck and they capture a component of gamification. An example of a game mechanic is awards.
- **Game Pattern.** These are the light blue cards in the deck and they represent complex game mechanics that may depend on two or more game mechanics. An example of a game pattern is feedback.

A set of cards containing 52 cards in total were provided. An example of each type of cards is shown in Fig.1.

Fig. 1. MyNeighbourhood Gamification Cards

3.2   Gamification of Services

The MyNeighbourhood gamification methodology described above has been tried out in the project by all the pilots. Gamification workshops consisting of group work among the pilots were conducted, where each pilot considered how they could design gamified services; an example is shown in Fig.2. Some of these services revolved around the use of the ICT platform, MyNeighbourhood platform, and the services available from it. Some examples of gamified services that were designed by the pilots are described in this section of the paper.

Fig. 2. Group work during gamification workshops

One of the services that was identified by the Lisbon pilot was called "EDU4ALL" where citizens could play the role of a teacher to teach another citizen something, meeting the need of one to improve their competences while the other has spare time to spend helping someone. Issues such as trust among the two citizens involved and continuity around this service were discussed, bringing forth ideas for gamification, where the engagement of the teacher to continue providing this service was identified as significant. Some of the ideas for gamifying this situation were to encourage the teacher by giving "Points" to the teacher for joining the MyNeighbourhood platform as a teacher and for the continued activity as a teacher. The points system works in such a way that the teacher gains points by inviting other teachers and inviting students or by accumulating a certain number of teaching hours. The teacher could win more points if s/he invites a teacher from a different area than his/her own as well as if s/he invites students for other teachers than for him/herself. The idea is to create a "pyramidal" system of invitations in which the teacher has an important role. As a "Reward", the points that are accumulated could then be exchanged for other services that the teacher might need.

Fig. 3. Using Gamification cards to co-design services

Another example is to engage volunteers to support the services for handicapped citizens living in care homes, identified by the Aalborg pilot. These services could range from paying a social visit at the care home to arranging an outing for the handicapped citizens where the volunteer takes the responsibility for taking one or more handicapped citizens outside of the care home, either for entertainment such as a cultural visit or to do their shopping. The main goal is to build and strengthen the relationship between these two groups of citizens. The game mechanics that were used in designing this service included "Points", "Awards" and "Power up"; see Fig.3. The volunteers received badges based on points indicating a tier, e.g. a super care taker. The different types of badges that could be earned were identified, e.g. a wheelchair badge or a bus trip badge, depending on the activity that the volunteer took part in. The recognition through the badges was an indicator to the mediators of this service (usually some one from the care home) how well a volunteer was progressing and this influenced the assignments that were given to the volunteer

4   Serious Game in MyNeighbourhood

Unlike the gamification of the MyNeighbourhood services and the MyN platform, the MyNeighbourhood Social Game is a serious game to convey the concept model that captures the use of ICT to support the close social engagement within neighbourhoods. Consequently, the purpose of the serious game is more about raising awareness and understanding of the concepts. Consequently, the serious game has become an effective dissemination tool that contributes to the uptake of the MyNeighbourhood platform.

The MyNeighbourhood Social Game is both a cooperative and competitive game, where the players take charge of the transformation of a neighbourhood. A maxi-mum of four neighbourhoods can play against each other, where each neighbour-hood may have one to three players working together to excel in the transformation of their local community. The transformation is achieved through the gradual successful executions of activities, which are governed by three distinct elements:

1. **Karma.** The Karma represents the level of social capital within a particular neighbourhood. The result of successful activities yields karma, but in the case of poor events, karma may be lost and in any case, most activities require the expenditure of karma.
2. **Money.** The money represents the funds available to a player to invest in the execution of activities. In some cases, successful activities may result in a monetary return.
3. **Population.** The population represents the number of people in the neighbourhood, which in some cases determines whether a particular activity may take place or not. The population may increase or decrease proportionally to the karma.

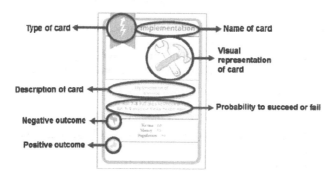

Fig. 4. Meta-representation of a MyNeighbourhood game card

Each activity is represented by a card, which meta-representation is captured in the diagram of Fig. 4. A player can choose a card to use, where a probability is tied to the successful outcome of the associated activity. The use of a card implies always a cost, in terms of karma and money, constrained by population.

There are two types of activity cards, one is for the organization of events (e.g.: a fair for the local businesses) and the other are direct actions to undertake in the neighbourhood (e.g.: a hackathon with purpose of identifying developers). In addition to activity cards, there are stakeholder and service cards. The former represent the identification of key community players, whom may have a positive influence on the outcome of activities carried out and the latter correspond to services running in the neighbourhood that generate income and karma, which ultimately may attract an increase in the population. The relationship between the different cards is captured in Fig. 5.

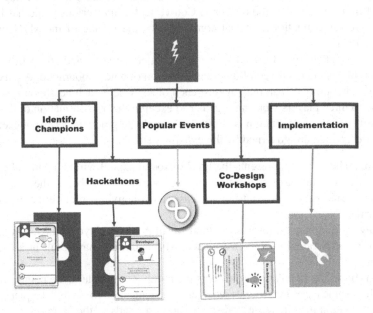

Fig. 5. Relationship between the different cards

The two-types of activity cards can be broken down according to their outputs:

1. **Identify Champions**. The aim is to organize workshops where one identifies champions in the neighbourhood, which ease the probability of success of future activities.
2. **Hackathons**. Through a hackathon, one identifies local developers, which improve the probability of success of future implementation activities.
3. **Popular events**. The main purpose of these activities is to contribute to the karma of the community.
4. **Co-Design Workshops**. The co-design workshops allow the player to choose a particular service to implement rather than it being randomly selected at implementation. In addition, by having a co-design result, the implementation has greater chance of success.
5. **Implementation**. These are activities to instantiate and deploy a service for the local community.

The game is turn-based, with each turn consisting of players moving along the board of Fig. 6 and using activity cards.

Fig. 6. MyNeighbourhood Social Game

When moving around the board, if the player lands on a blank square, their turn is finished and the next player from another neighbourhood starts their turn. If the player lands on a square with a card or a quarterly square (karma, service upkeep, revenue), they follow the instructions.

In addition, as the players achieve certain intermediate goals, they receive awards, such as organizing successfully five popular events. To win the game, the players within a neighbourhood need to collaborate to achieve and sustain a particular threshold of karma for a period of time

5   Serious Games or Gamification

Based on the experiences of using serious games and gamification in the MyNeighbourhood project, we have been able to distinguish these two concepts in many following. The serious game is created to convey the concept model that cap-tures the use of ICT to support the close social engagement within neighbourhoods. Citizens could play this game, without the support of an ICT platform, to raise their awareness and understanding of the social infrastructure and engagement in their neighbourhoods, which in turn will attract new users to the MyNeighbourood platform. On the other hand, gamification is done on the ICT platform, to engage its users and to encourage (or discourage) certain types of behaviours.

A serious game is designed based on a certain set of rules and actions that users can take; the scoring in a game is based on these rules. While both serious games and gamification engage users, the serious game does this implicitly though its design in a more holistic manner, where a total score is based on the overall behaviour or performance of the player in the game. Unlike this, gamification engages users in specific behaviours and does not require this incorporated within a game; i.e. gamification can exist without a game. It employs elements (one or more as desired) in everyday situations to motivate and engage users. Similarly, a game usually implies a winner (and a loser), with players competing among each other. However, in gamification, depending on the elements of games that are used, the element of competition need not always be. Rather, the game elements may be used to encourage a user to strive to achieve better irrespective of the performance of other users. The use of these two concepts could be quite different as in the case of the MyNeighbourhood project. In the design of the ICT platform, serious games and gamification has been seen as concepts that can support two different things. Gamification can be used to encourage specific behaviours of individual users, such as contributing content to the plat-form and thus their communities, or taking part in neighbourhood activities. Examples of these are illustrated in the previous sections. Such individual behaviours are rewarded implicitly by recognising them via the platform; for example by the use of functionalities such as "like" or interest around them. The serious game, on the other hand is designed to create a collaborative and community spirit among the neighbours while competing with other neighbourhoods. Thus, a synergy exists between the social game and gamification, where elements of the game encourage the outcome of the gamification and vice versa, utilizing the strengths of both serious games and gamification.

6   Conclusions

This paper discusses the concepts Serious Games and Gamification, highlighting their differences through examples from experiences of using both concepts in the European MyNeighbourhood project. The MyNeighbourhood project aims at strengthening the social bonds within a neighbourhood through the use of ICT and Serious Games and Gamification have been used as means for engaging citizens in social innovation, to find solutions to their problems.

A serious game brings together a set of rules and actions in a cohesive manner, where players score and compete with one another. The game can be based on individual players or teams of players, where the latter encourages collaborations and could facilitate a community spirit. Gamification on the other hand uses elements from game design, but is not a game. Gamification can encourage and engage users, where users can compete with one another or simply challenge ones own self to improve own performance.

The MyNeighbourhood project illustrates the synergies between the two and brings together the strengths of both serious games and gamification by using both in a manner where users are engaged and motivated through the two mechanisms. The MyNeighbourhood ICT platform will be launched in the near future. The future work in the project will evaluate the outcomes of using these concepts, distinguishing further their distinct roles and producing empirical evidence from their use.

Acknowledgements. This work has been conducted within the MyNeighbourhood European project grant agreement 325227. The authors wish to thank the project partners for their contributions during the gamification workshops

References

1. Gee, J.P.: What Video Games Have to Teach Us About Learning and Literacy, 2nd edn. Revised and Updated Edition. Palgrave Macmillan (2007)
2. Djaouti, D., Alvarez, J., Jessel, J., Rampnoux, O.: Origins of Serious Games. In: Ma, M., Oikonomou, A., Jain, L. (eds.) Serious Games and Edutainment Applications. Springer (2011)
3. Rivera, J.: Gartner's, Hype Cycle for Emerging Technologies Maps Out Evolving Relationship Between Humans and Machines. Gartner Press Release (2013), http://www.gartner.com/newsroom/id/2575515 (retrieved May 30, 2014)
4. Zichermann, G., Cunningham, C.: Gamification by Design. O'Reilly Media Inc., CA (2011)
5. Kim, A.J.: Gamification 101: Designing the player journey. Google Tech Talk (2011), http://www.youtube.com/watch?v=B0H3ASbnZmc&feature=youtu.be (retrieved June 30, 2013)
6. http://www.forbes.com/sites/gartnergroup/2013/01/21/the-gamification-of-business/
7. Kapp, K.M.: The gamification of learning and instruction: game-based methods and strategies for training and education. Pfeiffer, San Francisco (2012)
8. Deterding, S., Dixon, D., Khaled, R., Nacke, L.: From Game Design Elements to Gamefulness: Defining "Gamification". In: MindTrek 2011, Tampere (September 2011)
9. United Nations, Department of Economic and Social Affairs, Population Division: World Urbanization Prospects, the 2011 Revision: Highlights, New York (2012)
10. https://www.gov.uk/government/news/government-launches-big-society-programme-2
11. http://my-neighbourhood.eu/
12. Francisco, A., Luis, F., Gonzalez, J., Isla, J.: Analysis and Application of Gamification. Paper presented at the Interaccion 2012, Spain (2012)
13. http://www.playgen.com
14. Schonfeld, E.: SCVNGR's Secret Game Mechanics Playdeck (August 2010), http://techcrunch.com/2010/08/25/scvngr-game-mechanics/
15. Oliveira, M., Petersen, S.: Co-design of Neighbourhood Services using Gamification Cards. In: Nah, F.F.-H. (ed.) HCIB/HCII 2014. LNCS, vol. 8527, pp. 419–428. Springer, Heidelberg (2014)

Author Index